SHATTERED IMAGES

SHATTERED IMAGES

The Rise of Militant Iconoclasm in Syria

Fred A. Reed

Talonbooks
2003

Talonbooks
P.O. Box 2076, Vancouver, British Columbia, Canada V6B 3S3
www.talonbooks.com

Typeset in Adobe Garamond and printed and bound in Canada.

First Printing: October 2003

The cover image of the miniature, "Mohammad and Ali cleansing the Kaaba of idols," is reproduced with the permission of Bildarchiv Preussischer Kulturbesitz, Berlin, Germany.

National Library of Canada Cataloguing in Publication Data

Reed, Fred A., 1939–
  Shattered images: the rise of militant iconoclasm in Syria / Fred A. Reed.

  ISBN 0-88922-485-4

  1. Islamic fundamentalism—History. 2. Iconoclasm—Syria. I. Title.
BP55.R43 2003   320.5'5'0917671   C2003-910964-X

The publisher gratefully acknowledges the financial support of the Canada Council for the Arts; the Government of Canada through the Book Publishing Industry Development Program; and the Province of British Columbia through the British Columbia Arts Council for our publishing activities.

Canada

" ... the history of every individual, of every social order, indeed of the whole world, does not describe an ever-widening, more and more wonderful arc, but rather describes a course which, once the meridian is reached, leads without fail down into the dark."

W.G. Sebald, *The Rings of Saturn*

Contents

Acknowledgements

In the researching and writing of this book, I contracted debts of gratitude and hospitality to many. First of all, to those who critically read portions of the text—Hassan Abdulrahman, Ammar Abdulhamid, Cilina Nasser and David Sherman—my deepest thanks. Karl Siegler, my indomitable publisher and editor, helped sharpen the text where necessary, blunt it where appropriate; his commitment helped keep the project afloat in moments of doubt, and saw it safely into port.

In Damascus, in addition to those named in its pages, I received welcome assistance from Dr. Iman Abdulrahim and her adjoint Anass Kouli at the Ministry of Tourism; from Professors Sultan Muhesen and Professor Jamal Sadek al-Azm; from author and translator Memduh Adwan; from Dr. Adbal Razzaq Moaz, Directeur Général des Antiquités et des Musées, who arranged for access to Syria's museum system, and from Hassan Hatoum, Directeur des Antiquités de Suweida and Muhammad Bashir Shbani, Curator of the Prehistory Department of the Aleppo Museum; from Eng. Mohammad Shahrour; from Salah Kuftaro, Director of the Abu Nour Islamic Foundation; from Riad Seif, member of the People's Assembly now serving a prison term; from Yaser Olabi, Elias Zayat, Ms. Daad Mousa, and Ms. Khowla Dounia; from Maurice Bachour, reverends Metri Haji-Athanasiou, Joseph Saghbini, Yuhanna Ellaty and Jean Kawat; from Ms. Rawa Batbouta of Chamtours; from Ms. Marina Laker of the Canadian Embassy. In Aleppo, I spent several rewarding hours in the company of Nihad Kiyata.

Professor Raymond Hinnebusch, whom I had the pleasure of meeting while in Damascus, shared with me his time and deep knowledge of Syrian political institutions. Dimitri Avgherinos and Sylvain Fourcassié, of the Centre Culturel Français de Damas, put their encyclopedic knowledge of Syrian culture at my disposal. The staff of the Institut Français d'études orientales granted me access and guidance to their excellent library.

Many others contributed in significant ways to my work, but for obvious reasons cannot be named. I trust that they will ultimately receive this anonymous expression of thanks.

In Lebanon, particular thanks are due to Nizar Harissi Dagher, whose unforgettable hospitality made every visit to Saïda feel like a trip home. As well, I owe thanks to Dr. Ahmad Issa of the Imam al-Sadr Center for Research and Studies; to Hussein Nabulsi; to Nayef Krayem of al-Manar TV; to Hani Abdallah, for arranging for me to meet Sheikh Hussein Fadlallah; to Robert Fisk, who took time out from a hectic schedule for several encounters that helped me clarify my view of the forces at work in Middle Eastern politics. Had it not been for Cilina Nasser, who quickly took my project to heart, the time spent in Beirut and in excursions to south Lebanon would not have been so fruitful.

In Istanbul, Faris Kaya and Cemal Ussak extended their gracious hospitality during the last days of Ramadan, 2001. Their colleague, Dr. Ibrahim Abu-Rabi, provided me with several key introductions among his wide network of colleagues.

In Tehran, Hassan Abdulrahman, Mohammad Raja'i-Moghadam, Marjan Marandi and Ali Arabmazar all contributed to making my stay productive and pleasant.

The research and writing of this book have been made possible by the generous assistance of the Canada Council for the Arts. Thanks, too, to the late Marcel Desjardins, managing editor of *La Presse*, who published my first reports from Syria and Lebanon. Without the moral support of David Homel, who saw me through bouts of writer's near-panic, it is far from certain I could have held to a difficult course.

Professor Eric Ormsby, of McGill University's Institute of Islamic Studies, was as generous with his erudition as with his time.

Closer to home, I wish to acknowledge the contribution of my son Anthony Reed, who created the map that graces these pages; of Fadi Dagher, who devised the index; of my wife Ingeborg who, on a rainy afternoon in Aleppo, generously gave me the insight I needed to shape the stories that make up this book.

Lengthy discussions, voluminous exchanges of e-mail, and the comments and criticisms of many oriented, corrected and guided me in my work. But its conclusions, judgements, oversights and inevitable errors are mine alone.

Finally, *Shattered Images* is dedicated to Jacques Bouchard, indefatigable neohellenist, gifted translator and loyal friend.

Preface

T HIS BOOK WAS TO BEGIN with the story of a vanished world, of a defeated but stubborn idea, of an ill-fated, quixotic and almost successful effort to purify the religion of the "people of the book" of the dross of visual representation. It now ends with that tale. Its starting point is instead a random inquiry into an encounter of civilizations in a land that may soon have ceased to exist as I had come to know it.

This is why.

With all the deliberateness of the inexorable, as I travelled to Syria and took up temporary residence in Damascus, my best-laid plans began to unravel, then to reorder themselves in ways I might have suspected but could not fully account for. There I met a broad spectrum of Syrians, some close to the regime of the Baath Party; some as far at odds with the ruling establishment as was reasonably commensurate with keeping one's head atop one's body. Still others had just been released from years of imprisonment.

What they told me, and what I inferred from the unspoken subtext of conversations held in traditional coffee-houses, in formal anterooms, around convivial tables laden with plates of *mezze*, or squatting cross-legged on the carpeted floors of ancient mosques, gradually obliged me to question the received wisdom that posited a movement known as iconoclasm—the willful shattering of images, my original point of departure—as little more than an obscure doctrinal or theological dispute within the confines of early Christianity, another of those irrational historical outbursts that, being difficult to explain, are left unexamined or at very best are taken up by small groups of harmless, scholastic erudites.

Everything I heard turned this naive and one-sided view of shattered images upside down.

I should not have been surprised that Syrians take a proprietary view of a phenomenon that they see as having arisen from the ancient soil of their civilization, as a chain of events that had been set in motion by its sudden emergence at the core of the first Islamic Empire.

This emergence, as sudden and overwhelming as it was catalytic, was at once the product of the forces released by the new social, political and religious teachings of the Prophet, and of its encounter—made up of equal portions of dialogue and conflict, those two faces of the same cross-cultural coin—with the Christian world at its far periphery that had impinged upon these new teachings only to be radically impinged upon.

These were the forces that clashed before the walls of Damascus, that were embodied in the construction of the great Umayyad Mosque, and that reached a climax of warring yet mutually defining ideologies in the rise and triumph of the iconoclast movement. They are forces that are quite alive and at large in today's world, as the Western counterattack against the last prophetic dispensation of the Abrahamic tradition assumes a form both aggressive and invasive at the borders of Syria.

In order to understand the world in which the original Byzantine iconoclasts flourished for more than a century, it was necessary for me to grasp the wider world that nurtured them. Such was the realization that grew as I wandered the narrow lanes of Damascus and Aleppo, and of smaller towns and cities in between, visited desert ruins burnt by the sun, or stood atop crumbling, windswept citadels.

In Syria I believed I had found the beginnings of that understanding. Not surprisingly, it defined itself against the conventional wisdom of the academic establishment which, as in the days of the Sultan's court, takes as its principal task to fill the mellifluous mouths of its expounders with gold coin. But now as then, the coin is debased and the mouths that gape open like the beaks of hungry gulls to receive it, rotted.

* * *

BETWEEN THE INCEPTION of this book and its completion, other factors would intrude. The work I had conceived was to trace Iconoclasm from its violent beginnings to its last theoretical vestiges in the present day. But by the time I had come to write, reality had overtaken my quiet project in a grim and shattering way.

In the summer of 2001, the Taliban movement then ruling Afghanistan bombarded and destroyed the immense stone Buddhas of Bamyian. The Taliban were, we recall, the hardscrabble fundamentalists who, with generous assistance from the United States, funneled through its Pakistani ally, had captured power in the vacuum left by the previous generation of proxy rulers, those great and good "freedom fighter" friends of Ronald Reagan and the Iran-Contra cabal. They were, we recall, the putatively Islamist cutthroat desperados of the *mujahidin.*

Iconoclasm was news again. Front page, prime-time news. As the bearded, turbaned alumni of Pakistani seminaries trained their howitzers on the statues at Bamyian, a chorus of earnest protest welled up. Intellectuals fired off anguished petitions, UN officials issued pronouncements, the government of India offered to purchase outright and transfer the monuments to Indian soil, Muslim leaders condemned what they termed, accurately in the event, a perversion of Islam.

"You will pay to save the statues," the Taliban leadership chided their critics, many of whom had not disdained to discuss possible pipeline projects with them. "But you will not pay to feed our starving people." No offer was forthcoming, nor would it be. Down came the Buddhas in billows of dust, completing the work begun by British troops who had used them for target practice more than 125 years earlier. Who could have doubted, at that moment, that the poor and dismal Taliban, having outlived their usefulness, would soon follow.

But, in the minds of some Islamists of a breed as modern as the globalized economy and as ancient as the impulse for religious purity, the work begun by the Taliban had yet to be completed. There were plenty of idols still to be smashed, and they were of another order altogether. Opinions differed, of course, as to the exact nature of those idols and on the precise means by which they might be brought low.

That was before September 11, 2001.

On that day another pair of great idols came crashing to earth in a series of apocalyptic explosions. No longer was iconoclasm merely a theoretical issue. It was to be a matter of life and death, perhaps of societies, perhaps of worlds. Suddenly, there was a new urgency in writing of, and in attempting to understand, events that took place not today—there would be a string of hastily-written journalistic accounts of the mysteries of Usama bin Laden and his al-Qaʿida network, of Jihadism and terrorism, of Islamic "fundamentalism" —but on a day almost one thousand three hundred years ago. The mentalities that created those cataclysmic events, and the profound societal and spiritual currents that reflect and express them, were no longer a forgotten page in a crumbling history book. They were, and would be for a suddenly unforesee-able future, bodied forth by living actors on a bloody stage.

Just how bloody began to be revealed with the American punitive expedition against Afghanistan. That country had been identified as host and refuge to the men designated as terrorists who had struck down the twin World Trade Center towers and breached the walls of the Pentagon, supreme icons of American economic, cultural and military domination. Just how brutal, overwhelming and relentless this American retaliation was to become would be demonstrated by the *Blitzkrieg* invasion and the ensuing eradication of the cultural heritage of Iraq. This act of rapine was meant to demonstrate the fate that lay in wait for all those who might be seen, or dare to consider themselves, as a countervailing force against the current world order as the "coalition of the willing" imagined it.

This military occupation of an essential segment of the Arab and Islamic heartland was to be more than retribution, more than the modern-day equivalent of gunboat diplomacy or the classic punitive expedition, more even than the ambition to control of Iraq's vast petroleum reserves, though it partook of all these things. It was to be the end of the Sykes-Picot geopolitical architecture that had been created behind closed doors in 1916 and certified at Versailles, and the first step in a thorough re-ordering of the existing international (read West-imposed) order in the Middle East.

Viewed as a discrete event, the end of the Sykes-Picot system would be as welcome as the fall of Saddam Hussein al-Tikriti's wretched and despotic house, and as the fall of each of the Western vassals created by the final liquidation of the Ottoman State in 1918. Its geopolitical successor regime, the contours of which are currently being drawn up behind closed doors in Washington, London and Tel Aviv, can even now be apprehended not only as an attempt to consolidate Western domination over the Arab heartland, but to go far beyond.

The conquest of Iraq may prove to have been the opening shot in a more ambitious campaign to eliminate Islam as the last, almost adamantine obstacle to the triumphal march of the American Empire, in its self-appointed role as champion of the Christian West, toward world hegemony, the process that is to confer on globalization its ultimate and singular meaning.

* * *

THE ORIGINAL ATTEMPT TO SUPPRESS the creation and worship of images had been as daring as it was unprecedented: to transform, not by alchemy but by political fiat, human perception of the divine. Of that attempt—whatever it may have been—a single word survives: *iconoclast.*

Today the term enjoys a raffish, pseudo-rebellious half-life of its own, remote to the farthest extremity of estrangement from its original context. In present-day parlance "iconoclast" denotes that person who dares to breech convention, to strike out in original and innovative ways, who challenges established beliefs and systems. One finds the term applied indiscriminately to computer graphics designers, to contemporary dancers and multi-media performance artists, to writers with a fondness for literary transgression, and to the more daring of fusion cuisine chefs.

Autres temps, autres moeurs. What once struck fear into the sanctimonious and shocked the pious now, in an age of speed, merely titillates or intrigues. What once proposed a fundamental re-ordering of the relation between depiction and the depicted now promises a ruthless rhetorical slash-and-burn metaphorically comparable to the plunder of the biosphere. Of the prototypical meaning—the smashing of religious images—only the notion of challenge to orthodoxy remains, and even it is skewed.

For more than a century, from 717 to 867, an iconoclast dynasty held sway in Constantinople. Hardly could that dynasty have been defined as a bold challenger. *It* was the imperial establishment of its day. And yet, in its attempt to reshape dogma, the Isaurian Dynasty had thrown down the gravest of challenges before a religious establishment that clung fast to both its ideological dominance and to its worldly prerogatives.

This, however, was not the only paradox.

The City—as Constantinople was then known, as if there were no other—though coveted by would-be contenders for domination of the world that centered on the Mediterranean, held fast to its position as the political, military and cultural power against which all others would measure themselves in might, influence and opulence. That it did so, argue some scholars, could be attributed to the iconoclasts who, by subverting the religious orthodoxy of its day, saved the empire.

That the iconoclasts bequeathed little to posterity but the enmity and opprobrium of those who were ultimately to overcome them was not entirely their fault. To the vanquished, who had smashed heads as well as images, the victors applied an even more violent corrective: eradication as total as it was relentless. Of course there could not have been an iconoclast iconographic tradition to smash in revenge for the indignities which had been visited upon holy pictures. The iconoclasts had done their work too well.

In the absence of pictures, their texts were expunged, their books burned in the fires of anathema, their names smeared with the excrement of revenge. The grim, baleful eyes of Christ Pantocrator that glared down from the domes of

Orthodox basilicas would pierce their souls to the depths, then send them hurtling into eternal hellfire. One can almost hear the accompanying throaty and sanctimonious chorus of amens chanted by a coven of unctuous, self-satisfied archimandrites straight out of a novel by Nikos Kazantzakis.

For, with the victorious return of images, the sacred could again be depicted, and was with a vengeance. And, as the iconoclasts had rightly intuited, the depiction ultimately became the thing it purported to depict. It became once more the object of veneration, and the medium for framing perception.

The history of the iconoclast conflict is the distillation of victor's justice. If I hoped to reconstitute the logic of the perpetrators of the war of the images that shook and redefined Christianity as no other internal conflict before or since, I would have to fall back upon the polemics of those who prevailed. I would have to intuit the theological subtlety and force of the iconoclast argument from the virulence of the polemics of those who denounced and overcame it. Ultimately, I would have to navigate waters for which all charts have vanished, with nothing but the rusty astrolabe of conjecture to guide me.

As I wandered deeper into my subject, I encountered the contemporary critical discourse on iconoclasm. Before me it laid bare a historical field rich in cultural collision, one in which multi-layered complexity overwhelms anything so simple as a cause and effect relationship, so innocent as linear reasoning; one in which theological imperatives overweigh historical evidence that in the end seems little more tangible than heat haze.

Upon this field not only complexity was to be found. As with any historical canvas, it proved to be a mirror as well, in which are reflected the doctrinal imperatives or the hidden desires of pseudo-exegetes, the barely veiled anathemas which even today thrust the upstart image fighters—εικονομαχοι, as the Greeks call them—deeper into damnation and oblivion, supposing the two to be equivalent.

Orthodox obfuscation of all that smacked of iconoclasm was only a first obstacle to my inquiry. Beyond it lay a second one, a perspective that, though "objective" in a narrow sense, posited the singular viewpoint of the religious victors and their lay acolytes as the invisible field, a glaucous fog of totalitarian ideology. And in this sense, it bore an uncanny resemblance with our own image-intoxicated age where the traffic in and of depiction is increasingly ordered by an international directorate of transnational conglomerates expanding like mutant viruses.

These were some of the things that had originally conspired to draw me to an investigation of the iconoclast conflict, to the war of the images that shook the Mediterranean world of 1,300 years ago. I confess as well to an odd and near life-long fascination for the contrariness of the movement's instigators, for their appeal to a spiritual purity unsullied by representation, for their fierce literality, and their strangely antique post-modernity.

What most engaged my curiosity was the enmity of the victors, the same sleek, unctuous and self-satisfied Orthodox establishment that was, centuries later, to be challenged by the revolutionary Zealot movement in Byzantine Salonica. These, we recall, were hard-headed men (and perhaps women) who resented the wealth and power of the monastic establishment, and who, for a few short years, established an egalitarian regime in the Empire's second city.

I was also drawn to the iconoclasts and their movement because so little is known about them. How was I to construct a credible account of more than a century of acute ideological, religious and social strife when almost all primary sources had been effaced, shrouded in the ground mist of historical conjecture, archeological uncertainty and textual ambiguity? When the only reference to the iconoclast theologians was to be found in the doctrinal, ritual denunciation of them by the Orthodox victors?

To the charge of absurdity in attempting to understand a movement buried so deeply in the past as to be beyond disinterment, I reply: precisely because it is impossible, it must be done. Nothing I discovered in Syria made the task any less impossible. But as I progressed, the imperative became even greater.

But simply understanding from the outside was not enough. Increasingly, I found myself seeking to grasp and to describe the contours of their world not from the historical and geographical perspective of the Westerner—though that is what I am. No, I had to attempt to enter the mindset of the iconoclasts, and to do so from an easterly direction.

* * *

SINCE THE NAPOLEONIC INVASION of Egypt in 1798, the military, social and cultural equivalent of hijacked aircraft had been impacting on the region we eurocentrically label the Middle East. Time and again they struck, in wrenching, near-freeze-frame slow motion, out of a clear sky. Bonaparte, the man who would share France's militant version of the Enlightenment with the world, whether the world wanted it or not, brought with him heavily-armed, technologically advanced forces that crushed Cairo's Mamluke defenders at the Battle of the Pyramids. He likewise brought the instruments of scientific and cultural inquiry, the learned orientalists, tomb robbers and asset strippers who have ever since been a constant in the Western project.

In the post-Napoleonic Orient, resistance to military occupation flared first in France's North African colonies, later in British-ruled Egypt and the Sudan, and ultimately, in the post-Sykes-Picot regime of League of Nations mandates. The Syrian patriots who opposed their French overlords, the Iraqis and Palestinians who sought to resist their British tutors, they all directed their efforts to expelling the foreign presence.

These efforts would come to be called "terrorism," a practice that can boast a fine and noble pedigree of unequal combat and sacrifice.

It was and remains a practice available to all. Militant Zionist gangs used it to accede to power in 1948, when Lord Balfour's promise of a national home-land for the Jewish people in Palestine metamorphosed into the state of Israel. It was only a matter of time before Palestinian response to the *naqbah*, as this catastrophe is known in Arabic, would be dismissed as terrorism. As would that of Lebanon in the aftermath of Israel's 1982 invasion and sub-contracted massacre of Palestinian refugees in the Sabra and Chatilla camps, and later, in the struggle of Hizbullah to expel the forces of occupation.

Over time, subtleties of meaning had fallen away. The right of occupied populations to resist was subsumed into an absolute scheme that offered either total submission or total stigmatization. To paraphrase George W. Bush's "You are either with us, or with the terrorists," terrorism would henceforth be defined as all action, speech and thought that opposes United States and, secondarily, Israeli, British and French interests.

The same conceptual framing device proved useful to the Arab regimes that grew under the tutelage of Western political and economic preeminence, clustered as they were around access to and control of oil, trade routes and geopolitical sensitivities. As franchisees and guarantors, theirs was not a policy of nuance. Resistance to these Western-sponsored entities, likewise cast as terrorism, could only have a fatal outcome.

Within a constellation of states defined by political, social and economic fealty to the West and to its interests, counteractive ideological vectors arose. Roughly classified, they were of two kinds. The first sought salvation within the Western tradition itself. Such were the socialists, the Communists and the hybrid variants that flourished in the region after World War II, not to mention the out-and-out westernizers. The Arab Party of Rebirth, known as the Baath, was the outstanding paradigm of the attempt to co-opt Westernism, recruit it to the national cause, and wield it as a weapon. Less than twenty-five years after its founding, the Baath had seized power in both Syria and Iraq, in the name of a curious amalgam of Arab nationalism and pro-forma cultural

Islam, a twin-headed monster that bore the names of Hafiz al-Asad and Saddam Hussein.

Earlier, generations of Muslim thinkers, both from among the *ulama* and the non-clerical elites, had pondered the ways in which the Islamic heartland could grasp the calamity that had befallen it. Powerful movements like the *Ikhwan al-Muslimin*—the Muslim Brothers—challenged for power in Egypt, fought the Zionists in Palestine in 1948, and went down to crushing defeat in the 1982 Hama uprising in Syria. They too would be branded as terrorists and exterminated, in Egypt with the direct, on-the-ground assistance of Kermit Roosevelt of the CIA.

Intellectuals like Saïd Qutb gave resonance to the ideal of a recaptured proto-Islamic purity, and wrote of a present that he defined as a new *jahiliyah*, the "time of ignorance" during which Arabia had no dispensation, no inspired prophet, no revealed book.[1] Here was a situation rife with idols to be overturned, as 'Ali ibn-abi-Talib had done when he climbed atop the shoulders of his father-in-law Muhammad and swept the statues from atop the Ka'aba, Islam's holy of holies.

Terrorism, as my work progressed, seemed increasingly to be conflated with the struggle to define, then overturn idols, the 'war' against it, to restoring, re-installing and protecting them.

* * *

THE ANCIENT CITIES OF DAMASCUS AND ALEPPO utter conflicting claims to be the oldest continuously inhabited settlements in the world. At their cores, in the narrow streets that wind between high mud-plaster walls to open unexpectedly onto tiny squares, broader thoroughfares and teeming *suqs*, the texture of life cannot be entirely unlike that of, say, three thousand, or one thousand four hundred, or two hundred years ago. Timelessness hangs in the still air like the ever-present dust.

One balmy spring night I and two Damascene companions, the novelist Ammar Abdulhamid and the poet Ma'an Abdulsalam, made our way deep into the labyrinthine network of the Old City. Ammar was somewhat of an icono-clast: American-educated, a man with a quizzical eye and a mordant sense of humor. He had invited me to visit the place where he and a few friends would soon be celebrating his thirty-fifth birthday. Ma'an, the free-thinking son of a religious scholar from the traditional neighborhood of Salihiyah, on the lower slopes of Mount Qassiun, knew the caretaker, a secularist Alawite.

The door we had halted before was low-linteled and quite unremarkable, a venerable wooden door like the hundreds one passes in the old precinct, with a tarnished brass knocker in the shape of a hand. Just as Ma'an knocked, a man carrying a plastic bag came up to us and greeted him, key in hand. He was the caretaker whom we sought.

We followed him through the door, stooping, into a shadow-filled space open to the sky. In the darkness I could hear the tinkle of falling water. The scent of jasmine hung in the air. Damascus, treated by the Baath Party hierarchy as a conquered city, has relatively little of the light pollution that accompanies urban development. An unexpected benefit, the stars winked high above. The moon was late.

The caretaker slipped through another doorway and with the click of a switch dim lights flickered on. We were indeed in a small courtyard. Thickets of flowering jasmine lined the walls; water trickled from the spigot of a small wall fountain.

"Don't you think this space is a bit cramped?" Ammar asked me. From the touch of archness in his voice, the rhetorical flourish, I intuited that more was to come.

Before I could answer, he led us through another portal. Again the only source of illumination was the starry firmament, and a low cloud of dust-refracted light that seemed to hover above the surrounding rooftops. By now, my eyes had grown accustomed to the darkness, and my skin to the expanded space that we now found ourselves in, to the warmth still radiating up from the paving stones. Again, lights flicked on in our passage.

We were in another courtyard, a larger one with a decoratively inlaid floor, a central fountain, and what appeared to be orange trees. They, and the softness of the air combined to remind me of the ceremonial tomb of the Persian poet Ha'fez, in Shiraz, on a December night long ago.

"This is better, don't you think?" said Ammar.

It was indeed, I replied.

"But it still may be a bit cramped."

So saying, he led us across the courtyard and through another gateway. We emerged into a broad space, broader than a courtyard. On its periphery I could make out arcaded balconies and staircases and the delicate tracery of fretted balustrades. Then, as I turned my head, I saw the dome of the Umayyad Mosque floating above the rooftops, brilliantly, breathtakingly illuminated against the dark bulk of Jabal Qassiun, the mountain that looms over the city, and against the purple sky thick with stars.

"Now, this is more like it," chuckled my guide.

The space could accommodate hundreds, with room to spare.

My friend was indeed a popular man, and I an amused and willing dupe.

"This is the Maktab al-Anbar," Ma'an explained. "It was built by a rich Jewish merchant who lost it gambling. Later, it was turned into the first secular school in Syria."

Though I did not realize it at the time, the nocturnal visit to the Maktab al-Anbar in the company of my two friends had implanted in me what would become the conceptual germ of the book that I had come to Syria to write. Almost eighteen months later, at the close of a bitter, rainy winter afternoon, as my wife Ingeborg and I took coffee in the lobby of the Beit al-Wakil, a traditional hotel in Aleppo, the shape of the book jelled at last.

As you wander through the labyrinth of Syria's ancient cities, your footsteps carry you past high walls of stone or sunbaked mud. Sometimes, far overhead, tufts of leaves are visible, or tendrils of vine. But the flatness and anonymity of the walls conceal all else. Portals, low-hanging doors made of heavy timbers fixed with iron bolts, are set into these walls at irregular intervals. Like the walls, they reveal nothing of what lies behind them.

But when you insert the key in the rusty lock, push one of these doors ajar and step through, bending low, you enter into a self-contained world that replicates, in symbolic miniature, the great world without. The entrance may be simple or it may be complex, it may open directly onto a broad inner court or a narrow antechamber; the interior spaces may be vast, open to the sky, or minuscule and claustrophobic, the vegetation rich or meagre; the structures that give onto the central court may be luxurious or humble; there may be hidden passageways.

Each space has its own particular story to tell, a story inscribed on the building and paving stones, in the melodious tinkle of water and in the whispering of leaves in a gentle updraft; in the shifting patterns of sunlight and shadow and in the exquisitely wrought decorative elements, the exacting geometric patterns of Damascene inlaid stone-work, the humble quotidian objects; of fleeting human presence, or absence. Each space is ramified, turns in upon itself, unfolds and leads you deeper and deeper, as though you are making your way through a mirrored hall of indeterminate depth and unmeasurable dimension, a succession of rooms and dependencies whose ultimate depth seems to be that of time.

As you read this book, imagine yourself wandering between high blank walls, then stepping through a succession of ancient doors and into interior spaces open to the sky. Imagine each of these interior spaces as narratives, each one branching, multi-faceted and inconclusive like the tales told by a story teller in a traditional Syrian tea house—and yet linked by a common thread. Follow me, for as you do you will be exploring the city and the civilization that gave birth to iconoclasm, to Islam before Islam, and to the Islamic Empire born of the first encounter between Christianity and the dispensation of Muhammad.

Damascus–Montréal, July 2003

0 50 100 km

Tigris

TURKEY

• Adana

Mediterranean Sea

Antioch

• Aleppo

• al-Raqqah

Lattakia

• Siffin

• al-Rusafa

• al-Qardaha

Jabal al-Nusayiriyah

al-Sheikh Badr

Misyaf

• Hama • Salamiyah

Krac des Chevaliers

• Homs

Orontes (al-Asi)

• Palmyra

Euphrates

LEBANON

• Damascus

Jabal al-Arab

IRAQ

• Yarmuk

• Suweida

ISRAEL

JORDAN

PALESTINE

SAUDI ARABIA

Syria

Map by Anthony Reed

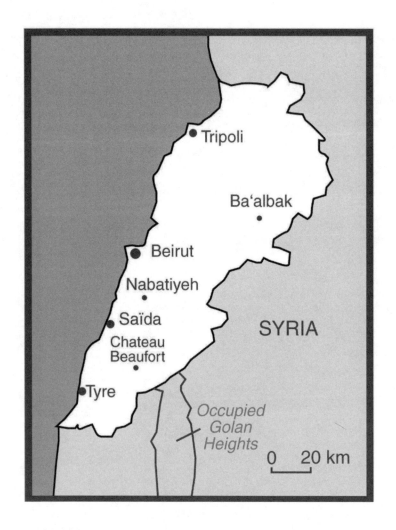

Tripoli

Ba'albak

Beirut

Nabatiyeh

Saïda

Chateau
Beaufort

Tyre

SYRIA

*Occupied
Golan
Heights*

0   20 km

Lebanon

Map by Anthony Reed

1

Farewell, Syria

CRUMBLED RAMPARTS THAT ONCE GUARDED a city older than history, demolished by the battering rams of time and war, plowed under by modernity, reduced in the end to a state of virtuality, the walls of Damascus are no more. Before them civilizations had met and clashed. If the past is a reliable indicator, they are likely to do so again.

I had come to Syria on a wide-ranging investigation into the first, fateful encounter between nascent Islam and the Christian world, and into their impact upon each other. That impact, both peaceful and violent, begun at the feet of these virtual walls, continues up until this day and now threatens the cradle of civilization itself.

The encounter, I believed, would illuminate the ultimate goal of my self-ascribed mission to Syria: to penetrate the mystery of the iconoclasts, the semi-legendary, all-but-forgotten icon smashers of Byzantine antiquity. I was convinced there was more to them and their movement than an outburst of pent-up theological frustration. I'd caught the scent of cultural dialogue as armed conflict—or was it vice versa—and traced it to Damascus. Now, at last, I was here to put my hunch to the test.

Every evening at sunset thousands of birds rise from the trees in the garden of the National Museum, wheeling and chattering in the darkening sky. That their flight coincides with the evening call to prayer from the minaret of the Teqqiyah al-Suleymaniyah mosque next door was no coincidence. Surely they are driven aloft by the voice of the aged muezzin, which sounded like the creaking of a rusty water pump.

The mosque, built by the Ottomans who ruled Syria for four centuries, had included within its perimeter a Sufi lodge. Its original residents would have been members of the Bekhtashi dervish order that provided spiritual guidance to the elite Janissary corps, the shock troops of the Ottoman army. Though they, like Syria's erstwhile Ottoman overlords, have long since vanished, there are parallels between them and the current tenants, the Syrian Armed Forces. Like the Bekhtashis, the minority Alawite sect that seized control of Syria forty years ago and rules it today through the Baath Party regime owes its pre-eminence to the art of arms, and to its ability to find shelter in the shadowy corners of the house of Islam, in the darkest nooks and crannies of dissimulation. Appropriately, the cells and garden have been transformed by the regime into a military museum.

Beneath the scraggly pine, eucalyptus and acacia trees of the compound are displayed rusting pieces of military hardware: trackless vehicles, cannons, tanks, even some samples of the Russian-built combat aircraft that served long and ineffectively in the country's air force. In one far wing of the museum, forlorn as a holy relic abandoned by the faithful, is displayed the re-entry capsule in which Syria's only cosmonaut—the Arab world's first man in space—successfully returned from his orbit about the earth.

It was in this garden that I found myself strolling among the military relics one morning in early winter, a year before captured civilian airliners had been flown into the World Trade Center and the Pentagon, a year before evil axes and who's next lists had been officially promulgated in Washington. One of the weapons, I noted on an explanatory signboard, was a French-made howitzer "used under the command of General Gouraud in Maysaloun Battle in 1920, against Syrian forces, on which was written 'victoire' or victory, which was for the Syrians in 1945."

General Henri Gouraud, the devout Catholic who belonged to the "whiff of grapeshot" school of pacification that the French had perfected in the course of their North African mission *civilisatrice* and hoped to apply to Syria, had cut down the small band of patriots led by Yussef al-Amzeh at the village of Maysalun, in the Barada gorge southwest of Damascus. The shots fired there in defeat are considered the first in the twenty five-year campaign to rid Syria of the French mandatory authority, and the men who died there the first of the martyrs in the long, bitter fight for an independence. The fight was all the more remarkable in that it came to a region that had existed as a crossroads of religion and culture almost as long as culture and religion could be said to have existed, had known many masters, worshipped many religions, but had never been a nation in the contemporary sense.

Inside the museum, the showcases were crammed pell-mell with pistols, swords, muskets and regimental banners; burned-out light bulbs had not been replaced. Everywhere, a thick layer of dust smudged by finger- and nose-prints coated the glass. Poorly typed English translations of the Arabic explanatory text had been placed—or had fallen—in such as way as to render them unreadable or invisible. Some exhibits were disintegrating outright; photographs had come unpinned, drooped or curled; documents were yellowed and crumbling

One of the halls housed a series of crude historical dioramas that looked to be made of cardboard and plasticine. Though they purported to demonstrate the glorious continuity of Syrian arms, their message was more complex, more politically charged.

Beneath one three-dimensional exhibit displaying a section of the former city walls, I read a description of General Khalid ibn-al-Walid's defeat of Theodore, brother of the Byzantine Emperor Heraclius, at the battle of Yarmuk. Following his victory, Khalid camped before Damascus. His forces used catapults, trébuchets, manganels and other siege engines to fling "iron, fire and naphtha" against the city's defensive perimeter. Then, "in one night they bridged the moat, scaled the walls and took the Byzantines by surprise."

The taking of Damascus, concludes the caption, was "a decisive step in the conquest of the Near East and the march westward." This much was true: the fall of the city removed the greatest obstacle to the spread of Islam. And while some sections may have resisted, other parts—along with most of the Syrian hinterland—fell to the compact, fierce and God-driven armies of Islam like a ripe fig into a wide-open mouth. Much more had happened in front of the walls, I was soon to learn, than the exhibit cared—or dared?—to let on.

The flimsy diorama possessed some merit in that it presented the names of the two protagonists whose careers intersected and whose armies clashed on the field of battle for the soul of a land and, though they did not know it, for the shape of their world: Heraclius the Byzantine Emperor, and Commander Khalid ibn-al-Walid, the "Sword of Allah." It was an encounter that was to be repeated symbolically a century later, culturally, and not militarily, when another Byzantine ruler, this one of Syrian origin, attempted to appropriate the conceptual tools of Islam to purify Christianity of its accumulated residue of Hellenic paganism, the better to defend it. To Syrianize it, in a word. His bold action would launch the century-long Iconoclast conflict.

* * *

DR. BASHIR ZUHRI, chief curator of the National Museum, is one of those engaging polymaths of a certain age who populate the Syrian cultural establishment. Fluent in French or English and often both, he and other men and women like him provide a cultivated interface between the foreign visitor and the harsher, inward-leaning, some might say cruel countenance the regime reserves for its subjects.

We met in his office just off the Museum's main entrance. Syria is hardly a prime tourist destination, and the hordes of camera-wielding cultural consumers that one might encounter in Egypt or Jordan are unlikely to descend upon Damascus any day soon. The atmosphere at the ticket-office *cum* souvenir shop was relaxed. When I presented myself one bright winter morning for the appointment arranged for me by the nearby Ministry of Tourism, there was nary a luxury motor coach in sight. The museum's grounds keepers were sweeping the night's bird droppings from the paths among the outdoor exhibits with all deliberate speed. The ticket-taker/souvenir salesman slid from behind his counter and guided me behind the massive iron gates to Dr. Zuhri's door.

Nothing about the wiry, spritely man with whom I spent several pleasurable hours sipping Arab coffee laced with cardamon, nibbling chocolate candies and chatting suggested anything less than sincere hospitality. His forty-year tenure at the Museum would have provided him with an ideal vantage point from which to view, and to assimilate, the vicissitudes of Syrian cultural politics, the hierarchical order of the dignitaries who passed through the gate and the occasional foreign cultural delegation.

Over the course of our discussions Dr. Zuhri became the first but not the only of many Syrian interlocutors to lay before me a more nuanced view, both of the manner in which Christianity had been supplanted by Islam, and of how both religions could trace their origins to the social and cultural history of Syria.

"The Syrians of Damascus opened wide the Bab al-Sharqi—the East Gate—to Islam," he told me, with a broad, reassuring smile. "The Byzantines had behaved cruelly toward them because of their monophysite beliefs. So when the forces of Islam came, people experienced it as a liberation from the Byzantine yoke."

Dr. Zuhri's comment set my amateur investigator's pulse throbbing. This was not the message conveyed in the crude diorama I had seen next door.

The monophysites of whom he spoke were Christian heretics who refused to accept the Church dogma of the dual nature of Christ as both God and man, or even that of a single divine nature. They were Syrian, and they had been legion. Dr. Zuhri was not a Christian, and even less a theologian. The arcana of Ecumenical Council debate and the infinite refinement of Byzantine Christology concerned him only slightly more than a whit. But as a broad-minded Muslim, and, I intuited, perhaps a Sufi, he was sensitive to one of Christianity's most acute dilemmas: the nature of its Prophet/Messiah.

Among the hunches that had brought me to Damascus was that disaffection among the Christian populations of the East, particularly in Syria, had been one of the prime driving forces not only behind the rise of Islam, but behind the battle to banish images from churches that climaxed in the Iconoclast conflict that broke out a century after the fall of Damascus to Islam. It was not an interpretation generally encountered in the literature.

One of the central articles of faith of Christianity, articulated in the Gospel according to Saint John, posits Christ as the Word made flesh, as God assuming the attributes of the physical world and becoming thus accessible to the apprehension of the senses and ultimately, to depiction. Inconceivable to the Jews, for whom the creation of images would mean imitating God, the doctrine of the incarnation troubled the Christians of Syria, as it would repel the followers of Muhammad for whom it constituted nothing less than *shirk*, idol worship.

As Dr. Zuhri explained it, Byzantium's failure to hold its Syrian provinces could be traced to Christianity's inability to resolve the conundrum. "When Islam appeared, the Christian population believed that it was a new Christian doctrine. Some time was to pass before they discovered that it was truly a new faith."

More than the apparent reversal of the divine order inherited from Abraham that Christianity seemed to represent was at issue. Within a social context structured in what could be described as exclusively doctrinal terms, human concerns and desires—including the timeless reflex of resistance to tyranny—found expression in them.

"When there are grave problems in a society, the imagination of the people creates a savior," he told me. "At that time, a time of oppression, expectations were great indeed. In Islam, people found what they had been yearning for. Transmitting the new faith was easy. There had always been communication between the Arabs of Syria and those of the Arabian peninsula."

The absolute authority that can lead only to oppression has its inconveniences. Byzantium's problems in Syria had come to be embodied in the person of Heraclius, a seditionist who seized power in 610 and instituted a new dynasty[2] which was to endure until the rise of Leo III the Isaurian—and iconoclast—in 717. Heraclius was, according to some historians a model ruler who had proclaimed that "power must shine more in love than in terror."[3]

Tell that to the Syrians, one is tempted to say. But I am getting ahead of myself. Let us instead stroll through this complex but essential digression at a leisurely pace. Precipitation is, after all, the enemy of reflection.

Determined to cast himself as a second Alexander, Heraclius undertook to expel the Persian Sassanids from the lands of Syria. Where the Macedonian could claim that he had marched eastward to avenge the Persian invasion of Greece and the affront to an Athenian democracy for which he cared little, Heraclius couched his campaigns in the language of crusade. His was a crusade that combined Christianity and Hellenism, the twin seals of Byzantium.

Politically, it had few long-term prospects in the Syrian lands.

These had migrated from Roman to Byzantine rule when Constantinople supplanted Rome as seat of the world empire and became its cultural heart. The Sassanids, not adverse to invoking their own imperial legacy, and that of their Achaemenid predecessors in particular, had marched westward in an expansionist frame of mind.

First they took Antioch, then Damascus in 611, one year after the new emperor's seizure of power.[4] Constantinople could ill afford to forfeit its eastern territories, least of all to its main contender for domination of the Eastern Mediterranean, the area that then as today stood for the "world."

The towering indignity was the capture and sack of Jerusalem three years later, after which the Persians absconded with the remains of the Holy Cross, perhaps the most precious relic in Christendom. To make matters worse, the massacre of the city's Christian population by the Zoroastrian Persians was aided and abetted by the Jews. The practitioners of disincarnate monotheism could hardly be blamed for their unforgiving mood after the calamity of witnessing their greatest false messiah, Jesus of Nazareth, transformed into the focus of a new and aggressively expanding faith.

To the lists of names, dates and battles and betrayals that constitute the ledger book of conventional history we must now add another factor, this one unquantifiable, tainted by legend, calumny, fabulation, hearsay and superstition: that of belief. Ever since Christianity had supplanted the rich variety of pagan and semi-pagan dispensations that flourished in the bustling commercial towns, desert caravan stops and harbors of the Eastern Mediterranean and Mesopotamia, it had hewn in these parts to a interpretation of religion devoid of divine incarnation and free of depiction, if for no other reason than to set itself apart from the polytheist creeds that swarmed about it.

So said my Syrian friends and informants. Dr. Zuhri had been first among them, but he would be far from the last.

Schematically put, the notion that Christ was not possessed of two natures had two competing, mutually exclusive interpretations that had nonetheless dovetailed in the popular mind into an oppositionist, or purist position. On the one hand, the followers of a certain Nestorius of Antioch believed that the Virgin Mary must be considered not the "Mother of God" but the "Mother of a man." This meant that Christ could not have incarnated God, could not have been the Word made flesh. For all its apparent complexity, the distinction would prove to be a crucial one in creating the public mind-set in which iconoclasm could emerge and prosper.

On the other, the monophysites (from the Greek *mono*, one, and *physis*, nature) held that Jesus Christ possessed but one nature, and that nature was divine. Either way he was not, and could not, be both.

The Persians had early on recognized the usefulness to their interests of sheltering and fostering the Nestorians. They, under the protection of eagle-winged deity Ahura Mazda, were able to expand far into Central Asia and India. It was hardly surprising that for the monophysites, the Persian conquest—the sack of Jerusalem notwithstanding—brought relief from the centralized religious tyranny of Constantinople.

As the third decade of the seventh century opened, Heraclius's reduced dominion had not only suffered a catastrophic amputation of territory, it was in danger of losing the proverbial battle for the hearts and minds of its subjects.

There is an aching familiarity, that of eternal recurrence, to the story. Heraclius, an able administrator and dynamic commander, organized the counterattack, routed and dispersed the Persians in classic set-piece engagements, killed the Shah Khosrow Parviz, and returned the Holy Cross to Jerusalem. To climax his triumph he declared himself Basileus. Greek, the language in which the Bible had been given definitive written form, had finally replaced the Latin title of imperator.

The triumph was as hollow as the victory was short-lived. Within less than a decade the emissaries sent by an obscure Prophet operating in the wilds of the Arabian Peninsula had infiltrated his Syrian dominions. Arab forces dared to occupy Damascus. It was not to be long before Heraclius would become the greatest victim of his triumph.

Simultaneously, he had become the principal though unintended ally of the Arabs, and of Islam. Fatally weakened by the Byzantine wars, the Persians could offer no significant resistance to the lightening campaigns of Sa'd Ibn-abi-Waqqas, one of the Companions to whom the Prophet had promised Paradise in recognition of his bravery.[5] It took but fifteen years for his ragtag troops to bring what had once been mighty imperial Iran under Muslim Arab domination.

Overextended, exhausted, and yet swaggering and arrogant in their short-lived victory, the Byzantines could not parry the double-pronged thrusts of Islam. The two—social/religious, and military—converged at Damascus in February, 635, and would reshape the ancient city as Islam was soon to be reshaped by it.

Dr. Zuhri's version of the fall of Damascus—or of its accession under Islam to the rank of dominant city of the Mediterranean world—was schematic of course. As was the primitive diorama in the Military Museum which it contradicted. But their very schematic nature had the virtue of revealing the clank and hiss of the primitive mechanisms at work beneath the gloss of scholarly historiography.

The siege lasted for six months. Commander Khalid ibn-al-Walid would have had ample opportunity to reflect upon the steadfastness and courage of the defenders. While his forces kept up the military pressure attitudes in both camps were shifting. Alongside war, politics.

Though we cannot date with precision Khalid's master stroke, it would have come toward the end of the siege. The Byzantine garrison had fled, supplies were almost spent, the citizens were on their own. The months spent before the city walls must have also taken their toll on the Muslim commander's troops, more at home in the hard-riding cut and thrust of mobile warfare in the open field. In a message to the citizens, he drafted a document which would become a model for conquering Islam's arrangements with the cities of Syria and Palestine:

> In the name of Allah, the compassionate, the merciful. This is what Khalid ibn-al-Walid would grant to the inhabitants of Damascus if he enters therein: he promises to give them security for their lives, property and churches. Their city shall not be demolished, neither shall any Muslim be quartered in their houses. Thereunto we give to them the pact of Allah and the protection of His Prophet, the caliphs and the believers. So long as they pay the poll tax, nothing but good shall befall them.[6]

According to legend, among those who led the delegation of welcome that threw open the gates at Bab Sharqi in early September, 635, was the financial controller for the Byzantine administration, a certain Mansur ibn-Sarjun, Sergius in Greek. A descendant of his would, as John Damascene, emerge as one of the most eloquent defenders of sacred images while at the same time remaining among the most faithful servants of the caliphal establishment.

We cannot read onto the past the approximate knowledge of the present. There is little to indicate that the defenders saw their besiegers for what they were. For Christians of the day, Islam must have appeared as a another secessionist movement from Orthodoxy—or perhaps a militant monophysite sect—than the radically new and dynamic yet closely similar creed that it was.

Perhaps Heraclius realized that his cause was lost, perhaps he did not. He mustered his forces and placed them under the command of his brother Theodore. The decision was taken in the clarity that attends desperation. There could be no turning back. One year later, the two armies clashed.

On the plain near the banks of the Yarmuk River, amid the torrid heat and blowing dust, neither the psalmodies of the Byzantine clerics nor the presence of their Armenian and Christian Arab allies availed the empire's host of more than 50,000 men. In fact, as believers in the monophysite doctrine, the soldiers themselves may have been loathe to die for Byzantium. By the end of that calamitous day, what shreds of the Byzantine forces remained alive were fleeing in panic. The Emperor's brother had perished on the field of battle. Gazing upon the wreckage from his distant vantage point of Constantinople, Heraclius waxed elegiac: "Farewell, O Syria, and what an excellent country this is for the enemy."[7]

How excellent it was took only a short time for the land's new masters to capitalize upon. Damascus, its crown jewel, lay at the center of al-Ghuta, a verdant oasis watered by the Barada, the crystalline spring-fed stream that rises in the Anti-Lebanon a few kilometers to the northwest of the city. Its soil was rich and productive, its orchards bountiful, its summers hot and dry, but more moderate than either the furnaces of Mecca and Medina or the steamy infernos of southern Iraq.

True to his word, Khalid demolished no houses, and quartered no Muslims amongst the civilian population. He and his followers, upon entering the city, almost certainly proceeded along the Via Recta, the Street Called Straight, to its center point where stood the Basilica of St. John the Baptist. There, in a corner of the immense courtyard, facing southeast toward Mecca, he and his followers offered their prayers. Islam had come to Damascus. It was never to leave.

Several aspects of this account may be true. Some may be imagined or invented. As my stay in Damascus lengthened, and as I made the acquaintance of intellectuals, historians and men of religion, what seemed at first a straightforward matter of chronological accuracy was rapidly transformed into a multifaceted complex of conflicting perspectives, a kaleidoscope of political imperatives and differing histories. The stuff of legend, the greater truth.

Running through them was a hidden tension: the question of images, of depiction, of idols and in the unspoken and ultimate instance, of the nature of Christianity's namesake. They were, I had imagined when I first travelled to Syria, questions of a primarily historical and cultural order. By the time I had departed Damascus for the last time, they had become questions of immediate and violent pertinence.

* * *

DAMASCUS, ONE YEAR LATER.

Dr. Abdel Aziz Allun eases his venerable black Mercedes sedan beneath the acacia tree on the sidewalk on a sunlit hillside. We'd been introduced earlier that day by a colleague of his at Syrian State Television, where I'd been dispatched by the Information Ministry to follow up on my unconventional quest.

"I have just the man for you," said the colleague. "Let me call him right now."

One hour later I was sliding myself into the front seat of the Mercedes outside the entrance to State Television headquarters at Umawiyin Square. From there we headed up the Wadi Barada, past the tea houses that line the refuse-clogged channel, past the pharaonic presidential palace built to accommodate the singular immodesty of Hafiz al-Asad, the man whose likeness even in death—like an omnipresent idol—is never far from view in Syria.

The books that lined Dr. Allun's living room walls revealed a man of broad tastes with a leaning toward the visual arts, both Western and Islamic. As he set tiny cups of cardamon-scented Arabic coffee on the mother-of-pearl inlay table between us and opened a box of minuscule, buttery baklava I rapidly learned more. My host, a compact man in his mid-sixties with an expansive manner and an easy laugh, was a producer of cultural programs for Syrian Television, as well as a sometime lecturer with a lively interest in history. He had also been for several years the official interpreter to the president before giving up the job. The pursuit of art had proved the finer and perhaps less stressful goal.

"We are interested in criticizing the way history is written about Syria and the Arabs," he tells me with a smile that was designed to moderate the implied criticism of his words. This was not an unreasonable position for a regime that had cast itself as a front-line combatant in the struggle to rid the Arab world of the imprint of colonialism, and adopted nationalism as the weapon of choice. But the longer we chatted, the less he seemed bound by the predictable pan-Arabism of the Baath, the party in power, and the more an exponent of the idea of a supra-national Syrian identity antedating both the rise of the Arabs and the advent of Islam.

(This I would later come to recognize as one of the distinguishing features of the Syrian Social Nationalist Party, an organization that favored the creation of a Greater Syria which would include even Cyprus. I would not be so careless as to suggest that Dr. Allun had any connection with the semi-proscribed SSNP. Surely though, its Syrian supra-nationalism had appealed to intellectuals close to the regime upon the collapse of pan-Arabism that followed the crushing Arab defeat at the hands of Israel in the 1967 war.)

My meeting with Dr. Allun was a succinct introduction into the diversity of opinion that existed in the shadow of the semi-monolithic official ideology of the state. Unless it was a component of that ideology designed to reinforce it by creating the illusion of tolerance.

"If you ask me, to talk about Syria is to talk about civilization," he said.

By then I had already travelled extensively in what was once known as Greater Syria, from the abandoned desert city of al-Rusafa to the ruins of Halabiyah high above the banks of the Euphrates and to the lush Palmyra oasis; from the Citadel of Aleppo to Ugarit, from Ba'albak to Byblos in what is today Lebanon. No leap of imagination was needed to appreciate Dr. Allun's aphorism, and only slightly more effort to accept its premise. Here was a civilization that generated gods as others produced poets, and yet others, far more primitive, secreted strip malls, energy broker Ponzi rackets, media conglomerates, human cloning schemes and wars of aggression in the name of "freedom."

"Most of the gods that were worshipped in Arabia were engraved and sculpted in Syria," he told me. "Certainly, they never would have been accepted had there not been a relationship between Syria and the people of the desert."

"Mohammad, the Prophet of Islam, first encountered Nestorian Christianity in the person of the uncle of Khadija, his first wife," he added, as my ears perked up. The uncle, a certain Waraq ibn-Nawfal who was also a clergyman, blessed the union between the older, successful businesswoman and her studious, punctilious and gifted protégé, and gave her counsel when her husband first began to receive the divine revelation.

"Mohammad's opponents accused him of taking ideas from the Christians of Syria. He indeed took counsel from holy men, and studied the Old Testament. Then there was Salman al-Farsi, 'the Persian,' one of the earliest converts to Islam and one of the first among the companions. Salman had previously been a Zoroastrian priest, then a hermit in a Syrian monastery.

"The prime influences on Islam were Syrian. Those who were martyred in the famous Battle of the Ditch, at Medina (627 CE), were Syrians, not Ethiopians. That is to say, they were not Copts, but the followers of Syrian sects. In fact, their names were carved on the walls of the basilica of St. Sergius at al-Rusafa."

Those names are no longer visible on the walls of the al-Rusafa basilica, which time, wind and shifting desert sands have reduced to a skeleton of stone. I could attest to that. Sources differ on the origin of those who died in the engagement of the Ditch. Salman al-Farsi is viewed by the Alawite sect that rules Syria through the Baath Party as the third member of its apocryphal trinity. But when the message is that which we wish to hear, it beguiles the ear as the tiny sweetmeats that Dr. Allun has served as an accompaniment to the coffee do the palate. By now, the winter sun has swung high enough to shine in through the curtained window of the villa. From the garden comes the sound of birds chirping energetically.

The land has always prided itself on its immense cultural fecundity, and on its fierce resistance, he insists. "Syria has never been empty. There have always been people here, never a void. Our archeological remains span the entire cultural history of humankind. Some historians are obsessed with the immigration of tribes from Yemen and the Hijaz. But we should talk about Syrian influences in Arab lands, not the reverse."

Syria, in early Christian times, was a crucible of coexisting and contending faiths, he insists. "There were hundreds of temples for hundreds of religions. It was as if each caravan brought with it its own gods: Adonis, Azana, Targatis, Artemis, Zeus, Aflad, Mithra, Jupiter, and of course, the God of Christianity."

If this was the case, I asked, what had brought Syria, land of many Gods, so decisively into the orbit of Islam, pinnacle of monotheism? "Syrians had accepted Christianity over Judaism because of its emphasis on peace. Don't forget, it was the indigenous religion. The Byzantines were looked upon as hostile on account of their doctrinaire behavior. The Syrians, who had given Christianity its 'soldiers' felt betrayed by Byzantine domination. It is no mystery why they turned to Islam."

Syria had been the bitter battleground between the Sassanids and Byzantines. So immense had been the depredations, so great the turmoil, that the Syrians "were prepared to accept anyone who might bring them relief. So, when the Arabs arrived from the desert, their beliefs harked back to early Christianity, when Christ had no divine substance, had not yet been crucified and risen. Only the ruling establishment of the day, the Byzantines, believed in the divinity of Christ; almost certainly not the Syrians. When the Arab armies arrived, it was all over in a matter of weeks."

The telephone rang. Dr. Allun grunted assent, jotted down a name and an address, glanced at his watch. It was nearly noon.

We parted company on his doorstep, and I strolled down to the main street to catch a microbus back to the President's Bridge terminal. There, into the clamor, into the humdrum, grimy everyday world of workaday Damascus, I returned to my room along al-Barudi Street, just behind the Teqiyah al-Suleimaniyah. Booksellers had set out their wares directly on the sidewalk. On display were tattered German fashion magazines, ancient back issues of *Newsweek*, and piles of Arabic-language mathematics, chemistry and physics manuals, cookbooks and religious works.

As I passed the mosque, the midday call to prayer rang out. Ramadan had ended, and nothing at that moment seemed quite so appealing as a hot *felefel* sandwich washed down by a glass of foamy *ayran*, the tangy yogurt drink beloved of Syrians and Turks. Strolling down the acacia-shaded street of stationery stores and offset printing shops, I ordered my spartan fare at the corner lunch-stand, elbowing for a place at the counter with errand boys from neighboring offices, schoolgirls in their khaki uniforms and Islamic headscarves, and local shopkeepers.

Halbony, where I had taken up residence for the duration of my stay in Syria, is a densely populated quarter where most of the residents are traditionalist Sunni Damascenes. It functions as a kind of urban barrier separating the outer fringes of downtown Damascus from the perpetual din and roil of the Baramke bus and service taxi terminal, the State Hospital from the once elegant and now derelict Hijaz Railway Station. In its narrow streets I rapidly located all I might need or want: barbershops, a laundry, purveyors of sweet biscuits of the sort that perfectly accompanied afternoon coffee, fruit and vegetable stalls, tiny convenience stores that sold eggs, milk and yogurt, along with 1.5 litre plastic bottles of locally bottled soft drinks; mini stores in which no more than three people could squeeze themselves that sold coffee beans and the cardamon seeds to grind with them; specialists in Islamic, non-alcoholic perfumes; hole-in-the-wall restaurants that offered only *hommos* and, on bitter winter nights, *ful*, the traditional worker's snack of boiled fava beans seasoned with salt, cumin and lemon juice. There were tiny shops specializing in the repair of radios and televisions, a store that sold typewriters, dying relics of the industrial age; several schools; and a state-run emporium displaying cheap electric appliances where on warm nights the salesmen made their beds in the courtyard in full public view.

As the seasons changed, pushcarts heaped with used clothing, with nuts and dried pumpkin seeds, with pomegranates, imported bananas or tiny, succulent Damascus apricots from the orchards of al-Ghuta plied the streets. And during the three days of *Eid al-fitr*, the feast that marks the end of Ramadan, the itinerant operators of mini-amusement parks set up their crude swings at intersections while pre-adolescents peppered passersby with firecrackers, causing the plumpish *hijab*-clad matrons of Halbony to jump in mock fright. Not far away was a twenty-four hour *qnafe* stand, patronized by passing taxi-drivers and late-shift workers, who would wolf down portions of this concoction of sweet shredded wheat with an underlayer of melted white cheese while standing on the sidewalk, then hurry off into the night in search of a fare or home to bed.

There was a neighborhood mosque as well, and in a semi-basement, a workshop that produced baklava, the buttery scent of which wafted down the street in the early morning hours. Inside a commercial passage was the Sudanese students' social club which had abruptly closed its doors after September 11, though Sudanese students continued to frequent the district. Rents were relatively low, so I often saw theological students in the streets, loping along with their robes aflutter, knitted skullcaps atop their heads, disputing the fine points of Qur'anic exegesis while hurrying to a seminar in Islamic jurisprudence—*fiqh*—given by one of the city's multitude of resident sheikhs.

The district's warren of narrow lanes also sheltered multitudes of tiny offices, two of which I would come to know well. The first, two doors from the terminal, was nestled above a bookstore specializing in Islamic subjects. There, I made the acquaintance of Shukri Abukhalil.

Mr. Abukhalil was a professor of Islamic history. I had come knocking at his door in the company of my interpreter, a young woman named Salam, a working archeologist and daughter of a Druze family from the southern Syrian city of Suweida. She had been recommended to me with the assurance that she was unconnected to the regime's omnipresent security services. I was, I told her, an amateur archeologist of ideas.

If there was such a thing as a distinctly religious perspective on the events that had transformed Damascus into the center of the first Muslim empire, I hoped to hear it from Mr. Abukhalil. I'd come with an introduction from Dr. Abdul-Razaq al-Munis, a ranking official at the Ministry of Religious Affairs, a portly man in his forties who wore the robes of an *alim*, a religious scholar. I had contrived to catch his attention when I spoke the name of Saïd Nursi, the Turkish mystic.

A professor of Islamic history at the University of Damascus who had studied in Azerbaijan, Mr. Abukhalil seemed ill-at-ease in our first encounter. Though we met twice subsequently, that feeling never dissipated. Had he been given to understand by those who exert ultimate control in Syria that it was advisable to speak to me, a Western writer, but was doing so under slight duress? Was he one of those Muslims who prefer to avoid non-believers? Had he assumed that I was hostile to Islam? Had I mistaken shyness for diffidence?

On the table between us Mr. Abukhalil, a slender, rather severe man of Palestinian origin who wore thick-lensed spectacles and smiled thinly and with some effort, had placed several books. "These are mine," he says. "They give my opinions about Islam, about forgiveness, understanding and living, and about the need for dialogue between the Islamic world and the West." As our meeting progressed, it became clear that the historical record interested him less than attempting to convince me how compassionate, humane and reasonable was the religion revealed to Muhammad. That was a claim I had not come to dispute. I was interested in Islam's approach to the world it encountered as it grew. What I found might provide clues to how it would respond to the violent encroachment of the West under the guise of free trade, free markets and democracy.

"Christianity," he said, "is not a logical religion. But for the people of Syria, the new religion, Islam, was logical and scientific. It encouraged people to think. If the new faith can answer questions, why should people not accept it."

Reaching over, he pulled a book from the shelf and showed it to me. It was an Arabic translation of Thomas Arnold's *The Call of Islam*. Not his own historical research, but the writings of an Englishman sympathetic to Islam would surely convince me, he must have reasoned. It was as though only a Westerner could validate that which Muslim jurisprudents and thinkers had arrived at on their own, often well before the rise of the West as a culture conscious of itself and of its power. I had encountered the same syndrome in Iran, a bending over backwards in the name of cultural accommodation.

This added an element of complication, not to say confusion, to his elucidation. As he spoke, was Mr. Abukhalil paraphrasing Arnold, or was he expressing his own views? Or were the two identical?

Salam threw me a glance, as if to say: what should we do now?

We would listen.

For Mr. Abukhalil, the battle of Yarmuk had been the decisive engagement. Following the battle, two Muslim armies besieged the city, he explained. One of them was led by Khalid, whose forces scaled the walls at the Bab Sharqi. When the Christians realized what had befallen them, they hastened to conclude a peaceful surrender with the commander of the other army, the victor of Yarmuk, Abu Ubayda ibn al-Jarrah.

"On the orders of the Caliph Umar, they divided the sanctuary into two parts. It was later transformed into a mosque when the Muslims exchanged all the space for granting permission to the Christians to build five churches. Even though," he said, leaning toward me, "the Muslims had every right to occupy the entire mosque area."

"But," I interjected, thinking back to my meeting with Dr. Zuhri at the Museum, "could the peaceful entry have been by the eastern gate?" Mr. Abukhalil rejected the idea with an emphatic wag of his index finger.

Who was right? Who wrong?

Was I pursuing chimeras? What difference did it make if Damascus had opened its gates after an undertaking of fair treatment by Khalid ibn-al-Walid? Who cared?

Contemporary Syrian thinkers do. Beneath the apparent futility inherent in revisiting the past, a hard nub of essence seemed to lurk. What interpretation was to be given to events that were to transform a primitive though dynamic new political, ideological and religious movement into a world government? Were they to be seen as the peaceful cooperation of the hard-pressed citizens of Damascus with those who would be be their new masters? Or as the arrival of a conquering dispensation that bestowed mercy upon the conquered? My first reaction was to see in Mr. Abukhalil's gloss of those momentous events the kind of flexibility that one might encounter in, say, the fine tempered steel from which sword blades have long been fashioned in this city. But as the discussion continued, I began to understand that his argument was a schematic, symbolic one. What we might call the "time line" was of less concern than the relationships between the brotherly adversaries, the Arab Christians discontented with their Byzantine overlords, and the Muslims.

What took place before and within the walls of Damascus could not be thrust into the pigeon-holes of either/or. They partook of both: of war and peaceful negotiation, of intimidation and accommodation. Scholarship here was less an issue than a wider program which I took to be political, in the sense that Islam itself cannot be dissociated, for better or for worse, from the political.

The conquering army of Islam had indeed attacked and captured Damascus, but at the same time the Damascenes, whose language was Arabic and whose Christian religious beliefs were closer to Islam than they were to the doctrine of the Byzantine state church, accepted the guarantees that the new faith promised and introduced it, willingly, grudgingly or both, into their midst. They were shortly to participate in the refinement and redefinition of that faith, and to become among its most steadfast defenders.

The meeting with Mr. Abulkhalil had been brief and inconclusive. We agreed to meet several days later, at his home.

* * *

WHETHER IT PRECIPITATED OR CONFIRMED the fall of Damascus, the battle at Yarmuk eliminated the Byzantine threat to the nascent Arab-Muslim state. Within a year Abu Ubayda, one of the most esteemed Companions of the Prophet, was promoted to high command in Syria by Caliph Umar, who apparently sought to curb the powers of the charismatic general Khalid. Plague was ravishing the land, and Abu Ubyada was soon carried away, as was his appointed successor, Yazid ibn Abi Sufyan. That left Yazid's brother Mu'awiyah, as the logical if not sole candidate for *wali*, or governor of the newly annexed Syrian territories.[8]

The appointment by Umar of the Meccan aristocrat Mu'awiyah was to place upon the house of Islam what some now consider the fateful seal of violence and illegitimacy. My years among the Shi'a in Iran and later, my several visits to Lebanon, had well acquainted me with the accusations levelled against the founders of the Umayyad dynasty—not to mention the first three "rightly guided" successors to Mohammad, the Caliphs Abu Bakr, Umar and Uthman. Now, in Damascus, I would, I hoped, be exposed to the mainstream Sunni view of events.

Before Mu'awiyah, "a late convert without early merit in Islam,"[9] could ascend to the caliphal rank after which he lusted, he had first to shove aside the last obstacle to a restoration of his clan, the Quraysh, the Meccan aristocracy which had shunned, scorned and even spat upon Mohammad during the early years of his prophethood, and only rallied to his cause when it became politically advantageous and commercially profitable to do so.

Against them stood one man, 'Ali ibn-abi-Talib, cousin and son-in-law of the Prophet. On assuming office as the fourth caliph in June, 656, 'Ali had finally achieved what he and his supporters had felt had always been rightfully his due: the succession to Mohammad. He had done so at enormous cost to his personal prestige, out of devotion to the greater good of Islam, and in recognition of a lack of support among those influential in the early Muslim community.

But 'Ali faced a deadlier foe in Mu'awiyah who, writes Wilferd Madelung in his remarkable dissection of the tragically flawed succession, had "developed a taste for despotism of the Roman Byzantine type. While endowed with a natural instinct for power and domination, his judgement of human nature was, contrary to his reputation, limited and primitive. He had come to understand that in statecraft, whenever bribery or intimidation would not reduce an opponent, murder, open or secret, was the most convenient and effective means."[10]

Mu'awiyah proceeded thus: he publicly accused 'Ali of the assassination of Uthman, the third caliph. Produce the murderers, he challenged 'Ali, or be seen as an accomplice and forfeit the caliphate.[11] Only war could settle the issue, a war that would forever rend the fragile fabric of Islamic society.

Though the battle itself took place far from the city walls, it was a battle waged by and for Damascus, a battle in which the deadliest weapons were words, and copies of the Qu'ran held high atop brandished lances. Had the battle been lost by Mu'awiyah and his henchmen, Damascus, their seat of temporal power and the source of their immense riches, would have been irreparably diminished.

Southwest of a bend of the Euphrates, on the road to the abandoned desert city of al-Rusafa, Siffin today is a place of desolation unmarked on most maps, where dust-devils whirl across an arid, scree-strewn landscape, and the sun beats down with relentless fury.

I had visited the battlefield—sped by, more properly—on a trip eastward to the banks of the great river. No monument stands to mark the place where the troops of 'Ali, who had marched up from Kufa, in Iraq, faced those of Mu'awiyah. Neither army was prepared for all-out hostilities, and for days only scattered skirmishes took place. Finally, in late July, on a day similar in its heat to Yarmuk, the battle was joined. 'Ali's forces were at the point of victory when Mu'awiyah's commanding general Amr ibn-al-'As, the conqueror of Egypt, ordered his cavalry to affix copies of the Qu'ran to their lance tips. At the sight, 'Ali's troops hesitated, then came to a halt. The gambit saved Mu'awiyah's army, preserved the ascendency of his clansmen of the Quraysh, and paved the way for his ultimate ascension to the caliphal throne. God's revealed book, not force of arms, would henceforth decide the outcome.[12]

The two sides appointed arbitrators, each authorized to act and accompanied by four hundred witnesses. In January, 659, they convened. As with many key events in early Islamic history, conflicting accounts abound. Some claim that 'Ali's appointee declared the caliphate of his master null and void. But these sources are primarily Iraqi, and reflect their deep hatred of Umayyad Damascus and all its works, argue orientalists with an unconcealed admiration for Mu'awiyah.

"The majority of Muslim annalists cannot but pay involuntary tribute to this remarkable ruler, to this most eminent among the political figures of Islam, who, in replacing the theocratic oligarchy inaugurated by Muhammad and maintained by Umar with a regular, organized government, contributed more than any other to create a firm basis for the domination of the Qu'ran," wrote the French Jesuit Père Henri Lammens at the beginning of the twentieth century.[13]

Lammens, a proponent of strong central government for Syria—under French rule—goes on to illustrate the character of the man for whom he felt such boundless admiration: "Four circumstances—Mu'awiyah was to declare later—granted me superiority over 'Ali. I took every precaution to conceal my intentions, while he made his public knowledge. My troops were better equipped and more disciplined; his were mediocre men, who cared for naught but rebellion. At the Day of the Camel, I allowed him to debate his enemies. If they were to win, they would show themselves, of this much I was certain, to be more accommodating than he; should 'Ali prevail, it would be at the expense of his prestige. Finally, I enjoyed the greater sympathy of the Quraysh."[14]

In the end, the final decision mattered little. 'Ali's rule was crippled. Most probably the arbitrators decided to depose both men. But Mu'awiyah, a provincial governor, had no caliphate to lose. The outcome raised him to a stature equivalent to 'Ali's. This was the victory he had schemed for. 'Ali's decision to agree to arbitration on Mu'awiyah's terms had been the worst option. The governor could now depict Siffin as a victory, though in military terms in was a defeat averted only by a clever stratagem. Perhaps as crucially, the respite from combat gave Mu'awiyah time to consolidate his grip on Syria.[15]

Two years later, on his way to the mosque in his capital city of Kufah, 'Ali was struck down by the poisoned saber of a killer belonging to the purist Kharijite sect. These distant precursors of what Westerners would later call "fundamentalism" criticized and ultimately destroyed 'Ali for having accepted arbitration which, they claimed, belonged only to Allah.[16] Mu'awiyah, now liberated from any constraint, asserted his claim to the caliphate.

The death of 'Ali placed its seal upon the chain of events that had been set in motion by the Prophet's death. In the dominant Sunni tradition, Mohammad left no designated successor. His assembled followers had chosen Abu Bakr, the first caliph, through a process of consultation called *shura*. The practice has been often invoked since as proof of the inherently democratic nature of the faith revealed by Allah to Mohammad. The Shi'a (the "party" of 'Ali) argued then, as they argue today, that 'Ali had been appointed by his uncle and father-in-law through divine ordinance, and that he possessed, by this fact, certain attributes of the Prophet himself. These were qualifications that far outweighed the suspect and partial consultations of men with a material and, some say, tribal interest in power in the emerging community of the faithful.

The battle at Siffin and its tragic aftermath raised questions and claims that struck to the very heart of the fracture within Islam, and continue to do so to this day. The traditionalist view, to which most Sunnis subscribe, holds the reign of the first four caliphs as being just, republican and righteous in nature. A condition to be aspired to anew. The Shi'a view lays all emphasis on the sanctity of 'Ali's blood ties to Muhammad, and upon the superior spiritual qualities that were his by inheritance.

Though the fourth caliph had been defeated and reviled by his tormentors, his spiritual heirs were to influence the history of Syria in strange and unsuspected ways. No physical monuments survive his troubled reign. Islam experienced under his leadership none of the expansion that would be unleashed when Mu'awiyah consolidated his power. Yet the name of 'Ali can be found everywhere in Syria today, especially among the heterodox minorities who invoke his unique moral and metaphysical qualities. And in a society dominated by Sunni Islam with its rigorous dislike of human images, idealized pictures of 'Ali are frequently encountered, the only one of the caliphs to be so depicted. Were they to be seen as icons?

* * *

"OF COURSE, THE ACCESSION of Mu'awiyah to the caliphate was illegitimate," said Mr. Abukhalil, as Salam and I settled into armchairs in his living room. After one postponement, our meeting had been rescheduled to a Saturday evening. From behind a closed door we could hear the clink of tea tumblers. At a tap on the door our host got up, opened it, received the tray and placed it before us on a low table. Salam, my interpreter, was wearing no headscarf. Beyond the door was Mr. Abukhalil's wife whom, in accordance with strict Islamist etiquette, we would not see.

"Islam declined after the inauguration of the dynastic principle," he says. "Everything 'Ali did was positive; he was an exemplary figure. But, it was Mu'awiyah who brought about the organization of the state, imposed the succession, and took control of the treasury."

Was there not a fatal flaw at the heart of the new regime that Mu'awiyah founded in Damascus? I asked.

"Yes, and this is why it fell. Mu'awiyah's seizure of the caliphate marked the end of democracy in the Islamic world. The first caliphs respected their duty of consultation; he did not."

If ever paradox was inscribed upon a political system, it would be upon the first Muslim empire. An illegitimate caliph who consolidated the power seized by his fellow clan members at the expense of 'Ali, Mu'awiyah presided over the further expansion and consolidation of a state that was to reach, at its pinnacle nearly one hundred years later, from Toledo to Samarkand, from the walls of Constantinople to what is today Pakistan. "Unlike the empires founded by world conquerors like Alexander and Genghis Khan, those regions captured by the armies of Damascus have remained Muslim to this day."

"The reason for this expansion, and for the persistence of Islam, is not due to the Umayyads, and the Abassids who followed them, but to the message they carried with them wherever they went. Even when Muslim military authority withdrew, the people did not return to their previous beliefs. If Islam had not been in harmony with people's lives, they would not have served and adopted it."

"Islam," he said, "touches the inborn nature of all people. It recognizes human inclinations and desires, but organizes and regulates them, and respects the unchanging aspect of human nature. That which made Damascus eternal was the thought carried by those first Muslims."

Theological and historical disputation are all well and good, an entertaining way to while away the idle hours over a glass of tea. But as nine o'clock drew near, Mr. Abukhalil became more fidgety, almost apprehensive. With increasing frequency he glanced at his watch, shifted nervously in his chair. Had Salam's uncovered head offended his religious sensibilities? If so, why now and not before? At five minutes before the hour, we discovered the reason. A German Bundesliga football match was being broadcast live on Syrian television, to begin on the hour, he said sheepishly. Bowing to the inevitable, Salam and I made a discreet exit.

I made my way back to my room, passing beneath the stone walls of the Damascus citadel and in front of the bronze equestrian statue of Salah al-Din al-Ayyubi, the Kurdish warrior known in the West as Saladin who liberated

Jerusalem from the Crusaders. Certain things snapped into sharper focus. Lurking in the dust, or beneath the ruined ramparts of Old Damascus surely lay the ghost of Muʿawiyah, true founder of the Islamic city it became and remained. He—as much as its architects, holy men, political dignitaries and wealthy merchants—had set upon it the indelible seal of blood which has become part of its heritage.

Give him his due: Muʿawiyah was an empire builder, the founder of a dynasty, and a gifted administrator. He possessed a instinct that set him apart from his predecessors and successors. His admirers attributed to him the quality of *hilm*, an untranslatable Arabic term that denotes the ability to "resort to force only when force was absolutely necessary."[17]

But he was also ruthless and cold-blooded, utterly dedicated to the promotion of himself and the interests of his tribe, the Quraysh. He placed his half-brother Ziyad in command of a 4,000 strong elite guard unit that acted as spies and police, tracking down anyone who dared favor the descendants of ʿAli, or speak ill of the caliph. The kind of man a historian like Père Lammens—who wrote his *Short History of Syria* at the urging of none other than General Gouroud—could cast as a Muslim Bonaparte, projecting upon him the qualities of iron-handed brutality and enlightened rationality he would later recognize in the General himself.

Muʿawiyah must answer to the charge of having destroyed the theocratic caliphate, and of replacing it with a *mulk*—a state of temporal, not heavenly sovereignty. While the first three caliphs, Abu Bakr, Umar and Uthman, have been presented as deriving their legitimacy from *shura*, or consultation, in the choice of their successors, the Umayyad descendants, the usurpers of ʿAli's legitimate succession, created a dynasty.

Perhaps, I wondered as I crossed the street in front of the Citadel, there was something about the city, a quality of the dust of its ancient walls, that created a fertile environment for such men. Hafiz al-Asad, who ruled Syria with an iron and implacable hand for twenty-six years, possessed the same unscrupulous quality, the same cold-blooded dedication to the promotion of the interests of his Alawite co-religionists and clansmen in the guise of imposing Arab Socialist Baath Party dogma on the state. His brother, too, commanded a force of elite guards whose only duty was to do the despot's bidding.

As Muʾawiyah's penchant for cruelty was balanced by his administrative capacities and his role as empire builder, so too could the sanguinary excesses of President al-Asad be explained away by his single-minded dedication to building the modern Syrian state. But that was where a comparison between the two enterprises ended.

I have long believed in the *genius locii*, the spirit of place that exercises decisive influence over the lives and affairs of men. But perhaps I had it backwards. Perhaps it was not the air or the dust or the stones of Damascus that had created the two tyrants. How much more likely that the name of the city itself, the resonances it carries, its venerable age, its wealth, its indestructibility, its reputation as a bejewelled royal harlot, had drawn them to it.

Who better than a steel-willed founder of empire like Mu'awiyah—or Hafiz al-Asad, the self-assigned creator of a modern nation-state where none had existed before—could understand the need to discipline, to purify, to master and to have his way with the courtesan that was Damascus, to impose discipline upon this figure of intrigue and treachery, debauchery and perversion? To bend it to his sovereign will, and to imprint upon it neither monuments to culture nor even to commerce, but the remembrance of fear driven deep into the bone, and the legacy of dissipation, profligacy and cruelty?

Contemporary Syrian critics of the ruling regime will surely reply that where Mu'awiyah created a world empire, the late tyrant left nothing but a black hole of non-politics, non-society and non-economy. Their point is well taken. The resemblance between the two men lies not in their accomplishments, for Hafiz al-Asad has played a grim farce to Mu'awiyah's majestic betrayal, but in their absolutist impulse to project upon an entire society their overweening selves.

I had long ago learned this much about the Islamic world: writers about it should be wary of the Western temptation to impute to their subjects the dark, impulsive proclivities we seek to repress in ourselves and in our historical vision of our own culture. Those who, like Père Lammens, were to study and to write about Mu'awiyah's career attempted to clothe the mountebank and usurper in the garb of a statesman, the better to disguise their preferences for the kind of strong, decisive leadership that they could project onto their own imperial objectives. The procedure has a certain resonance in our own day.

"Undoubtedly, Islam can be proud of the success of the Umayyads: the victory of 'Ali would have perpetuated anarchy within; his sons [Hasan and Hussein] would inherit the negative qualities of their father."[18]

So overwhelming had been the legacy of Mu'awiyah that his son could never have matched, let alone surpassed him. Yazid did prove more licentious, dissolute and cruel than his father. Bloodier, too, and with none of his father's sense of utilitarian restraint which could be disguised as statesmanship.

Where Mu'awiyah had set in motion the series of events that consolidated the stranglehold of the Quraysh on Islam and sealed the humiliation of the Banu Hashim, those original and most devoted followers of the Prophet, his profligate spawn was to earn eternal opprobrium for the murder at Karbala of Imam Hussein, the son of 'Ali, grandson of Muhammad and Lord of Martyrs.

President Bashar al-Asad, the son and anointed successor of the late dictator, may be spared the indignity of killing the sons of his adversaries. That, his father had already attended to. In January 2002, by way of advising American intelligence on the best ways to eradicate "terrorism," the heir to the virtual Syrian throne proposed nothing less than the symbolic re-extermination of the regime's dead foes, the Ikhwan al-Muslimin, better known in the West as the Muslim Brotherhood.[19]

In May of the following year, when American Secretary of State Colin Powell arrived in Damascus to deliver an ultimatum, Mr. al-Asad was confronted with a far less attractive dilemma. He had been ordered to deliver the severed head of Hizbullah, the Shi'a resistance movement whose outstanding contribution to "terrorism" was its expulsion of Israeli occupation forces from Lebanon.

To accede to his visitor's will would be betrayal. But there was little in the family history to suggest that he would recoil in horror at the prospect.

* * *

ON THE OTHER SIDE OF DAMASCUS, well beyond the ancient perimeter walls, in the center of a landscaped park, lies an institution built to offset the dispirited lassitude, dilapidation and dustiness of the Military Museum. The October War Panorama is the regime's monument to itself and to its sole founding father. Where a visit to the Military Museum sets the visitor back a puny five Syrian pounds, the equivalent of twenty cents, at the Panorama, the entry ticket for foreigners is a bracing $10 (US).

Where the visitor can wander through the Military Museum, and even imagine the life and times of its original lodgers, the Bektashi dervishes, there can be no mistaking the purpose of the Panorama. Ostensibly, that purpose is to display the only significant military "victory" ever won by Syrian forces against the Israeli army in the October 1973 conflict known in the West as the "Yom Kippur War." But even before the visitor, who must join a guided group, enters the immense drum-shaped building he is informed by smartly dressed, youthful guides in civilian clothes that the entire enterprise is a hymn to "the glory of the eternal leader," that inescapable, omnipresent and once omnipotent Mr. al-Asad.

The secular pilgrim, the seeker after patriotic indulgences, must follow a meticulously charted, ascending path, beginning with a series of paintings illustrating great moments in the history of Syrian political and military achievement housed in a circular hall. But here the content and sequence differs from that of its threadbare downtown cousin.

Huge canvases depict the first diplomatic treaty, which is claimed to date back to the seagoing city of Ugarit; Queen Zenobia, who carved out an autonomous desert principality in Palmyra in the third century of the modern era; the Caliph al-Walid accepting tribute from conquered Spaniards in the courtyard of the Umayyad mosque; and the great Arab champion Salah al-Din, astride his horse as he liberates Jerusalem.

Something about the paintings catches my attention, something I cannot immediately put my finger on. Then I understand the anomaly. The faces of Zenobia's retinue, of Salah ad-Din's warriors, of al-Walid's courtiers all have a pronounced east-Asian character. I step forward to look more closely at the paintings. The artists' signatures are all written in Korean. Noting my curiosity the guide steps over and crisply informs me: "All the paintings here were done by artists from North Korea. They were the only ones who knew the secret of creating the effect of three dimensions."

By then, since I had come alone, I had attached myself to a group of Lebanese Shi'ites on a short excursion to Damascus. One of them, a bright-eyed young woman from Ba'albak, volunteered to translate for me. Although I appreciated her kindness—and we managed to chat about the tribulations of her homeland—the experience spoke for itself.

From the hall of paintings we made our way upward to a small auditorium. There, after standing for the national anthem, we were shown a short film that evoked the war: canons firing, rockets being launched, MiG jets taking to the air, Soviet-made surface-to-air missiles streaking upward, the full military might of the nation unleashed against the Zionist foe. Then, from amidst the sound and fury, emerged the victorious commander, Hafiz al-Asad.

At the conclusion of the film, the screen retracts to reveal a diorama of the commando assault on the Israeli observation post atop Jabal al-Sheikh, as Mount Hermon is known in these parts. The work of the Korean artists is extraordinary. The foreground, littered with the detritus of war, blends seamlessly into middle-distance where Syrian troops advance uphill under withering fire, and on upward to the vapor trail-streaked sky where Syrian MiGs do brave battle against the technologically superior Mirages and Phantoms of the Israeli Air Force.

All this was but the *hors d'oeuvre* that precedes the main course, the immense Panorama itself, a 360° canvas of the battle for Quneitra, of which we occupy the precise center. As the spectators' section rotates slowly, the eye is drawn from the far horizon to the heroic carnage unfolding at our feet. The uncanny verisimilitude is heightened by the presence of wrecked tanks, blasted concrete, twisted metal, spent shells. Everywhere the Syrian forces press forward, standard bearers striking heroic poses, officers urging their men on. Everywhere the Zionist aggressors are in retreat; some of them cower as prisoners, hands over their heads; others flee. In the sky, Syrian planes streak southward from Damascus while SAMs bring down Israeli jets as helicopters carry elite troops toward their positions.

Never having experienced combat, I could not say whether the Panorama would convince a soldier, much less a veteran of the battle itself. Never having seen nor smelled a bloated, dismembered corpse of the kind Robert Fisk is always stumbling over as he covers the Lebanese Civil War, I could not say with absolute certainty that this was warfare expurgated of its horror.

The Syrian victory in Quneitra was brief and bloody. On October 6, Egyptian forces had crossed the Suez Canal, and quickly overran Israeli defenses on the East Bank. At the same time, Syrian armor and infantry crossed the 1967 ceasefire line in the Jaulan, as the Golan Heights are known in Syrian Arabic, recapturing the city. The Israelis counterattacked, and six days later had reoccupied Quneitra. Though defeated, Arab arms had not been humiliated, as in 1967. Syria suffered massive losses and damage to its infrastructure, but it remained pugnaciously combative. The success of its failure was that of Hafiz al-Asad, and it would, he vowed, be properly commemorated.

That the immense canvas is a masterpiece of *trompe-l'œil* was beyond dispute. The team of eight Korean painters had labored six years to create their 45-meter-long *chef d'oeuvre*. Through the young lady from Ba'albak I learned that they had declined all payment for their efforts. Surely their contribution to Syrian-North Korean friendship, plus a daily bowl of rice, had been more than sufficient remuneration.

If the epic Panorama was the main course, surely the final exhibit—a great hall devoted entirely to the life and times of Hafiz al-Asad and his family— must qualify as a *pièce de resistance* to satisfy even the most gargantuan appetite for self-aggrandizement. Here the Korean artists had surpassed themselves. At the extremity of the immense chamber opposite the door, the visitor's gaze is led along a ceremonial passageway of traditional Syrian inlaid stone to a larger-than-life portrait of the Eternal Leader who greets us, open hand raised above his head. Standing tall, dressed in a blue suit, under a perfect and cloudless sky, he is surrounded by the adoring multitudes surging forward, beatific smiles on their faces. There are sturdy yet attractive peasant women in national costume, doughty Druze and Alawite mountaineers, light-footed Bedouin tribesmen, nubile Damascene girls with bouquets of flowers, school children in uniform, workers in well-pressed factory dungarees, soldiers, sailors and aviators, even, in the middle-background, two token clergymen, a Christian and a Muslim, faces suffused with inner radiance as though they had stumbled upon the Second Coming.

Only when I turned to look behind me did my eyes fall upon the triumphal portrait of Hafiz al-Asad and the late North Korean despot Kim il-Sung, their clasped hands raised high in joint salute. The symmetry was perfect: the Eternal Leader, in company with the Great Leader was greeting himself. Anything less would have been an anti-climax.

The lateral walls of the chamber were devoted to aspects of the Leader's life, from his modest beginnings in the dirt-poor hill town of al-Qardaha to his boisterous days as a street brawler in Lattakia, his youthful career as a flyer, his rapid rise to influence in the Baath, and finally, the seizure of power in the Corrective Movement of 1970, which gave Syria, as some friends assured me, "at least a stable regime." Surrounding a larger-than-life portrait of the entire al-Asad family, including his mother Naessa and his five children, is an inverted rogues' gallery in which Mr. al-Asad meets the high and mighty of the modern world, as if to persuade the visitor that he indeed wheeled and dealt with them on equal footing. I note photographs of him chatting with the late Richard Milhouse Nixon and his cohort "Doctor" Henry Kissinger, the criminal mastermind to whose duplicity can be attributed a substantial part of the tragedy of Palestine and the unfolding agony of the Middle East.

When the Syrian heirs, in whatever shape or form, to their iconoclast forebears, enter this place with hatchets, sledgehammers, knives for slashing, buckets of whitewash, or jerry cans of gasoline for burning, they will surely rush into the coagulated slice of time that is the portrait gallery and there, begin their work of obliteration.

It will be a pity, for Hafiz al-Asad's commemoration of himself is far from unique in its delirious excess. In fact, it is of a piece with the age. What he attempted, near successfully, to inscribe upon Syria, men of far greater ambition, men who profess Christianity and Judaism, now stand poised to impose upon the entire Middle East.

2

In the Shadow of the Mosque

DAMASCUS TURNS ON A SINGLE PIVOT, the great Umayyad Mosque that lies at its heart, which concentrates and simultaneously radiates a symbolic, synthesizing power at once religious, political and physical. Its function is that of an aleph, one of those points in space that contains all other points, and which are said to "take the shape of a man pointing to both heaven and earth, in order to show that the lower world is the map and mirror of the higher."[20]

This fulcrum, this point in space, this figurative pointing man has, since the beginning of the city, been sacred, as if the hallowed quality of the ground itself pervades everything built upon it, as if it contains all history and all potentiality.

It had begun perhaps ten centuries before the the modern era as a temple to Hadad, the Aramaean god of storms, of rain and of the harvest, and perhaps before that as a place impregnated with the inchoate connection between earth and sky.

When the Romans arrived, sucked willingly into the vacuum left by the demise of Alexander's short-lived empire, they constructed there a mighty temple to Jupiter which conserved some of Hadad's attributes, preserving the structure's monumental dimensions. Not long after Christianity had seized control of the empire from within, Theodosius, Emperor of the East, in 379 caused to be built atop the ruins of the the pagan temple which he had ordered destroyed a basilica dedicated to St. John the Baptist.

The Macedonians, the Romans and after them, the Byzantines, had brought with them, along with their gods, the Hellenic esthetic in which the human form represented the ultimate measure of beauty and perfection. The rise of Islam, and the iconoclast conflict, suggest that in the Orient in general and in the *Bilad al-Sham* (as the Syrian lands were then known) in particular, this conception was to remain symbolic of foreign domination and foreign belief.

In its triumph, Islam was to sweep that symbolism aside, and to integrate it into its own belief system centered on a God who brooked no partners and tolerated no likenesses.

When the Muslim army entered Damascus in 635, its brilliant commander Khalid ibn al-Walid, accompanied by several of the Prophet's companions, proceeded to the ancient *temenos*. There, in a corner remote from the church they offered their prayers facing Mecca, to the southeast. So it was that Islam came to this most ancient of sanctuaries, the holiness of which the new religion was to preserve intact yet alter almost—but not quite—beyond recognition.

The duty of a visitor to Damascus is, above all others, to pay a respectful visit to the mosque. And so I did, on a luminous winter day not long after I'd arrived in the city, in January 2001. From outside the Old Town, its graceful dome and three minarets dominate the skyline, seeming to float above the rooftops of the low gray and ochre buildings that enfold it. Illuminated by night, the venerable structure gleams like a lode-star in the galaxy of lesser mosques that dots the cityscape.

In the Islamic city, commerce and faith blend seamlessly. Though no commercial activity is tolerated within the sanctuary of the mosque, intense activity goes on all around it as befits Islam's origins as a faith of townsmen and traders. As with the Friday Mosque of Isfahan and the Suleymaniye complex in Istanbul, here in Damascus the hubbub of buying and selling, of tea-drinking, story-telling and negotiation surrounds the sacred precinct.

As I approached through the sunless bowels of the Suq al-Hamiddiyah, an enveloping labyrinth of minuscule stores, tiny workshops, storehouses, offices and sweetshops where itinerant vendors hawk their wares and carpet merchants' touts attempt to hook the rare tourist, the dome of the Great Mosque vanished from view but its magnetic power seemed to guide me inexorably toward it.

Arriving at the eastern extremity of the covered market, I emerged into an open space occupied by pushcarts laden with clothing or personal grooming accessories, amid the impromptu stalls where dry goods hung from cords strung between the marble columns that survive the pagan temple. In front of me loomed the massive wall, and towering above the parapet, the north-west minaret.

Non-Muslims may enter the mosque, but only through a small gate at the opposite end of the enclosure. Ticket in hand, I stepped through that portal and into the courtyard, shading my eyes against the scintillation of the polished marble paving stones.

The great ceremonial structures—the churches, mosques, and temples that represent the summit of human architectural achievement—share a common trait. They touch off spatial resonance, focus the sky as would a magnifying glass on a patch of earth, organize volumes of space in such a way as to make empty air hum with the immense Brownian movement of life itself, evoke the unknowable divine.

Like all these great structures, the Umayyad Mosque simultaneously touches off in the visitor a powerful sense of insignificance and of its opposite, the impression that one has returned to a well-known, familiar and welcoming place. I paused at the threshold, an ant-like presence at the edge of the courtyard that could easily hold ten thousand. (As many stood in this very place, in 1911, when the Turkish Islamic revivalist Bediuzzaman Saïd Nursi delivered his famous Damascus sermon.) Yet I was enfolded by a welcoming intimacy, a sense of belonging.

Mosques have a devotional function, but they are also public space, offering sanctuary for social intercourse, discussion, debate, often for the exchange of confidences, even for the planning of acts that may be construed as political, acts of authority, and of resistance to illegitimate authority. No subject is too small, none too great. In the warm climates where Islam arose, these spaces are open to the winds, the rain, the sunlight. But all of them, from China to Kosova, from Tatarstan deep into Africa, provide shelter for the offering of prayer, the rhythm of standing, kneeling, prostration; and to the business of the community of believers.

Before me, a knot of sightseers wanders beneath the portico arches, another group is hurrying purposefully across the bright paving stones. By the women clad in black chadors and the men with their stubble beards I could identify these figures in middle distance as Iranians, come to pay homage to the severed head of Imam Hussein, by legend buried here beneath the western wall. Flocks of pigeons take to the air with a whir of wings, then flutter back to earth in a constant, harried to-and-fro. Behind me, outside the walls, as if forgotten, lay the marketplace of which the mosque is both continuation and antithesis. I feel myself poised like the proverbial dervish, halfway between eternity and infinity.

* * *

IF GENERAL KHALID AL-WALID and his adjutants had been the first Muslims to offer prayers in the enclosure in the heart of Damascus, another al-Walid, this one a caliph, indelibly imprinted upon the city its Islamic character. The first Umayyad rulers had been less concerned with physical monuments, more with the survival of the newly-founded faith, and even more with the consolidation and expansion of their own earthly dominion. As the community of believers grew, exponentially in its first upsurge, it found need of ceremonial spaces that would match its imperial dimensions, its universal purview and ambition.

Mu'awiyah, the first Umayyad caliph, had been content with a monumental palace that gave onto the remains of the pagan temple where the Christian basilica stood. Worship ranked none too high on his priority chart. A generation later, the sons of Abd-al-Malik, the "father of kings" had brought Damascus to the pinnacle of its prosperity and power. Islam now reigned supreme from the Atlantic to the marches of China. The time had come for his city to be endowed with a monument to its prosperity and power.

The first of those sons, al-Walid I who ascended the caliphal throne twenty-five years after the death of the dynastic founder, was the master builder of the Umayyad Empire. His antecedents were illustrious. In 691 his father had constructed the great octagonal monument known as the Dome of the Rock in Jerusalem. That monument, built atop the site claimed by the Jews to be that of Solomon's Temple, certified Islam's self-ascribed stature as the third and ultimate in the great chain of the Abrahamic religions and its ascendancy over its two predecessors. Furthermore, it had been the place from which Muhammad had departed on his night journey to heaven astride his steed Buraq. As such it soon came to rank as the third holiest place in Islam.

The son, who assumed rule in 705 upon his father's death, could be no less resolute in marking out the province of the new faith. He enlarged and beautified the great mosques of Mecca and Medina, and created in Damascus the building that was to become a beacon of Islamic belief and a model of Islamic architecture often emulated and never equalled.[21]

Truth and legend, fact and fiction lie so thickly encrusted about the Umayyad Mosque that it is next to impossible to separate them. Take the genesis of the mosque itself. Al-Walid may well have negotiated with the Christian faithful whose churches would have to be expropriated in order to build the mosque. Or he may not have.

One account, that of the scribe Ibn al-Faqih, claims that "when al-Walid decided to build the mosque of Damascus, he summoned the Christians of the town to appear before him and said these words: 'We wish to enlarge our mosque at the expense of your church which we propose that you erect upon another site which we will accord to you as you so choose.' The Christians cautioned him against undertaking such an action: 'Our Book says that he who would destroy our church will die a violent death.' Al-Walid replied: 'Then I shall be the first to destroy it.' The caliph, who was clad in a yellow robe, then began to destroy it, and the people joined in. The mosque was thus soon enlarged."[22]

Whatever the nature of discussion between the two unequal parties, the outcome was never in doubt. The Christians relocated their church further eastward, to that part of the Old Town near Bab Tuma that is now known as the Christian Quarter, and construction of the monumental structure began. Damascus by now had become an imperial capital with no earthly rival; it needed a ceremonial building to match its stature.

The work lasted nine years, and cost "400 strongboxes each containing 10,000 dinars."[23] Writes Finbar Barry Flood in his exhaustive study, "According to various accounts, 12,000 marble carvers and 10,000 individual pieces of marble were used in the embellishment of the mosque."[24]

A later visitor, the Andalusian traveller Ibn Jubair, would write (in 1194) that when al-Walid began to build the mosque, "he called upon the king of Constantinople to dispatch twelve thousand artisans from his lands, and threatened him with the most dire of punishments should he delay. But the king of the Greeks did has he had been ordered, with all the desired docility."[25]

Perhaps the Byzantines were motivated by admiration. Perhaps, characteristically, they sought to curry favor with their more powerful rival. Another scribe recounts: "the Byzantine (*rum*) emperor sent him then a gift consisting of one hundred thousand mithqals of gold and forty mule-loads (*waqr*) of mosaics together with a thousand laborers."[26]

We must remember that many were those in power in Constantinople who viewed the rise of Islam as an ephemeral event, a short-term disturbance created by a pseudo-Christian heretic, or, at worst, a scourge sent by God himself to punish laxity in belief which would, like any scourge, eventually abate.

Whatever the prevailing view, the Byzantines had good reason to be docile, or cautious. The power and prestige of their empire was at a low ebb. But they were not the only non-Syrians to contribute to the construction project which was by far the largest and most ambitious of its time. There were also Persians, incomparable masters of the ceramic tile, not to mention skilled craftsmen from those parts of India and North Africa that had passed into the Umayyad domain only a few years before. As the princes of Damascus funneled wealth toward their imperial capital, so too did artisans, masons, mosaicists, carpenters and hundreds of other skilled trades flocked to the city, answering the twin call of faith and livelihood.

During the early decades of its existence, the Umayyad caliphate's relation-ship with Constantinople had been ambivalent. Dazzled by the sophisticated, hellenized urban culture of Damascus, its new Arab masters had little choice but to employ the skills, and the language, of their new subjects. Greek had continued to be spoken in the royal court and in the civil service until the reign of al-Walid, who finally replaced it with Arabic.

Alongside their efforts at Arabization, the new rulers of Syria gradually formulated, in opposition to Byzantine predominance, "a visual culture capable of reflecting the ... specific needs of the Muslim *umma* while projecting the political aspirations of the Umayyad caliphate," writes Flood convincingly; " ... far from an homage rooted in feelings of cultural inadequacy, (the) evocation of Constantinopolitan topography was part of a subversive appropriation designed to project Muslim claims to the Byzantine empire."[27]

By the time the great mosque had been completed, the claim had become persuasive indeed. Al-Walid's successor Sulayman was soon to launch the third Arab onslaught against Constantinople, that which would be repulsed *in extremis* by Leo III, the Isaurian, chief of the iconoclasts. A visiting Byzantine delegation is said to have remarked, upon seeing the splendors of the completed mosque, that the Islamic kingdom had undoubtedly come to stay.

Impossible today to imagine the city without its spiritual and cultural beacon, only marginally less difficult would it be to imagine how construction of the great mosque would have been perceived by the Damascenes themselves. Perhaps seventy years earlier, Islam had come to the city. At first, the caliphs were content to worship in a makeshift mosque, perhaps like the reed and dried mud structures that had been hastily thrown up in places like Basra and Kufa, in Iraq.

Within nine years, all that had changed. The mosque imprinted upon the city "a permanent affirmation of Muslim hegemony"[28] that symbolically coincided with the real-world hegemony of the Umayyads. At the same time, it embodied the lofty position of Damascus among the cities of Islam. Was it not the city the Prophet himself had declined to enter, explaining that it too much resembled Paradise? Surely, no other city had been so caught up in the near-miraculous, explosive expansion of Islam, a feat as much spiritual and ideological as military.

This was the heady combination of forces that fashioned the Umayyad Mosque. Within its walls were concentrated, fixed for all time, both the material and political triumph—and the spiritual dignity of Islam. After the capture of Damascus, Khalid al-Walid and the Companions of the Prophet had offered their first prayers in the exact location where, according to legend, al-Walid caused the mosque to be built. A prayer offered at this precise spot, transformed into the prototype of the *mihrab*, or niche, has the same value as one offered at al-Aqsa Mosque, in Jerusalem. And on the day of Final Judgement Jesus the Prophet will, it is believed, return to earth here in Damascus, descending from the minaret which bears his name.

Caliph al-Walid was not a modest man. On completion of the mosque, he is reported to have addressed the citizens thus: "Inhabitants of Damascus, four things give you a marked superiority over the rest of the world: your climate, your water, your fruits and your baths. To these I wanted to add a fifth: this mosque."[29]

Shortly before his death, he would preside over the event that marked the zenith of the Umayyad state. In February of 715, his leading general, Musa Abu-Nusayr entered the city at the head of a triumphal procession. Fresh from his conquest of Spain, Musa had marched an entire cohort of captive Visigoth nobles across North Africa to pay homage to God's vice-regent, who received the victor and his captive supplicants in the huge courtyard of the mosque. For the first time, blond-headed Europeans bowed their heads in submission before the Commander of the Faithful, at only a few removes a son of the desert. This was the event reproduced, in all its curious reverse-orientalizing splendor, in Hafiz al-Asad's immense military panorama.

Ultimately, the call of the desert from which they had sprung proved too powerful for the Umayyads. While Damascus continued to be the capital, Sulayman transferred the caliphal residence from the palace adjacent to the great mosque to the desert city of al-Rasafah, which before had been called Sergiopolis. There, in the blinding sun, the heat, the unceasing wind and blowing sand, the last of the Umayyad caliphs lived, turning their backs upon the city that had provided the backdrop for their cruelty, corruption, licentiousness, arrogance, daring, piety, administrative and military genius but, with few exceptions, little in the way of spiritual accomplishment.

By 750 the house that Mu'awiyah built lay in ruins, brought low by the Abassids who had stormed out of Khorassan under the black flag of revolt against the regime of impiety. In a tomb in al-Rasafah they came upon the embalmed corpse of Hisham, one of the most illustrious of the late Umayyad caliphs. His body they disentombed, scourged eighty times and burnt to ashes.[30] As the bonfires of disgrace burned high, the single survivor of the one-time rulers of the world, Abd-al-Rahman ibn-Mu'awiyah ibn-Hisham was fleeing westward in disguise across North Africa, to found the second Umayyad dynasty in Spain. Imprinted upon his memory he bore the prototype of the great mosque of Damascus, which had by then become the model for the entire Muslim world.

* * *

BY LATE APRIL, the Damascus sunlight is strong enough to discourage idle standing about in unshaded spaces. Of a late morning on one such day, I met Faruq Akbiq in the shade of the main portal of the Umayyad Mosque. He waved aside the objections of the door-keeper, who protested that I was a tourist, and we stepped inside, removed our shoes, and entered into the welcoming coolness of the *haram*, the great prayer hall that stretches the full 130-meter length of the building.

Mr. Akbiq and I had been introduced by mutual friends, and we rapidly discovered strong affinities. Although he was a partner in a small medical supply import-export firm located at the foot of the steep slope of Jabal Qassiun, his true vocation, I soon learned, was that of chief interpreter for the Grand Mufti of Syria, Sheikh Ahmad Kuftaro. Mr. Akbiq combined an exquisite command of English with a courtly manner and a rich baritone voice. He was a man whose modesty caused his talents and bearing, accentuated by his height and slender build, to appear almost mundane. They were anything but.

Shoes in hand we strolled slowly down the carpeted hall beneath the great dome, a wonder of Islamic architecture surpassed only latterly by those of Sinan the Ottoman and the architects of the monumental mosques of Isfahan, in Saffavid Iran. Beneath our stocking feet were the paving stones, if not the carpets, upon which caliphs, some iniquitous, fewer devout, had trodden as they made their way from the ceremonial entrance to the raised platform reserved for them adjacent to the *minbar*. It was from this pulpit that their name would be spoken at the Friday congregational prayer, as befitted the ruler of the Islamic state and God's vice-regent on earth.

Around us small groups of faithful were praying, some close to the *mihrab* wall as if to draw as close as possible to that which separated them from the Ka'aba, the black stone in Mecca to which all Muslims direct their prayers, others far to the rear of the hall. The call to midday prayer would not sound for at least an hour. Several women were praying in a space often thought to be an exclusively male preserve. The caliphs had long vanished, and the modern-day secular pharaohs who ruled would come here only on the rarest of ceremonial occasions. It had become the preserve of the humble.

The spot Faruq—we had soon come to first-name terms—chose for us to sit down had, for all I could see, nothing in particular to recommend it. Yet it was perfect. We could talk in normal tones, disturbing no worshipper and yet remain acutely conscious of the hum that pervaded the hall; we were slightly removed from the main axis of foot traffic but could observe the comings and goings of the faithful and the curious; the morning light was slanting through the stained glass windows set high in the south wall in such a way as to cast upon the carpet richly luminous rectangles that almost, but not quite, reached our knees; to our backs, the brilliant reflection of the sun glinting off the paving stones of the court shone through the wide-open doors.

"After the Muslims had captured Damascus, they shared this space with the Christians. Each worshipped in his corner of the ancient temple, but each could see what the other was doing," he said, with an open-handed gesture. "But fifty years later, the Muslims had increased, and sought a larger place of worship. Caliph al-Walid requested that the patriarchs of the Church relinquish their one half of the shared space in return for fair compensation. Four churches which the Muslims had previously taken were returned to them in return for the space claimed by the caliph. This was the ruler whose power extended from Iran to Spain."

Though Faruq's version differed from several I had seen, and was at odds with contemporary accounts, it had a ring of plausibility that reflected his sense of himself as a believer in a region where coexistence has at times been strained but never ruptured. "When Muhammad came," he confided, leaning toward me to emphasize the point, "he brought a teaching that recognized and incorporated both Moses and Christ. When the Christians understood the nature of Islam, they found in it an affinity with their own beliefs."

As we talked, I looked around me at the worshippers, the ever-present cohorts of Iranian pilgrims, small groups of tourists wearing the rough cotton robes they must use to cover their irreverent dress, and, adjacent to the shrine of St. John the Baptist—he to whom the original Christian basilica that occupied this space was dedicated—whose severed head is also reputed to lie beneath the paving stones of the prayer hall,[31] a line of men kneeling on their haunches, rocking slowly backward and forward, their fingers clicking over the beads of their *tasbis*, on which they tell and retell the ninety-nine names of God.

"They are Sufis," said Faruq. "This mosque is like a home to them."

The invisible spiritual city that radiates out from the Great Mosque has long been, and is today, a favorite dwelling and meeting place for dervishes, those who see in Islam not a doctrine of proscriptions and legalistic rigor, but one of clemency, mercy, beauty and harmony, of proximity to the *Haqiqa*, the divine reality that lodges in every single thing. This spirit of exotericism is most concentrated in the mosque itself. It is here, claim some authorities that "every Friday at dawn, a council of Syrian saints (*diwan awliya al-Sham*) takes place; it is they who protect and govern the city and the surrounding area, though they remain invisible to the uninitiated."[32] Who, I wondered, were those initiates able to see them, and perhaps overhear their deliberations? Was Faruq among them?

An hour or more had passed. The call of the muezzin echoed from the ancient minarets. Faruq excused himself to perform his midday prayers. When he returned, it was high noon. As we parted, he invited me to attend the Mufti's sermon that coming Friday. "I will meet you at the main entrance of the Abu Nur mosque."

I would be there. I had learned that the Mufti was a controversial figure in post-Hafiz al-Asad Damascus. For some, he had been a beacon of compassion during the darkest night of a cruel regime. For others, he had been the passive accomplice of that regime for failing to denounce its abuses. Still others whispered that he had contrived to exert some influence, and maintain a form of autonomy, within the totalitarian system. Few would deny that he was a man to be reckoned with in Syria and within the wider Islamic world.

The appointed hour and day arrived. On Friday morning, the normally traffic-clogged downtown streets were all but deserted, except as my taxi approached the religious institution that was my destination. I got out of the car—it was an Iranian-made Saipa—and walked the last two blocks, passing the sidewalk fruit stands and sellers of religious trinkets and devotional objects that had agglutinated around the mosque in expectation of a brisk after-prayer trade.

The Abu Nur Foundation, a massive work in progress built up over the years by the slow process of accretion, like a corral reef, dominates the skyline of upper Damascus. Where once stood a humble congregational mosque there now towers an eight-story raw concrete structure that houses classrooms to accommodate its 5,000 regular and 7,000 part-time students.

Within easy walking distance of Abu Nur—named for a lieutenant of the illustrious and pious Kurdish liberator of Jerusalem, Salah al-Din—are the ancient *madrassas*, mosques, graveyards and *teqiyah* of the venerable Salihiyah district. The quarter had been first settled by refugees expelled by the

Crusaders from their villages in the Nablus region of Palestine. They were folk who followed a narrow, doctrinaire interpretation of Islam. Later came itinerant Andalusian mystics, the foremost of whom was the great Mohid al-Din al-Arabi, whose underground mausoleum is today a place of modest pilgrimage, and of coolness on a hot day.

What more propitious a place could be found for an ambitious young clergyman to found a congregation? Here it was that Mullah Musa, the great-grandfather of the present Mufti, settled. He was seeking to expand his religious knowledge by taking counsel from the area's numerous religious teachers, whose fame extended throughout the Arab-speaking provinces of the Ottoman Empire. The family itself had originated in what is now south-eastern Turkey, in a village near the mountain-top town of Mardin that overlooks the Syrian plain.

Right on time—Syrians have a well-deserved reputation for seriousness, courtesy and punctuality, except where overworked, underpaid civil servants are concerned—Faruq stepped out in front of the portal in which he had been waiting, as knots of worshippers filed into the building. From deeper within the huge structure I could hear the murmur, insistent, of many voices speaking softly. We moved rapidly through a lobby, down a series of corridors and to an elevator which whisked us up to the third floor. We had reached the prayer hall level. There we removed our shoes, and I followed my host down the central aisle through a crowd of several thousand worshippers toward a large, stuffed divan-like armchair placed beneath the *minbar*, the pulpit that abutted the wall. Turning to the right, he found me a place to sit, then hurried off to his interpreting booth in a glassed-in gallery two floors higher.

A young man edged over on all fours and handed me a headset and backrest. Not far away, another young man was chanting a rhythmic incantation that sounded for all the world like the *dhkir*, the term which denotes both calling God to mind and invoking Him and, for the Sufis, "symbolizes the Covenant sealed between God and man in pre-eternity, before man's arrival on earth."[33] A faint smell of rosewater wafted through the room. Sunlight shone obliquely through the high windows, and ceiling fans rotated lazily high above.

Around me men wearing the traditional long robes and turbans of the *sheikh*, or religious authority, sat or squatted. Some were of venerable age, some in the prime of life, some just this side of early maturity. The nature of the place was unmistakable: if these men were not Naqshbandi Sufis, in behavior remarkably like those whose constant company I had kept in Turkey, then I had indeed fallen in with skilled imposters.

Looking upward, I caught sight of Faruq behind his microphone, and across the cavernous space, another gallery filled with women. Excitement rippled through the hall, and a deep bass humming welled up in the room, the threnodic repetition of the word *huw*, Arabic for "He," as the Grand Mufti made his way slowly through the crowd of believers. The chanting, I was certain, referred not to the Mufti, but to God.

Mardin, the Kuftaro clan's place of origin, is the city where Saïd Nursi had circumambulated the parapet of the minaret of the town's Great Mosque in 1892, and encountered militant Islamic reformers. Saïd's path had led him to Istanbul where he admonished the Sultan and, eventually, to hardship and exile at the hands of Turkey's republican dictators. The path of the Kuftaro family had brought it to Damascus, and to the summit of religious prestige and authority.

Both men were Kurds, those irreducible, irascible, untamable and resilient odd-men-out of empire; proud, disputatious, ready to fight at the merest pretext, and deeply attached to the freedom of their mountain valleys. Both men were also members of the Naqshbandi order.

Mullah Musa sent his son Emin to study with the local scholars who congregated in Salihiyah. After a rapid and distinguished passage through the complexities of the traditional Islamic education system, Emin began to preach in the tiny mosque that then stood on the site of the present-day Abu Nur Foundation. Soon after, he married and started a family that would be made up of five boys and two girls. One of the five was Sheikh Ahmad, who seems to have been, from birth, his father's favorite.

Now, the man who in Syria wielded a spiritual influence greater than the president's made his way slowly, laboriously before me, a tiny, ancient figure bent lower than the Pope, supported by a group of his devoted handlers. As the throaty, droning hum reached a climax, they helped him clamber into his padded throne, smoothed his robe, then sat cross-legged on the carpets at its feet. Silence fell upon the huge room. Ahmad Kuftaro began to speak.

His words, conveyed by the headphones in Faruq's idiomatic translation, which tracked the unpredictable course of the Mufti's talk as a skilled canoeist would follow the invisible channel of a fast-flowing stream, were easily understood. But his method resisted comprehension at first. Perhaps I had expected a prepared and structured sermon, a text with a beginning, a middle and an end; a series of propositions, perhaps some timely advice or an exhortation to the faithful. It was instead to be a rambling homily, with no apparent internal logic, no conclusion, no lesson.

Once again I had been misled by my assumptions, though this I was only to learn over time, after attending several more of the Mufti's Friday sermons. For all the apparent formlessness of his remarks, he seemed to be speaking to me, and from the expressions on the faces of the members of the congregation, to each of them as well. Arabism, he began, as if to stroke the sensibilities of his listeners, was the essential component of Islam. The Persians and the *Rum*—the Byzantines—were the two Great Powers of the day. And yet in less than twenty-five years, thanks to the Teacher who taught all, everything had changed. "A humble mosque with a dirt floor brought forth a great people who changed the world around them."

I had been told that because of his frail health, the Mufti would speak for fifteen minutes. Forty-five minutes later, he was still going strong, eyes bright, piping voice firm. As the sermon finally drew to a close, Sheikh Kuftaro returned to his original proposition, seemingly to turn it on its head. "The enemies of Islam," he said, "have promoted Arabism to divide us. We must return to the Qur'an of true understanding."

* * *

FIRST AMONG THE CONTINGENT of master-craftsmen whom the Basileus had dispatched to Damascus at Caliph al-Walid's bidding was a group of mosaicists, practitioners of an art that had been brought to perfection in Constantinople. The new mosque abuilding would be unlike anything theretofor seen or imagined. It would, in the mind of its architect, transform the proudest of Byzantine art forms, that which it had inherited from its Roman ancestors and best identified it, into something new and unmistakably Islamic.

How remarkably successful the project was can still be measured today.

As I walked slowly across the courtyard of the mosque after parting company with Faruq, I looked up at the walls above the colonnade, where the fragments of those original mosaics still cling. Only a fraction of the original decorated surface of 30,000 square meters has survived the assault of time, fire, vandalism and earthquake. Restoration of doubtful quality has attempted to fill some of the gaps. But the remains of the dazzling mosaics that once covered both the inner and outer walls still gleam green and glint dusky gold in the meridian sun.

The mosaics, more even than the mosque itself, were an artistic challenge to Byzantium's symbolic supremacy. They are what representational religious art in Christianity—and ultimately in our culture—might have been had the

Iconoclasts prevailed. Respectful of the limitations on figuration inherent in Islamic teaching, they depict trees with luxuriant foliage, gardens, stylized flowing water, and complex groups of buildings. No living being can be seen, nor could be. The mosque's decorators had adapted the Byzantine pictorial vernacular the better to transform it. In their extraordinary mosaics, they demonstrated the potential of a distinctly Islamic approach to a religious art form of which Constantinople had been the unquestioned master.

Most scholars, and the many chroniclers who have described the Umayyad Mosque, believe that the images are those of the heavenly garden so often promised believers in the Qur'an, with its leafy bowers, fruit trees and the rivers that flow beneath it. But one, a scribe called al-Maqdisi, argues for a more mundane reading: "There can hardly be seen a tree or a city known to man that has not been represented on the walls of the Great Mosque. The mosaicist has set out to express the dominance of the Muslim caliphate."[34]

For others, "these motifs represent Damascus itself: its streams, its Ghuta, is vineyards and its houses."[35]

Was there really a contradiction? In Islamic tradition, Jerusalem had long laid claim to the status of terrestrial paradise. But it enjoyed no monopoly. The Damascus oasis, "on account of its fertility, abundant water supply and pleasant climate ... is frequently referred to as a paradise on earth."[36]

I was determined to test the hypothesis, to make an excursion into the oasis, to assess for myself the extravagant claims made on its behalf. But I was reluctant to do so on my own. Better to go with a companion, with someone who could act as a guide. Months passed. Then, on the final day of the *Eid al-Fitr* holiday, a few days before Christmas in 2001, my friend Abdullah and I hired a taxi for a foray into al-Ghuta, the precinct of orchards and gardens to which Damascus owed its reputation as "the earth's beauty spot, the betrothed of the world, the feathers of the peacock of paradise ... "[37]

The man who, for reasons easily understood in Syria, I will call Abdullah proved the ideal companion. He balanced an inquiring, modern sensibility with a barely concealed, somewhat self-deprecatory nostalgia for a bygone day, something I found startling but refreshing in a society where the attractions of Western modernity are hugely magnified by their remoteness and inaccessibility.

Modern Syrian poets to this day sing the praises of al-Ghuta, and of the Barada River, the waters of which flow down from the foothills of the Anti-Lebanon range to irrigate it, explained my friend. "Look," he snorted, "the Barada has become an open sewer, and they are burying al-Ghuta under concrete. These people are perpetuating a myth, that's all they are doing."

Not that I didn't believe him. Over the course of the months that we'd known each other, most of Abdullah's insights had proved well-founded. But I wanted to see for myself. We hailed a taxi in front of the Hijaz Railway Station, bargained briefly with the driver, and climbed in.

No clearly drawn boundary line divides the urban sprawl of the city from its surrounding oasis. Only five minutes after passing the Bab Sharqi, the Old City's eastern gate, scraggly groves and patchwork fields begin to appear, surrounded by mud-brick walls butted up against multi-floor apartment blocks. To our right, the road branches south toward Jeramana, once a village, then a satellite town, and now all but engulfed by the marauding city of four million. For all its absorption as an enclave, Jeramana has preserved its particularity as a kind of half-way station for Syria's Druze migrants on their way north to Damascus from Suweida, the Druze "capital" in the heart of the Jabal al-Arab.

Our trajectory is not south, however, but east. Through dusty streets, thick with the billowing plastic bags that seem to litter every square meter of the Syrian periurban landscape, we move ahead with all deliberate speed. Our driver is bemused. Instead of rushing to our destination, we are creeping along, zigging and zagging, with no destination. Instead of urging him on, we restrain him. Go right, we instruct him. Go left. Back up. Slow down.

Gradually we leave the populated areas behind. Down short streets we catch a glimpse of fields. Then, gliding imperceptibly from between multi-story apartment blocks and ranks of low-lying shops with shutters drawn tight for the holiday, we emerge into the countryside. Here, at last, we enter the semi-mythical al-Ghuta of Syria's anachronistic, laughably romantic poets. Was it also the vision of earthly paradise, the source of inspiration of the Umayyad mosaicists?

It was hard to imagine anyone more un-romantic than Abdullah. He is a man of sharply held views and strong sentiments: love or hate, and little in between, as if to mirror his own life as a man oscillating between a traditional background of modest means, and a danger-defying fascination for modernity. Once upon a time, he confesses with a wry smile, he had known such feelings. He remembered certain places amid the orchards and the irrigation canals, recalled the experiences of a decade before, when the city still knew its place. In the spring, he said, people would come here to enjoy the cool of the evening in the open-air restaurants and the tea-houses.

They are a fading memory now.

Pruned, tilled, trained, cultivated, fertilized and irrigated for millennia, al-Ghuta is a crazy-quilt of orchards—mostly cherry, apricot, peach and plum which, each in its season inundate the city's markets and pushcarts—; of tiny open fields planted to tomatoes, cucumbers, eggplant and zucchini, mint and tarragon, rocket and romaine; of groves of fast-growing poplar trees the trunks of which are used to this day, laid side-by-side and covered with a thick coat of native mud, to build the roofs of traditional houses.

In one orchard, among the bare-limbed fruit trees, fresh green grass had sprung up after a night's rain several days before. Now, as a shepherd looks on, back propped against a tree, his sheep forage placidly. The scene is one of pastoral contentment, like something out of a Middle Eastern version of Handel's pastoral *Acis and Galatea*. Only the happy nymphs and happy swains are missing. The monster Polypheme, disguised as urban sprawl, lurks offstage.

The ruling Baath Party's agrarian reform of the early 1970s had a particularly fierce impact here in the oasis. As it did throughout the country, the new regime sought the support of the independent small-holders—naturally enough, for the party's leaders were men of modest means, often from small towns, who saw in the Baath a remedy for their thralldom to the traditional Sunni landowners of the cities.

The idea was to ensure a steady supply of food to the city and to its factories, while putting an end to the traditional system of crop financing which lay in the hands of the wealthy merchants of the Damascus *suq*.[38] In social terms the goal seemed laudable, and it was achieved. The monopoly of the powerful merchants was shattered, touching off their decline as the city's principal economic and political force. But by breaking up the large estates, the land reform made the small-holders vulnerable in other, unforeseen ways to the pressures and attractions of the encroaching city.

From a nearby field comes the rhythmic putt-putt-putt of a water pump. Along the boundary lines dividing orchard from field we see Bedouin encampments. Black tents are flimsily pegged to the bare earth. Barefoot children, scraggly dogs and flocks of sheep trot along, dust rising from their feet. There is not so much as a sprig of green in sight. The pastoral calm of grazing animals had given way, in the space of a few kilometers, to the search for the odd tuft of dry nettles among the wintery hummocks.

Now we are rolling down curving, narrow lanes beneath the overhanging branches of the oak trees which throw a dappled shade on the road surface. Perhaps this is the place where, as a medieval chronicler relates, twenty fully armed men had once staged an ambush from their hiding place high in the branches of a single mighty oak.[39]

By the early 1920s, a dense network of narrow roads—surely the same that we were following today—had linked the villages of al-Ghuta. All goods were transported on the backs of animals. Its orchards and lanes were lined with mud-brick walls topped with branches to dissuade unwelcome visitors. The oasis had been transformed into an intimate, tight-knit landscape which provided an ideal environment for surprise attacks by the nationalist guerrillas who fought a running battle with the French occupation forces. During the Great Revolt, in 1925, the French Army destroyed most of these walls.[40] The pretext, of course, was "fighting terrorism," as a people's defense of its land against the usurper was called, then as now.

Smoke from a distant fire hung in the air, lending the wan winter sunlight a melancholy tone as its oblique rays penetrated the thicket overhead. Damascus could well have been dozens of kilometers behind us now. The horizon was all bare-branched trees, fallow fields, and the brittle yet enduring tracery of irrigation ditches and canals.

I felt myself succumbing to the seductive appeal of al-Ghuta, to the blending of truth and tall tale; on the verge of being trapped between the legend of paradise and the reality of the catchment ponds where the murky, polluted waters of the Barada, having accumulated the raw sewage of Damascus as it flows sluggishly beneath the city, lie stagnant. In the taxi, conversation had stopped. I noticed Abdullah glancing at me warily out of the corner of his eye.

The taxi veered left, and in the middle distance we spotted a minaret. Then, in quick succession, its dome and the unmistakable contours of urban blight: shop-lined streets, sidewalks planted with dusty eucalyptus, gray-ochre buildings that might well have been any downtown, posters of the al-Asad family peering into the future, torn between the self-assurance of power and the uncertainty of the tyrant who must always protect his back.

Midday, in this settlement which seemed almost to be holding its breath as it awaited the arrival of the spreading city, the streets were thronged with families out for a stroll. The Eid holiday, like Muslim society itself, is a family affair. Parents, children, in-laws, aunts and uncles are visited, tea and sweets consumed, lavish meals eaten while the sun still shines as if to quickly inverse the unnatural order of Ramadan. Boys cavorted in the alleys blowing off fire-crackers and firing toy automatic pistols, perhaps acting out the running battles between youthful Palestinians and the Occupation forces they saw every night on television. Here, a woman without *hijab* draws attention. Here, men with the proud bellies of prosperity and the self-assured swagger of a certain status could be seen, with their well-scrubbed families in tow.

Do not think that people here are particularly pious, said Abdullah, as if he had read my thoughts. He had done his military service in one such small town where he observed people's lives at proximity. They may look as though they are conservative, and the women may veil their faces, but underneath they are just like everyone else, he said. Tipplers, petty gamblers, adulterers and philanderers, should the opportunity arise. Put succinctly, dissemblers and hypocrites. That would make these pious citizens, leading their quiet, modest, difficult, or rewarding lives in the midst of al-Ghuta, people just like us.

Not that I was not prepared to accept my friend's judgement uncritically. Abdullah had a shrewd eye, not to mention a thin skin. But he was also no friend of religion, least of all the variety of visibly orthodox Sunni Islam that flourishes in the suburban neighborhoods of Damascus as it does in the new towns that promise one day to submerge the fertile oasis beneath a rising tide of concrete. In his summary judgement, I thought I detected a hint of the modernist malaise at the resurgence of faith that surrounded us so visibly, if indeed it was a return and not simply a continuation by other, more modern means of something begun long before among Syria's Sunni Muslim majority. In the climate of political repression that prevails in Syria, the only vector of opposition has remained what the West calls "fundamentalist" Islam. That it was the only critical discourse able to withstand westernizing totalitarianism that could take root in this environment seemed altogether plausible. Perhaps even inevitable. It would be clandestine; it would be cautious; it would be silent; it would be intractable.

We had reached the far extremity of al-Ghuta. Far behind us were the green and gold mosaics of the Great Mosque. Around us lay the grayness, dust, grit, hope half-fulfilled, half betrayed, halting pride and a dearth of future prospects. The oasis we had seen today was paradise no longer. Our taxi returned us to Damascus.

* * *

I MET HIM IN A CYBERCAFÉ. It was one of the dozens of hole-in-the-wall hangouts equipped with a handful of computers where Syria's fast-growing cohort of web-surfers repair for their daily—or weekly, for computer access is expensive—digital fix. A young man with a wispy beard, dressed in the threadbare garb of a Muslim religious student: white knit skullcap, flowing tunic and a silken shawl worn over the shoulders. What had caught my eye—I confess to having glanced shamelessly—was the boldface title of a document in English on the notorious defender of Islamic rectitude, Ibn Taymiyya, the thirteenth century scholar and polemicist. Ibn Taymiyya, who was born in Harran, the city where worship of heavenly bodies had been tolerated throughout the early years of Muslim rule and migrated to Damascus where he established himself among the city's most outspoken and rigorous sheikhs. There he inveighed against innovation, the worship of saints, and pilgrimage to shrines.[41] The name of Taymiyya, who is widely regarded as the spiritual forebear of the extreme Wahhabi sect that now rules Saudi Arabia, wields influence in large parts of Pakistan and has been linked with the extremist elements that coalesced to form al-Qaʻida, is often invoked by those whom we call "fundamentalists."

Did he speak English? I asked as he logged off and got up to leave. Yes he did, idiomatically too, with an American accent. Was he a religious student? Yes he was, at a *madrassa* not far away, in the heart of the Old City. Would he agree to talk over a cup of tea? He would.

In a quiet corner of a nearby teahouse, as shutters rolled down along the street, I listened to the young man's tale. (To protect his identity I shall call him Ahmad, though it is not his adopted Muslim name.) Born in the American Midwest, he converted to Islam in circumstances he declines to discuss, before migrating four years ago to Damascus. Here, in the ancient city he attached himself to a traditional theological establishment, learning Arabic in the process.

"Today, I've just about come to the end of my diet of mashed carrots. Soon I'll be able to begin eating the whole vegetable," he said, his modesty ill-concealing a pride of accomplishment I could not begrudge him. Ahmad was not alone. By his reckoning there are dozens, perhaps hundreds of foreign students of Islam in Damascus.

Many of them study at the Abu Nur Foundation; I had seen them in its corridors and classrooms. But Abu Nur wasn't to Ahmad's taste. The Foundation was too close to the power structure, he said, and had compromised its Islamic credentials by inviting Louis Farahkan to address the faithful. That had happened several years before, during the Middle-Eastern tour of the Nation of Islam's maximum leader, a circuit which also included embarrassments to Iran, not to mention Libya, where embarrassment in religious matters has become a way of life.

Ahmad had that kind of calm, bright-eyed intensity I'd come to recognize in the recently converted. Islam is a powerful spiritual, cultural and social force, and it can burn with a fierce, bright flame those who come to it of their own volition. "Fundamentalism," a concept which has been lifted straight from American evangelical Protestant religious practice and applied willy-nilly to Islam, does not really describe the outlook of a man like Ahmad. But it was clear enough that he had crossed over the cultural divide, a space at once infinitesimally narrow and yawningly wide, into another value system, one which was total, all-encompassing, nurturing. This system he would defend with all his soul I intuited as he spoke with reverence and familiarity of the great spiritual figures of Islam. What had brought him to the faith of Mohammad, he said, was the completeness, the wholeness of its spiritual universe. The vacuity, the crass banality of the life held up to young people in the West as the only possible future had, he suggested, helped speed him here.

While there could be no doubt about his sincerity, certain of Ahmad's beliefs struck me as aberrant, a reflection of the scholasticism which many claim has penetrated so deep into Sunni thought and doctrine as to render it, contradictorily, both fragile and immutable. "If I were to go to Iran," he told me rather melodramatically, when I mentioned my own travels to that self-styled Islamic state, "I would probably face death." How? I wanted to know. Since when had the Iranians become so thin-skinned as to threaten guests who did not share their doctrinal peculiarities? (What they were prepared to do to their own was another matter.)

"No, no! I've studied works by those who are under death sentence in Iran, because they reveal what is corrupt and un-Islamic in Shi'ism, how they curse the caliphs except 'Ali ... " What my young friend was telling me played to the perfect negative image of Sunnism propagated by extreme Shi'a thinkers, if one can call them thinkers. I wanted to ask Ahmad what really interested him: Islam, or the historical divergences, unresolved today and unlikely to be so tomorrow, between Sunni and Shi'a. I bit my tongue, but I was afraid I knew the answer.

From the tea house, we had migrated slowly to the empty taxi-stand in front of the West Gate of the Old City, at the feet of the citadel. The hour was late, the moon building to full after the first faint crescent that marked the end of Ramadan. Street cleaners swept around us. Drowsy beggars extended their hands perfunctorily, mumbling, then slouched on.

Syria's Christian minority was all too indulgently treated, he said, *sotto voce*, though there wasn't a soul within hearing distance. According to strict interpretation of law and custom, they should be required to dress in a manner deferential to their Muslim superiors and pay the obligatory head-tax. No construction of new churches should be permitted. But a few moments later, he was inveighing, as if to assure me of his moderation, against the extremist Wahhabis of Saudi Arabia, they of the medievalist near-sequestration of women, draconian interpretation of the *Shari'a* and ill-concealed support for the Taliban, not to mention a certain grudging admiration for their wayward brother, Usama bin Laden. These people were not espousing true Islam, certainly not.

To be fair to the young man whom I would be unlikely to meet again, his defense of Islamic law, the much feared and worse understood *Shari'a*, was trenchant and, to my inexpert ears, accurate. "*Shari'a* is not a system of punishments. It is a system of law. Take adultery, for instance." (The example was well chosen; few aspects of Islam touch off such *frissons* of voluptuous and horrified self-righteousness among Westerners as the Islamic view of sexuality and its regulation.) "The testimony of four eye-witnesses is necessary to obtain a conviction. Which means that, in practical terms, it's impossible to convict anyone. Where there are convictions, it is because the offending party has chosen to repent, admitted his or her guilt, and sought mercy."

In real life, things weren't so simple, and I knew it. In Iran, in poor and dusty provincial towns, women had been stoned to death, convicted under what would certainly have been claimed to be due and rigorous Islamic process. The condemned would not have been the corrupt and wealthy, but the destitute and desperate. Money may even have changed hands to ensure a verdict. And yet, Ahmad's point was well taken. Few Westerners would be likely, he suggested, to accept that the integrity of their legal systems be called into question, or rejected, because of an occasional or even systematic miscarriage of justice, to cast aside their civil and criminal codes because of a handful of corrupt judges, or, as in the United States, on account of the pervasive and endemic racism that has created a gulag for African Americans.

Since my encounter with Ahmad, my awareness of these young foreign students of religion—*taliban* in Arabic, the plural of *taleb*—was heightened. A few days later I spotted a young man walking along a lane in Halbony, my neighborhood in Damascus. He was caught up in an earnest discussion (God will surely forgive my journalist's indiscretion in involuntarily overhearing snippets of the conversation, as I had earlier caught a glimpse of the Ibn Taymiyya document) of the minutiae of certain *hadith*. (*Hadith* are those sayings attributed to the Prophet which Muslims, the Sunnis in particular, use to guide their behavior and thought. Some are reliable, some spurious. Their number is vast.)

The subject eluded me, but what did not was the intensity. I attempted, briefly, to imagine the grip of this environment over a young man far from his home and native culture, plunged into a new, powerful, enveloping system as demanding as it is consoling; the thrill of sudden certainty, of the feeling that, at last, the moral imperative that slumbers within us has found expression in a language understandable to the mind and the heart. I could imagine, too, the young man's vulnerability. And the temptation that lay before any scholar of religion who would, incautiously, inscribe words and ideas on such a blank, yet potently charged slate.

I mentioned the encounter with Ahmad when I met my friend Faruq a few days later. He shook his head with a hint of sadness: "Yes, there are some preachers here who are irresponsible. Their teachings are not what we mean by Islam. In fact, what they convey to these young men, who are impressionable, can be dangerous."

The danger seemed obvious. What seemed less obvious was why the Syrian state, which wielded tight control over all religious institutions on its territory, including the licensing of imams and the vetting of sheikhs, would permit the dissemination of ideas so totally at odds with the regime's advertised commitment to the struggle against extremism in any form. Dark rumors, of the kind that abound in a closed society like Syria's, spoke of a Faustian bargain struck by the authorities, to allow the pro-Saudi hyper-fundamentalist sects to prosper in return for substantial financial support from the Kingdom. But they remained rumors only, plausible—given the missionary zeal and deep pockets of the Saudis—but unverifiable.

* * *

THE SHADOWY WORLD of Islamist revival is nowhere to be seen at the far eastern extremity of al-Ghuta. The early January day was raw and blustery, with a hint of snow in the air. I was a passenger, not in a slow-moving taxi, but in a speeding, rattling pick-up truck driven by a spiritual boon companion.

On the overland journey from Istanbul that brought me to Damascus in the dying days of 2001 I had carried, along with my suitcase, a load of books: the multi-volume Arabic edition of the writings of Bediuzzaman Saïd Nursi. These I had been charged by my Turkish friends to deliver to an admirer in the Syrian capital. "Call him when you get there," I'd been asked. I did.

The voice at the other end of the line was a man named Muhammad Ridwan Majdalawi. He would meet me in a few hours to pick up the package. Thus began a friendship made up of theological dissertation and intellectual jousting, punctuated by spine-rattling, breakneck dashes in Mr. Majdalawi's battered pickup truck through the backstreets of Damascus that had both of us laughing, and me clutching the edges of my seat.

I soon came to call him Seyyid Ridwan—"Seyyid" means mister in Arabic; I was Seyyid Farid. He was a Palestinian who had lived in Trablous, the northern Lebanese port city also known as Tripoli, for several years before moving on to Damascus with his family. Our cross-town jaunts were always frantic. We were always a few moments late, but soon we came to realize that the journey was more interesting than the destination. On one such outing he confessed that while in Lebanon he'd owned a Mercedes-Benz. This he said as a sleek, late-model Benz of the kind driven by government or party officials, the only people in Syria who could afford such wheels, cut us off at an intersection.

"When I have such car, people pay attention to me," he laughed ironically. "Now, with this truck, no one sees me."

Better that way, I thought.

Our frankest, widest-ranging discussions took place in that truck. We were like strangers on a train, liberated from conversational convention, able to exchange confidences with the candor that thrives on fleeting proximity, on the need to speak one's mind rapidly for time may be short, and, given Damascus traffic, in danger. It was on one of our cross-town journeys that he revealed to me the deep personal crisis that had brought him from secular Palestinian nationalism to Islam, and from there into the orbit of the Sheik Ahmad Kuftaro. It had been a period of inner turmoil which he described in detail I undertook not to reveal under any circumstances.

My short-jaunt travel companion was a man engaged in a constant dialogue with his faith, this much I could disclose. Nothing was to be taken for granted, all was to be tested. One of those tests was the effort to bring others to that faith. So it was that as we waited in rush-hour grid-lock, or slalomed in and out of slow-moving traffic, my own beliefs were probed, examined and weighed.

"You are not minding I ask you these questions?" he had once asked, as we rounded a tight turn and came to a sudden, skidding stop behind a slow-moving garbage truck.

"I would mind if you didn't," I'd replied, jamming my foot to the floor against an imaginary brake. My own disposition tended to draw the question.

We laughed.

Not only had the book delivery brought me an excellent companion. Seyyid Ridwan was an expert in *fiqh*, Islamic jurisprudence, and in the interpretation of *hadith*, the sayings and actions of the Prophet Muhammad as collected and collated by scholars and shaped by generations of erudites and exegetes into the corpus that defines Islamic life and structures Muslim society. Surely I could raise with him the question of Islam's attitude toward the depiction of the human form.

"Yes," he said. "I will say you what I know. But we must find a man to interpret. For me, too difficult."

We agreed and shook hands on the deal.

He would find the man. I would find the time.

Today we had another destination: the country residence of Sheikh Ahmad Kuftaro, at the far reaches of the oasis not far from the Damascus Airport highway.

After I had attended several of the Mufti's homilies at the Abu Nur Foundation mosque, Faruq Akbiq had finally concluded the arrangements for our meeting. Sheikh Ahmad would receive us on Saturday, the day after his weekly sermon. By now I was convinced that the Mufti's apparent lack of method concealed an approach that was all the more methodical for being invisible, but that it was indeed a method that possessed the qualities of the finest aged wine, to coin a distinctly un-Islamic metaphor. All was subtlety, nuance, demi-tone, suggestion, allusion.

Over the weeks I noted how certain themes would recur, with slight variations. He had fleetingly referred to Arabism, to touch upon it again, critically, later in his talk. In his Friday homily the day before, he had been less restrained: "Arab nationalism has given us twenty-two states and the need for twenty-two visas. But what did Arab nationalism do for Islam? What did it achieve for the Arabs themselves?"

Religions, he went on to say, follow the same curve as life itself, from youth through maturity until old age, with its bent back, wrinkles and white hair. This he said with a smile, as if to certify that he knew whereof he spoke. Muhammad's prescription for the inevitability of degenerescence was to reassure the believers that God would send, at the end of every century, a renewer. "Such a man, more perfect than those around him, would attack the extremes which make religion unacceptable to humanity."

"Indeed, we have progressed," he said, his gentle irony settling lightly on the shoulders of the congregation. "In our egotism and in our ability to produce weapons of mass destruction."

As I glanced around me at the faces staring with undivided attention, I understood the Mufti's uncanny power. His was not the way of the traditional preacher brandishing certainties and calling down curse and anathema— though he could do that too, as he demonstrated when the United States attacked Iraq. Then, stepping out of character, he had authorized martyrdom attacks against the invaders, and called on the faithful to carry out armed resistance as a sacred obligation—*jihad*—where possible.

His method I witnessed in Damascus was rather that of the butterfly, flitting from one subject to another, from the worries and problems of one of the two thousand-strong congregation to another as if they were so many flowers upon which his words would alight with their dusting of spiritual pollen.

I snapped out of my reverie and into the present. In a cloud of dust, Seyyid Ridwan's vehicle swung abruptly from the winding al-Ghuta road, passed through an unguarded gate, roared down a long driveway and finally skidded to a stop just beyond a three-storey concrete building surrounded by vine-laden bowers from which dangled the shriveled remnants of autumn's grapes.

The Mufti's detractors accuse him of living like a king. But there was nothing kingly about his residence. The building contained, from my cursory examination, little more than the bare minimum needed for an old, infirm man to be looked after in moderate comfort. Far from luxurious, these quarters were somewhat Spartan.

As we stepped into the elevator, I reflected that they were quite in keeping with Sheikh Ahmad's public character, that of a man whose modesty stood in sharp contrast to the nouveau-riche exhibitionism of the country's Baath Party rulers.

Whose credentials, I mused, were the more genuine? Those of the al-Asad clan, parvenus from the Alawite mountains who had grabbed state power in a series of military cabals and bloody purges? Or those of the tiny, frail man of Kurdish descent whom I would soon find propped up in the large bed that occupied most of his reception room? It was a false dichotomy. The Mufti had no claim on the temporal, no craving for earthly dominion.

The tiny, creaking elevator reached the third floor. We transited a narrow corridor, then stepped into his room. Faruq Akbiq, who would be acting as the Mufti's interpreter, had already arrived. With us were two of Sheikh Ahmad's male nurses.

By now, the Mufti could recognize me. I had been a front-row listener at his Friday sermon for several weeks, and on several occasions our eyes had met. For all his frailty, his handshake was firm and warm. Hot tea soon arrived. I had not come for an interview, I explained through Faruq, but simply to pay my respects. The old man smiled.

I had asked Faruq to convey to him my concern that despite the best efforts of the world's spiritual leaders, an open clash of civilizations had now seemed to have replaced dialogue. That seemed to have been the principal result of the events of September 11, 2001. The reply, true to Sheikh Ahmad's method, was oblique, elliptical, flitting, suggestive.

"It is the will of God," he said, "that human beings should impart happiness to themselves and to others. This is the great example of the prophets. But when humans lose sight of this duty, they become like animals." If present-day people cannot grasp this simple fact, he argued, it is because they lack education, lack the direction that can only come from teachers with the true qualities needed to dispense the necessary instruction.

"Today," he continues, "we must convert the colossal sums spent on producing calamities into the creation of an earthly paradise until such time as our souls rid themselves of their shells, and gain release from the prison of egoism." How is this to be done? Through the application of reason and logic. Modern means of communication can multiply a single knowledgeable person one-million fold.

(The thought slides across the back of my consciousness: might the Mufti have too rosy a conception of the purported powers of communication to break down the barriers that divide humanity? What had these superior powers done for the population of the United States, mired in ignorance fostered and exacerbated precisely by the omniscience of communication?)

"The very idea of faith has been distorted, and we are the distorters. We think we have belief, but it is the result of our own intellectual folly. The people who propagate such folly are atheists, those who put salt in tea, causing all those who seek refreshment to reject it.

"But if a human being searches with dedication and devotion," he went on, "God will help him reach that which he seeks, as a reward for his sincerity. Were not the prophets humans like us, with eyes, ears, hands? But they were graduates of that school of wisdom and steadfastness. Until now, we are drawing nourishment from the crumbs of their table."

The Mufti's tone was identical to that of his Abu Nur homilies, but more intimate. His audience today consisted of a lone foreign writer and a handful of men who could not be described as friends, but whose feelings for him surely exceeded friendship. They were pupils, he the master; they the wayfarers, he the path.

"I see no difference between the West and Islam," he concludes, finally turning to my question, as I was certain he would. "Both arise from the same origin. How can a teacher teach one thing to some, and another thing to others, or abrogate what he has taught? If we have differences, it is because of blind mimicry, without reason, of the ways of others."

It seemed a gentle rebuke to his coreligionists. Such would have been the Mufti's way; to speak of the ills that afflict his own house before taking note of those of others. "Yes, the religion of Muhammad is the highest level, that of

PhD studies. But it would be wrong to mistake Islam for the status-quo of Muslims. They are in one valley, Islam is in another. Today, they have distorted their religion, which seeks mercy for all humankind."

Sheikh Ahmad paused, sighed, and took a sip of tea.

"God gave us life in this body as a seed to be planted, watered and tended, even under the most adverse conditions. If you are humble and modest, you will be lifted up, and the seed planted deep in the earth will become a source of beauty for others."

He fell silent. Many days, as the poet says, had passed in a very short time. I looked out the window. The leafless trees of al-Ghuta swayed silently against the slate gray sky.

From the vantage point of his ninety years or more (no one knows exactly how old Ahmad Kuftaro really is), he looked down upon humanity with the all-encompassing eye of the elephant. There, far below, conflict, death, horror and redemption played themselves out in the souls of humans craving for, denying, or fleeing from divine grace. It was as though in his eyes I could see the world as it must have appeared to him, like the mosaics that adorn the Umayyad Mosque, a bountiful orchard in vibrant tones of green and gold, with the swift river of time coursing, unquenchable, through it, as it had shown itself however fleetingly to me that day.

3

The Hama Rules

THE EARLY 1980S WERE YEARS of ferment and upheaval in the Islamic world. The beginning of the decade witnessed the thunderous collapse of a living idol, the self-styled King of Kings, Shah Mohammad-Reza Pahlavi. He who would have ruled Iran as the spiritual successor to Cyrus the Great was swept away by an unlikely revolution led by turbaned Shi'a men of religion.

Two years after the shah's fall, the whirlwind touched down in Syria. President Hafiz al-Asad had transformed the Baath Party into a vehicle for his personal ascension. As the respect owed the ruler metamorphosed into servility, as authority reshaped itself as tyranny, the coals of resentment began to glow, then burst into flame.

The blaze broke out in Hama. Why it did not inflame all Syria is a story that is only now, twenty years later, beginning to emerge from the still-smouldering ashes of the bonfire that consumed the ancient city on the Orontes.

On an axis with Aleppo to the north, and Homs and Damascus to the south, Hama is one of the four cities that form Syria's urban spine, the last rampart of civilization before the sand, gravel and stubble of the desert. In the later decades of the twentieth century, it had earned a reputation as "a city closed in upon itself, and a byword for landlordism, conservatism, religious zealotry and xenophobia."[42]

Summary and sweeping as the judgement is, it contains—as does any libel—a grain of truth. Hama had long been a traditional city where piety was prized, where women tended to be heavily veiled, and mosque-going popular. A nucleus of wealthy merchant-landlords exercized dominion over the surrounding countryside, populated by impoverished peasants held in their thrall. The arrival of modernity—that is to say, of the West—which not unfortuitously coincided with the collapse of the Ottoman Empire and the establishment of the French Mandate, overturned the old ways, emancipated the peasantry, undermined but did not destroy the pre-eminence of traditionalist Sunni Islam, and set Hama on a collision course with the onrushing juggernaut of secular Arab nationalism.

Hama today is a quiet city of shade trees, finely crafted stone walls, bustling *suqs*, and huge wooden waterwheels—the *norias*—that raise water from the river into the venerable irrigation network that once fed its rich and productive fields and gardens. A citadel which conceals beneath it the remains of a mighty neolithic tell looms over the town.

It remains a pious city, where a visibly larger percentage of women than in the rest of Syria wear an extreme form of *hijab* that covers all but the eyes.

I had stopped off in Hama on my way from Damascus to Aleppo late one afternoon in early spring. As the sun sank beneath the mountains to the west, I followed the winding path to the top of the citadel. The public park at the flattened summit was empty of picnickers and pleasure strollers. A chill breeze whispered in the trees. Stray cats darted through the undergrowth. From far below came the mournful squeal and creak of the *norias* that line the riverbanks.

I looked northward across the dark strip of the Orontes. There, shrouded by a deeper darkness set off by winking lights lay an empty quarter. I knew what it concealed: the remnants of the center of the old city, a monument to devastation.

* * *

LONG BEFORE I HAD even imagined that I might one day come to Syria, the name of Hama had registered itself on my consciousness. Terrible, inexplicable events had taken place there, that much I remembered. What they were, and who they involved escaped recall and comprehension. When I finally reached the country, nearly two decades later, it took very little time to realize that Hama was a city spoken of in hushed tones; a city that declines to speak. In a country where the president's every pronouncement is met with an avalanche of laudatory telegrams from civic and other ruling party front organizations, Hama maintains a tight-lipped conspicuous silence.

A Damascene acquaintance, a distinguished academic who lectures regularly throughout the country as well as abroad, told me that the same lecture that was greeted with applause in any other university would be met with stony silence in Hama. Where normally speakers would be peppered with questions, he said, in Hama no questions were asked. Hama is a city where, every year, on the occasion of the president's Ramadan amnesty, parents throng to the bus terminal in the hope that at last their missing children will be returned to them alive. Twenty years after an atrocity so terrible that it cannot to this day be spoken in the land, Hama remains a city in mourning. Why this is so remains a forbidden topic in Syria. Reliable eye-witness accounts are rare. The accepted version is deficient and necessarily partial; the contending version, like that of the iconoclasts, has been eradicated, banished and proscribed. For all of these reasons, and in spite of them, the story of Hama cries out to be told. I would, I concluded that night atop the citadel, attempt to tell it. The darkness looming at my feet, surrounded by the feebly twinkling lights of the city, was reason enough.

* * *

POWER DISFIGURES, physically as well as morally. The diet of wealth and abundance, the regimen of effortless comfort, the deference of vassals and the obsequiousness of subalterns cause a thickening of the features, a coarseness of the hands, an unfocused, humid brilliance of the eyes, a brusqueness of gesture, an abruptness of manner. The clothing of power is finely cut and sewn, its fabric carefully chosen, its accessories well matched, shoes shined to a mirror polish, its grooming faultless. But the blemish-free smoothness of its face cannot entirely conceal its cold reptilian stare.

I observed these things as I sat on the visitor's sofa in the office of Adnan Omran, on the eleventh floor of the Dar al-Baath, the Syrian ruling party headquarters building that overlooks the Mezzeh Autostrade on the outskirts of Damascus. Mr. Omran is Minister of Information of the Syrian Arab Republic, designated interlocutor for visiting journalists, mid-level delegations and second rank VIPs.

In the event, I was not a journalist, and certainly not even semi-important. But Munir Ali, the resourceful, chain-smoking director of the Ministry's foreign press office had cajoled an audience for me. If I were to write about Syria, I had explained, it would not do to report only criticism of the regime.

Mr. Omran's manner was at once expeditiously gruff and expansive, abstractly solicitous and impersonal. As he spoke in fluent English, my eyes strayed upward to the larger-than-lifesize portrait of President Bashar al-Asad gazing sternly yet benevolently down from behind his desk. I couldn't avoid the thought: Syria's Baath regime ruled through icons ostensibly profane, but which had a sacralizing function.

The ritual cup of coffee appeared, but Mr. Omran's set-piece presentation left time only for a sip, and by the time I could rest my pen (for it would be more impolite to appear anything less than fascinated by the words of a high official than not to partake of his perfunctory hospitality) the coffee was cold.

The date was late December, 2001. A scant three months had passed since the attack on the World Trade Center. The Minister was summarizing the Syrian regime's position:

"Syria was quick to offer its condolences. But we should not leap into transforming this event into the end of something and the beginning of something else. Wisdom is needed. You cannot destroy the world around you. There must be not less, but more adherence to international law.

"All international norms are being set aside and we see increasing use of hegemonic power, verbal and military.

"We have heard irresponsible statements. According to Henry Kissinger, the world is now divided into two camps: that of the tolerant, the forgiving and the civilized, and that of the terrorists. This was from the man who is today accused as a war criminal.

"Today, we are seeing a return of Samuel Huntington's clash of civilizations. It is the West against the Islamic world and China. This theory is a racialist one, inspired by an idea of superiority. It is also connected with Zionist ideology.

"The West, and primarily the United States, is using the events of September 11 as an instrument for greater hegemony over the region. But most people here predict that the result would be an explosion."

It was a cogent synopsis of regional and international politics, reflecting the Syrian regime's view of its interests, and of the region. Mr. Oman spoke with the full and unchallenged authority of the state. A few weeks before, he had been freshly reconfirmed in his position by President al-Asad in a cabinet shuffle the aim of which was to bring "new blood" into the government without putting the stability of the ruling establishment at risk. In Syria, the state took it as its absolute prerogative to speak on behalf of the citizens who, in July 2000, had elected their new president "unanimously in a plebiscite for a seven year term."[43]

There had been no contending candidate. The idea of a contending candidate would have been, in al-Asad Syria, laughable and mortal.

Less than two months later, in a meeting with a high-level United States delegation, this same Adnan Omran had assured his visitors that Syria's dedication to the fight against terrorism was was as unmatched as its pedigree was impeccable. Twenty years before, he is reported to have said, the country had faced a fierce domestic terrorist movement and overcome it. Now the Baathist regime was ready to share its anti-terrorist knowledge and expertise with Washington.

If the hard-eyed men who design and execute United States Middle East policy were not listening, they should have been. On second thought, how could they not have been listening?

The authoritarian regimes of the Middle East, those which stand on guard over the region's oil fields at the behest of their Western paymasters, boast a record of violent repression of their own citizens for which neither they nor their geostrategic backers can contrive to feel the slightest shame. To employ concepts like shame with regard to the men, and the handful of token women, who rule over this hermetically sealed system established by the Sykes-Picot accords is, of course, as laughable as it is naive. A summary catalogue, in the form of an *aide-mémoire*, follows:

In Egypt, then-president Gamal Abdul Nasir, with the connivance and direct assistance of CIA operative Kermit Roosevelt—the same man who would oversee the overthrow of Mohammad Mossadegh in Iran in 1957—carried out in 1954 the violent suppression of that country's powerful and influential Muslim Brotherhood.[44] The inimitable Saddam Hussein, long-time ally and protégé of both the United States, Europe and the former USSR, successfully eradicated several tens of thousands of the members of Iraq's Kurdish population, and, in the closing years of the Iran-Iraq war, used chemical weapons to eradicate the population of Halabja, not to mention the gassing of Iranian troops on the battlefield in the closing years of the Iran-Iraq war. The chemical weapons he employed were provided by a coalition of Western countries, headed by the United States. Jordan, the semi-protectorate on the East Bank of the Jordan River, turned the full power of its American-supplied military (which, since 1948, had never engaged Israel, its putative anti-Arab adversary) on the Palestine Liberation Organization in the events known as Black September, in 1970.

Syria, however, was a special case. This was the country that had cast itself as the principled defender of the Arab national cause, the leader of the "steadfastness front" against the Zionist aggressor, the regime that prided itself on its devotion to the Palestinian struggle, and on its commitment to recapturing the lands occupied by Israel during its war of aggression in June 1967. None of these considerations was of the slightest avail to the citizens of Hama, the country's third largest city, when the Syrian Muslim Brotherhood rose in revolt in the early spring of 1982. Contrarily, they were invoked by the regime to crush the uprising.

On direct instructions from Hafiz al-Asad, and under the command of his brother Rif'at, crack units of the Syrian Army attacked and destroyed the center of the historic city, killing between 10,000 and 20,000 people—as much as one-fifth of the population. The final death toll is unknown to this day.

In the operation tanks, heavy artillery and helicopter gunships—prefiguring Israeli tactics in Jenin and Gaza—were used, the fighting was bitter, block-to-block, house-to-house. Entire neighborhoods, *suqs*, mosques and public buildings were levelled in an orgy of indiscriminate destruction. No one was spared, neither women nor children, neither the old nor the infirm. Hama had nourished within its bosom a mortal aversion to the kind of state which Hafiz al-Asad was determined to bring to the people of Syria. His verdict—for he was accuser, prosecutor, judge, jury and hangman rolled into one—spoke the implacable and ruthless measure of the man. Hama, having failed to bend, would be broken.

Obliteration was not enough. The wreckage, the rubble-strewn desolation that still lies at the city center, the dark field of obliteration I looked down upon that evening, would be left untouched as a silent reminder to survivors and visitors alike of what happened here, and by extension, what would happen to anyone who dared challenge the regime.

These were the Hama Rules, the unspoken but universally recognized doctrine that governs Syria to this day.

* * *

IN ONE OF THE NARROW ALLEYS that lead through Halbony to the Baramke Terminal stands a block of traditional houses built during the last years of Ottoman rule. How they have contrived to survive the clearances inflicted by the French mandate authorities in their suppression of the Great Revolt, and later, the wave of pseudo-socialist urban renewal that transformed many of the traditional neighborhoods of Damascus beyond the Old City walls into concrete apartment block wastelands is hard to imagine, but survive they have.

On a cold, bright, breezy day in January 2002 I knocked at the door of one of these dwellings. A courtly, fastidiously-dressed man opened the door. Before me stood Haitham al-Maleh, a seventy-year-old attorney and founder of the tiny, struggling Human Rights Association of Syria.

Built for the long, hot Damascus summer, the old house offered little protection against the cold. Mr. Al-Maleh was wearing a sweater under his jacket, I kept my coat on. Successive cups of hot coffee only barely held the damp, penetrating chill at bay. On the walls of his office hung several framed extracts from the Qur'an executed in finely detailed bead-work. My host noticed me examining them. "I did those when I was in solitary confinement," he said with a laugh, as he translates. They enjoin steadfastness and devotion. Though they meant to speak of their artisan's ordeal they might well have described his character.

Haitham al-Maleh was arrested in 1979, on direct orders from Hafiz al-Asad, whom he describes as "a bloody man" who respected nothing but his own cunning and thirst for power. I found it impossible to disagree with his characterization of the man who sought to define himself as Syria and, by elimination of his adversaries, in the short term proved successful. Asad has long been described as, at minimum, a ruthless Machiavellian prepared to use any means to attain his more realistic ends.[45] That was only the half of it.

"You were either with al-Asad or against him," he said, wincing at the uncanny resemblance with certain prevailing attitudes in international affairs. "Islamists, Communists, Democratic Baathists, lawyers like me, engineers, doctors ... Everyone was suspect. Anyone could be arrested at any time. He set up military courts to try civilians. More than 15,000 prisoners were killed in Palmyra prison, another 3,000 at Mezzeh, here in Damascus."

Mr. Al-Maleh, along with several colleagues who had been arrested with him, was released in 1986, after seven years behind bars. They had never been charged, never brought to trial, never convicted.

"Arab Union lawyers finally brought pressure to bear, and expelled the Syrian Bar Association [which by then had been taken over by the state and transformed into a rubber-stamp "mass" organization]. Hafiz al-Asad had promised to release us in mid-1986, but he reneged."

Then a funny thing happened. A sometime Syrian agent of Jordanian nationality by the name of Nizar al-Hindawi had persuaded his Irish girlfriend to carry a travel bag full of plastic explosives aboard an El Al flight from London to Tel Aviv. The explosives were discovered, al-Hindawi was caught, and confessed.[46]

Several months later, during the trial at which al-Hindawi was sentenced by a British court to forty-five years in prison, a BBC report linked the affair with Syria's detention of Mr. al-Maleh and his fellow attorneys. They were released on October 30, six days after the London court brought down its verdict.

"From that date, I established contact with international legal bodies, including Amnesty International. Our demand was simple and it has not changed. All political prisoners must be released."

"Since my release, I haven't stopped working. No one has given us any financial assistance," he said with a rueful grin. As I looked around me at the peeling plaster and blotches of mold that stained the ancient walls, I could believe him. His office's threadbare upholstery, wobbly tables and a dormant oil stove that seemed to mock us in the bone-numbing dampness were hardly the appointments of an upscale legal firm.

Mr. al-Maleh is a practicing Muslim who makes no apology for his beliefs. His dedication to human rights and a democratic future are no less intense. "This is my country and my people," he said. "I am prepared to pay the full price for what I am doing. I am 70 years old, my life is at risk, but I do not care. Of course, what I do is legal. But if they want to arrest me or even kill me, they will do it. That is why this regime must go."

As if on a paranoid's cue, the doorbell rang. When I jumped, Mr. al-Maleh laughed. "Don't worry," he said. "It's not the *muhabarat*,"—the regime's feared and loathed secret police—"I want you to meet two of my friends."

(My alarm had been both justified and misplaced. Syria in early 2002, and for the foreseeable future, was and would be submitted to the martial law regime in force since 1963, when the Baath Party seized power in one of the series of bloody coups d'état that had ushered in regime changes since Independence in 1945. Until "regime change" ushered in by United States military intervention or political pressure came about, that is. But these days, as I had learned from political prisoner friends, the security services no longer came bursting into private homes in the small hours of the morning. They telephoned and invited the object of their attentions to drop by for a cup of coffee. "If you accept the invitation, that cup of coffee might end up lasting for ten years," another acquaintance—who himself had received such a call but not taken up the invitation—had quipped.)

The luncheon guests were two eminent alumni of the Syrian higher education system, as the illegal detention system for political prisoners is jocularly known. As Mr. al-Maleh introduced them, his sense of pride and respect was palpable, for though they were younger, they had greater "seniority" thus merited greater respect.

In his previous life Dr. Adnan Faez al-Fawaz had been a physician, and a member of Syria's small but influential Communist Party. Caught up in the purge of what the regime defined as anti-regime elements from what today are called the organizations of "civil society," Doctor al-Fawaz inhabited the shadowy realm of semi-persons. "Look," he said, as he thrust his identity card into my hands. "It says here: 'no civic rights.'"

My reading knowledge of Arabic did not go beyond newspaper mastheads and micro-bus destinations, but I believed him.

His companion was a nervous, smilingly ingratiating man wearing large horn-rimmed glasses. His name was Salim Kheirbek. Mr. Kheirbek's offense had been membership in the national association of engineers, an organization that had committed the grievous error of issuing a public appeal for democracy. Its members were rounded up and, like Mr. Kheirbek, thrown in jail without trial.

"In this society," he said, laughing, "it's better not to be able to vote. There is no one here I could vote for until we can change the situation, and find candidates to represent us."

Rarely had I met a more good-natured, laughter-prone group of men. These three veterans of Syria's special system of higher education by incarceration without charge laughed heartily and often. It was the laughter of mockery, of course: gentle mockery of themselves, bitter when it turned against their captors and tormentors, the faceless nameless conscienceless minions of the dictatorship who had carried out the orders. Mockery perhaps—though none would be so indiscreet as to suggest it—of "God" himself, the ultimate authority from whom all power flowed, whose icon adorned every wall, every shop window, every office, every public space.

(There was reason for this laughter, which I would learn several days later. The scene was the al-Rawda café in downtown Damascus, not far from the parliament buildings. Al-Rawda is a public house in the traditional Damascene style, open to the sky during the warm months when pine trees growing in the central court provide luminous shade, thronged from morning until late at night with card, chess and backgammon players, solitary *nargile* smokers, newspaper readers, and the occasional intellectual holding court with a group of acolytes. A place where the ambient din provides a suitable environment for limited confidences. I was drinking a tumbler of fragrant cardamon-scented coffee with a man whose name I will not disclose, an eminent post-graduate student of the al-Asad Academy, who had served seventeen years for crimes of opinion without ever being once brought before a court, the man who had arranged for me to meet Haitham al-Maleh. "Why do we laugh all the time?" he asked rhetorically. "Because after what they have done to us, everything else in the world seems insignificant by comparison. And funny.")

"Our situation," said Mr. Kheirbek, "is a totalitarian one, centered on the person of the president. But he himself is only a symbol of the ruling structure.

It is made up of the Party, the security forces and the state bureaucracy. In this country, everything else is excluded from life and is without value. Look at our parliament, our labor unions, the press. All of them are helpless and without influence. They simply transmit policy from the Trinity."

As if to demonstrate the futility of public institutions, two outspoken members of the Syrian parliament—seen by most Syrians as an empty shell, or as a cruel parody of the democratic ideal—had been arrested several months earlier and thrown into jail. Their offense had been to call for reform of the decision-making process, and for an end to official corruption.

"After 40 years of rule by the Baath Party, we Syrians can do nothing," said Mr. al-Fawaz. "We do not have the conditions for people to create their lives, no way to achieve anything. Our institutions and our lives have been crushed."

Mr. Kheirbek nodded silently. He was not laughing.

The last word belonged to Mr. al-Maleh. "I've forgotten how to be afraid," he said, pointing a finger upward. "In the late sixties, the regime wanted to recruit me to the government. They attempted to bribe me. I refused. I knew I was going to end up in prison. I was not for sale."

Messages of warning were sent, suggesting that he leave the country. That too he refused. "I thought they would kill me. But I believe in God, *ulhamdullilah*."

* * *

HOW HAD IT COME TO THIS? When Michel Aflak, a Christian, and Salah al-Din al-Bitar, a Sunni Muslim, founded the Baath ("Renaissance") Party in 1946, nearly all the Arab lands were under direct foreign control, or strong foreign influence. The two men, provincial school masters who had lived in France during the Popular Front years of the late 1930s, returned to Syria full of dreams and audacious plans for the social and political emancipation of the Arabs.[47]

A first step toward this goal in Syria had taken place during the war. The pro-Nazi Vichy régime had withdrawn from the moribund League of Nations and terminated the Mandate. Syria was now an occupied country. On the pretext that the Vichy authorities had allowed German aircraft to land, British and Free French forces occupied the entire country. Bickering between England and France flared. General Charles de Gaulle's forces appeared determined to maintain their grip despite promises of independence, a preview of what France would later inflict upon Indochina, Madagascar and Algeria.

But de Gaulle's Free French were not yet a government; their undertaking had to be guaranteed by Britain. Thus began the end of French rule in Syria. Under British pressure, the French restored the constitution and elections were held in 1943. The National Bloc, which had waged a decades-long political struggle against the country's French overlords, triumphed and formed a government. The outcome displeased de Gaulle, who brought in troops and bombarded Damascus. The outrage brought a sharp British response. A superior British force marched into the country, established control and escorted the mortified French out of the capital.

For the first time in its multi-millennial history, Syria could claim to be a state. But it was an enfeebled state, ruled by the wealthy landlord class which had inherited its privileges from Ottoman times and defended them ineffectively against France's colonial depredations. Its days were numbered.

Like many aspiring national liberators of their generation, Aflak and al-Bitar had welded their dedication to the cause of emancipation of the homeland to the socialist doctrines they had become familiar with in France. Communism, because of its emphasis on internationalism, would not be viable in the Arab world, they decided. The conscious Arab, they wrote, was the one who realized the dynamic and revolutionary nature of Islam. This consciousness was henceforth named Arabism. It was to leave a trail of short-lived triumph, long-term disillusionment, social and political disaster.

In the minds of Aflak and al-Bitar, and in its programmatic documents, Baathism was to have been a liberal, idealistic doctrine that would harness the latent power of Islam to the quest for the shimmering goal of Arab unity. In the minds of a generation of junior officers hardened in the cut and thrust of barracks politics, of plot, coup and counter-coup, it would become a weapon to be wielded in their irresistible ascent.

Faithful to its pan-Arab ideology, the Baath recognized no borders. It conceived of the Arab world as the "nation" within which and on whose behalf it would function and which it would ultimately set free from foreign control. The party's first success came not in Syria, but in Iraq, in February, 1963, when a group of officers overthrew General Abd al-Karim Qasim in a brutal putsch. This was the General Qasim, who had unhorsed and later had killed the British-installed monarch Faisal II in 1958. One of the conspirators was an eager, ruthless young man called Saddam Hussein, who had hastened back to Iraq from exile in Egypt, some say with the encouragement of the CIA. The agency had claimed that the Qasim regime had been infiltrated by Communists. Saddam, like Suharto in Indonesia a few years later, won favor as an anti-communist hitman, and is reported to have been provided with execution lists by the Americans who would ungratefully turn against him forty years later.[48]

Absent were the Arab masses on whose behalf the rebels had struck. Absent they would henceforth remain.

One month after Qasim's fall and death in Baghdad, a secret junta of six Baath officers seized power in Damascus amid a public reaction of fear and indifference. The party's pan-Arab strategy appeared successful; a new power alignment was taking shape in the most volatile region of the globe.

Three years later, yet another violent coup had brought into power radical "regionalists" who believed in consolidating what could be called Baathism in one country. The "nationalists", who hewed to the purist view of an Arab nation that transcended colonial borders fled to Baghdad. Overnight, the dream of Arab unity had been weakened; the 1967 war would deal it the final, devastating blow. In Iraq, Saddam finally emerged as strongman in 1979, on the eve of the Islamic Revolution in Iran. Perhaps it was appropriate that Michel Aflaq, the founder and spiritual guide of the Baath, was forced to leave his native Syria and take up residence in Iraq, where he died a bitter, broken man. The fate of co-founder Salah al-Din Bitar proved even more tragic.

If the recent history of the Middle East is constituted of equal amounts of perfidy and tragedy, the first brought about from without, the second produced by the gods who grind human bones, the story of the Baath is one of its most cautionary chapters.

Created to channel the gathering momentum of Arab self-awareness and pride into the great river of socialism and national enfranchisement, the Baath was instead captured from within and transformed into an agency for the promotion of the heterodox Alawite minority in Syria, and Saddam Hussein's equally minoritarian Sunni al-Tikriti clan in Iraq.

Questions remain to this day unanswered. Had the Baath militant leaders' monstrous appetite for power perverted what its founders had created, or was perversion inscribed in its very organizational fibre and fabric? Was the failure of the Baath a part of the deeper, endemic inability of Arab and Islamic culture to create what Westerners like to describe as liberal institutions, assuming the latter to be if not irreproachable, at least that goal toward which all reasonable humans must strive?

The history of colonialism, a somber trade at which the liberal, democratic West excelled and which created the context in which movements like the Baath arose and flourished, not to mention recent developments in the United States, have contrived to cast these certainties in an ominous half-light. As the penetration of the United States regime by a small, well-organized group of plotters who do not disdain to conceal their aims indicates, not even "liberal democracy" lies beyond the organizational capacity and inventiveness of unscrupulous men craving worldly dominion. No structure is immune, no ideology, no system of checks and balances, no structure of government inherently qualified to resist. To believe otherwise is to nourish the cruellest of illusions.

* * *

BY THE TIME I REACHED DAMASCUS, Syria's most celebrated political prisoner was not available for meetings with visiting foreign writers. After an exposure to freedom as intense as it was brief, Riad al-Turk had been arrested anew and cast back into the prison system where he had survived for twenty years, thirteen of them in solitary confinement. Although I never met the man many Syrians call their Nelson Mandela, I managed to do the next best thing.

It was the spring of 2001. I had made the acquaintance of Mohammad Ali al-Atasi at the home of a mutual friend who was active in the newly-created, short-lived Syrian civil society movement. Mr. al-Atasi spoke fluent French, and made no secret of his feelings toward the regime. We agreed to meet again, at the earliest opportunity.

That opportunity finally arose in Beirut, where I had stopped off for a few days on my return to Montreal. At that time, he'd shown me his video documentary on this extraordinary political figure: a man who has no public identity and yet is certainly better known, and more respected in Syria than any member of the government.

Mr. al-Turk, a leading cadre of the Syrian Communist Party, had been imprisoned twenty years earlier. Insurrection was in the air. The Muslim Brothers' campaign to overthrow the Alawite regime they saw as inimical to the very existence of Islam was gathering deadly momentum. In the waves of repression that each new assault on the power structure provoked, the authorities cast an ever-wider net. Once collaborators with the ruling Baath Party, the Communists had moved gradually into opposition.

At the time, little love had been lost between the Brothers and the Communists. Now, however, they faced the same enemy. In fact, a shared perception of the fact may have thrust Mr. al-Turk behind bars once more. Several weeks before his arrest he had joined a representative of the Muslim Brotherhood for a live panel discussion on al-Jazira, the Qatar-based Arab satellite television station that so irritated George W. Bush during the war in Afghanistan that its Kabul offices were bombed by United States forces.

(True to form, al-Jazira's Baghdad correspondent was killed by an American rocket while he broadcast a news commentary from the roof of the station's facility in the Iraqi capital. The building's exact location and purpose had been declared to the United States military command well before the invasion began.)

Mr. al-Atasi, a contributor to the prestigious cultural supplement of the Beirut daily *al-Nahar*, had been drawn to Riad al-Turk for several reasons. Among them were his subject's extraordinary resiliency and courage, and his attitude to those whom he left behind when he vanished into the Syrian penal gulag. There was a powerful personal motivating factor as well. Mr. al-Atasi's father Nur al-Din had been a former president of the Republic who had ended up, after years of loyal service, crosswise with Mr. al-Asad and spent the rest of his life behind bars, where he died.

What was most striking about the video, which I saw at Mr. al-Atasi's Beirut apartment on a humid evening in March, was the character of Riad al-Turk. Though an old man, he still had the fiery, piercing eyes of the single-minded, militant combatant. In order to survive, he had so disciplined himself that he obliterated all memory of his family, his friends and his party comrades. His entire being he would then concentrate on confronting—and not bending to—his captors. Throughout his years in solitary, his only human contact had been the prison guards who brought him food. From this food, or more properly from the tiny inedible fragments he discovered in it, he would fashion the instrument of his survival and his sanity.

The lentil gruel he was served three or four times a week contained hard black seeds. These he removed from his mouth as he ate and put aside, until he had amassed several tens of thousands. Then, using his bedsheet as a canvas, he began to "paint," using the seeds as a pointilliste would use color. At first he executed geometrical and floral patterns, developing them slowly over days and weeks, then went on to increasingly intricate landscapes which took shape over weeks and months. It was methodical work that demanded absolute concentration. Precipitation was the enemy. When the sheet was moved by his jailers, and the picture scattered, he began again. Lesser men would have gone mad. In Syria's prisons many, perhaps most, did. His resolve steeled, Riad al-Turk endured physical torture—which he described as "nothing" compared to that inflicted upon the captured members of the Muslim Brotherhood—and the psychological torment of total isolation, of the weight of time.

Mr. al-Atasi's camera revealed him as a man of seemingly total self-control. The appalling circumstances of his captivity had transformed his face into a mask as impenetrable, implacable and unyielding—and perhaps as cruel—as the unseen faces of his tormentors. What human emotion, what compassion could a man who had willingly suppressed the memory of his family and his comrades as the price of survival still possess?

Mr. al-Atasi knew well a son's relationship to an imprisoned father. He set himself the task of cracking the mask. Riad al-Turk is shown being reunited with the daughter he hardly knew. Confronted with the overpowering emotional charge of the moment, he stares mute at the camera and gradually tears appear, glistening, in the corners of his eyes, his defiant glare diffuse, blurred.

Mr. al-Atasi and I met more than half a year later, on Christmas Day 2001 in a Damascus café frequented by young people who would be considered upscale in dowdy Syria, where the sweet life is circumscribed to a few square blocks of the capital and select, well-insulated holiday resorts. Perhaps not surprisingly, while he travels with relative ease between Damascus and Beirut, digital video disk copies of Mr. al-Atasi's al-Turk video must circulate clandestinely throughout Syria where they are regularly confiscated by the *muhabarat* when discovered.

In slowly thawing Syria, some things can be said, and well-circumscribed criticism can be levelled in cultural matters with some cautious leeway. Not so in the realm of politics. As our cups of coffee emptied and the café filled with customers, the young men sporting billed caps, their girl friends tottering on absurdly thick platform soles, and most nattering into mobile phones, the discussion turned to the question of legitimacy.

"In Turkey," he told me, "Atatürk and his followers won theirs in the war of independence. But here in Syria, the al-Asad regime lost every war it fought. The regime has no legitimacy, and it knows it. President Bashar al-Asad's only qualification for office is that he is Hafiz al-Asad's son. Only he could have made it possible for his father's legacy to be perpetuated … and made it impossible for Syria to turn the page, to admit the crimes and errors of the past, to make a new start."

Whatever faint hope might once have existed, he explained, lies buried beneath the ruins of Hama, the city where everything came to a stop in March, 1982. There can be no reconciliation in our country until the Hama file is opened, said Mr. al-Atasi, who can by no means be described as an Islamic fundamentalist. We must not judge the criminals, he adds. We must try instead to heal the wounds that will not close.

"Hama is a time bomb. If it is not defused, it will explode," he said as we stood up to leave. "Its people must be allowed to speak their pain and their suffering."

* * *

NO ONE, ASIDE FROM the regime's hard-core apologists, disagrees that the events that took place at Hama in the spring of 1982 were awful beyond description. But disagreement still persists over the precise sequence of events, and over who should bear ultimate blame. Let us begin with the victims.

The city, it is fair to say, had won a reputation for resistance to the central authority represented by Damascus well before the al-Asad dynasty had been established. Everywhere in Syria, since the late 1940s, the shock forces of the militant Baath Party and the Muslim Brotherhood had been clashing sporadically, fighting for control of the streets and ultimately for the destiny of the land. In Hama, where the new ruling party's policy had attacked religious conservativism head-on, traditionalists were aching for revenge.

In April, 1964, street rioting there against the newly established ruling party had been met by violent repression. For the first time, firearms were used. The army had been called in to suppress the uprising. Seventy members of the Brotherhood were killed; many more slipped away, and disappeared underground. One of them was a man named Marwan Hadid.

Hafiz al-Asad seized power in the bloodless takeover known as the Corrective Movement of November, 1970.[49] The putsch brought stability to a country wracked by internecine strife, a country exhausted by years of violent coup and counter-coup as military, religious and political factions fought for power. Hopes in the new leader, the former commander of the Syrian Air Force and Defense Minister, had been high. In the early years, his regime had been met, if not with widespread support, at least with a sense of relief that the chaos and violence of the preceding decade had been brought under control.

Less than ten years were to pass before things fell apart. The Baath had long ceased to be the vehicle of social idealism envisaged by its founders, Michel Aflaq and Salah al-Din Bitar. In the iron grasp of Hafiz al-Asad, the party that was to have integrated Arabism and the Islamic social, cultural and political heritage of the Middle East, had become instead a vehicle for the promotion of a religious minority with questionable Islamic credentials. For the country's Sunni Muslim majority, the seizure of ultimate power by a once-despised heterodox minority was as galling as it was provocative.

Now the near-absolute ruler of Syria, Hafiz al-Asad found himself under fire from adversaries with whom no compromise seemed possible: the Muslim Brotherhood. Had the country's economy been robust, had war with Israel and civil strife in Lebanon not absorbed vital energy and drained the treasury, had the corruption inherent in totalitarian regimes not sapped his credentials, the new president's efforts to portray himself as a benevolent, pseudo-democratic despot might have succeeded.

1979—the year Haitham al-Maleh was arrested—was a very bad year. Three years earlier, Syria had intervened in Lebanon on the side of that country's Christian minority and long-time ally of Israel against the Palestinians and their supporters. Muslims, not to mention Arab nationalists, predictably saw the move as a betrayal. Within the country, powerful and influential voices began to call for the overthrow of a regime which had apparently traduced its own bedrock principles of Arab solidarity and in the process become increasingly intolerant of criticism or dissent.

The October 1973 war with Israel, the conflict immortalized in the gigantic excess of the Damascus Panorama, had restored some of the pride of arms that had been so devastatingly shattered by the defeat of 1967. In its aftermath, whatever economic gains, whatever timid progress toward greater equality and opportunity among citizens had been realized, had been frittered away, or simply confiscated by a new ruling caste that had rapidly learned to enjoy its impunity. "Partnerships grew up between businessmen and the military and political barons of the regime, spawning networks of patronage, corruption and cronyism,"[50] writes Patrick Seale, al-Asad's semi-official biographer.

The storm was gathering: "Children of old notable families stripped of political influence, merchants outclassed by new money, religious families downgraded by the secular climate of the times all seethed with resentment."[51]

Long in the forefront of critical opposition to al-Asad and the Baath regime, the Brotherhood had become its spearhead. In mid-June, 1979, a commando squad broke into the Artillery Academy in Aleppo and opened fire on the cadets as they were mustering for morning roll-call. Thirty-two young men were killed, according to the official report.[52] Up until then, the pattern had been one of seemingly random explosions and assassinations, of which most of the victims were Alawites in positions of authority. Whatever doubts may have remained were dissipated. The regime now understood, in the instinctive, visceral mode of the cornered beast, that its survival was at stake, and that it faced an adversary as ruthless as itself.

From 1979 until mid-1980, the armed religious opposition and the growing mass movement that supported it held the initiative. The cities of Aleppo and Hama, with their narrow, winding lanes through which military vehicles could not pass, had become fortresses of resistance to the regime. Close-knit networks built up around the mosques provided money, manpower and supplies to the insurgents and the hit-squads who ventured forth to kill high-ranking members of the regime, usually Alawites. The fighters of the

Ikhwan al-Muslimin—the Muslim Brotherhood—were the violent spearhead of the movement, but they were not alone. Entire neighborhoods rallied to their call. The forces of militant Islam controlled the streets. When they issued the call, backed up by muscle if necessary, the *suqs* would close. In March, 1980, the entire business quarter of Aleppo was shut down for two weeks.[53]

Hafiz al-Asad's policy of incarnating Syria in his person, begun with his seizure of absolute power a decade before, now faced its severest test. The country teetered on the brink of civil strife. It was to be the ultimate test of the president's cunning and brutality and, ultimately, of his fitness to rule in the narrowest social-Darwinian sense.

On March 8, 1980, the seventeenth anniversary of the Baath-led revolution, he issued what Patrick Seale describes as a "ringing declaration of Islamic faith": "Yes! I believe in God and the message of Islam ... I was, I am and will remain a Muslim, just as Syria will remain a proud citadel flying high the flag of Islam! But the enemies of Islam who traffic in religion will be swept away!"[54]

The appeal won him nothing but opprobrium from his bitter enemies. On June 26, a group of Ikhwan fighters penetrated the president's entourage in Damascus, firing machine guns and throwing two hand-grenades at the president himself during a diplomatic reception. Al-Asad himself kicked one of the grenades away; a bodyguard fell on the other and was promptly blown to smithereens.

A wave of fury swept through the Alawite community, writes Seale. Units of the special paramilitary Defense Companies commanded by the president's brother Rif'at were flown to Palmyra, where Ikhwan captives were being held. Early in the morning of the following day, some "sixty men were driven to the desert prison, split up into six or seven squads and let loose on the prison dormitories with orders to kill everyone inside. Some five hundred inmates died in their cells. (...) On 8 July membership in the Muslim Brotherhood became a capital offense."[55]

* * *

TWO DAYS AFTER my first visit to Haitham al-Maleh's office I received a telephone call from his secretary. Another meeting had been arranged; could I come the following day? His guest would be Khalid al-Chami, one of the highest-ranking leaders of the Ikhwan al-Muslimin to have survived the events of 1982 and the horrors of Palmyra prison. After nineteen years behind bars, Mr. al-Chami had been released in late October, 2001, as part of the president's annual Ramadan amnesty. Now he was prepared to meet foreigners.

As I neared the door of Mr. al-Maleh's office, I noticed a tall non-Arab striding purposefully toward me. He was, I was soon to learn, a journalist from the *New York Times'* Cairo bureau come to interview Mr. al-Chami. My experience with American journalists in the Middle East has, for the better part of two decades, been as revealing as it has been depressing. As the princes and princesses of the media establishment, they have come to expect deference, or worse, reverence. As the courtiers of the mighty, they combine a rare obsequiousness when in the presence of their masters with a streak of domineering and often cruel indifference to all those below their lofty station. They may well be, in many cases, more interested in gathering intelligence than information. They all, without a second thought, speak in the imperial "We."

I thought back to another Cairo bureau chief, this one from *Time Magazine*, who once told me, in Tehran, that his editors would be the ones to invite then-President of France François Mitterand for lunch, and not the other way around. Or to the deferential rustle, the whispers of "here she comes now" when Christiane Amanpour of CNN entered a press conference given by Iran's President Mohammad Khatami. A dignified and decent man who must have felt it galling to speak on cue as if he were a late-night talk show walk-on, Mr. Khatami would have been counseled by his advisors to do just that.

Mr. al-Chami had already arrived, and was chatting with our host. He was a short, plump, clean-shaven, good-natured man who corresponded not at all with the stereotype of the turbaned Islamic fundamentalist or the bearded terrorist mastermind. Like many Syrian former political prisoners, his English was competent. Like those of his fellow former prisoners I'd met, his delight at being among the living was palpable and infectious. Still, it was clear that his principles had remained intact, as had his humanity. When New York Times attempted to exclude me from the conversation by speaking in halting though serviceable Arabic, Mr. al-Chami not only answered in English, but painstakingly translated the question.

Mr. al-Chami owed his life to the vagaries of fate, that much was clear. His arrest had come on January 6, 1982, one month before his native city, Hama, was to implode. The conflagration had been long in coming.

The French had, as a matter of colonial policy, cultivated Syria's minority religious and ethnic groups, who were seen as less vulnerable to the appeal of nationalism, as a counterweight to the Sunni majority. Under French rule, these groups were encouraged to look upon military service as the pathway to social and political advancement. Meanwhile, in the eyes of the mainstream population of the country's major towns and cities, to serve in the French-organized *Troupes spéciales* was seen as serving imperialism. Nonetheless, under the Mandate, a tradition of military service had been established, and was to continue after independence, in 1945.[56]

In 1948, the founding of the State of Israel administered to the Arab world a shock from which it has yet to recover. Confronted with the enormity of the Shoah, the West discharged upon the Middle East, and upon Palestine in particular, its own repressed guilt, along with the poisoned heritage of its incapacity to impose upon the Jewish people its own universalizing vision.[57]

The shock was compounded by betrayal. Palestine, it must be remembered, had always been a part of the historical Syrian lands, the *Bilad al-Sham*, which had long "had critical importance due its pivotal geographical position and its importance in the Arab and Islamic worlds as a religious, cultural and intellectual center and a source of political ideas and movements."[58]

Modern Syria, Lebanon, Jordan and Palestine are, when viewed from this perspective, hardly more than artificial entities created by a combination of secret negotiation between the Great Powers of the day, and subsequent treachery hardly less concealed. Great Britain had held out to the Arabs the vision of a unified kingdom in return for their participation in the military campaign against the Ottoman Empire. Large amounts of gold had been funneled into the coffers of the Arab chiefs in payment for their fealty. The courier had been T.E. Lawrence. Instead, Britain delivered the promise of a Jewish homeland in Palestine to Theodor Herzl's international Zionist movement. With the establishment of Israel, the United Nations awarded fifty-seven percent of Palestine to the Jews, although in 1947 they possessed only ten percent of the land.

Twice betrayed, the Arabs declared war. Disunited and ill-prepared, they were crushingly defeated. The fiasco of 1948 was taken by Syrian officers as a professional as well as a national humiliation. It also constituted, writes historian Raymond Hinnebusch, a "watershed event in the radical policization of the officer corps. (…) The military assumed a permanent 'guardian' role in Syrian politics after 1949."[59]

Thus the stage was set for two turmoil-filled decades punctuated by coup and counter-coup, political assassination, and violent repression. The first assault on civilian government was a military takeover engineered by General Husni al-Za'im in 1948 with the support of the United States Embassy and the CIA. The United States sought Syrian acceptance of an armistice with Israel and ratification of an agreement to allow the Trans-Arabian Pipeline Company to build an oil pipeline across its territory to an outlet on the Mediterranean. The Za'im dictatorship acquiesced on both counts. Its fall, and the that of the military dictatorship set up by Adnan Shishakli in 1949, opened wide the gates for a generation of politicized, nationalist and politically radical officers. It was from these ranks that the Baathist and Alawite leaders, relatively unscathed in the internecine bloodletting that decimated the ranks of the Sunni-led officer corps, would be drawn, and gain mastery of the skills of conspiracy, treachery and assassination essential to gaining and holding power. Under their leadership, the populace was to be given rapid and intensive education in the superficial anti-Westernism that soon became the trademark of a succession of authoritarian regimes.

The catastrophic events in Palestine also created ideal conditions for the emergence of the organization that was thirty years later to challenge the Baath-Alawite ruling caste in a fight to the death: the Ikhwan al-Muslimin, the Muslim Brotherhood. On the one side, draped in the mantle of Arab nationalism, socialism and anti-imperialism, the ruling military establishment struggled to sculpt traditional Syrian society to match its absolutist version of modernity. On the other, the Muslim Brotherhood saw Islamic revival as both normative and natural in a traditional society whose majority had remained deeply attached to its Islamic beliefs and cultural heritage.[60]

Under the guidance of its charismatic founder Hasan al-Banna, the Ikhwan arose and thrived in British-ruled Egypt in the 1940s. Many of its leading members had fought as volunteers against Israel in the first, disastrous Palestinian campaign. Their courage and discipline under fire had stood in stark contrast to the demoralized, badly trained and poorly equipped soldiers of the Arab national armies.

In Egypt, the Ikhwan had proved its capacity to mobilize masses of people through its grass-roots organizations among the youth and in the workplaces. The Egyptian officers, headed by Colonel Nasir who seized power in 1952, had recognized in the Brotherhood the greatest threat to their hegemony. Seizing on an alleged attempt on Nasir's life in 1954, they violently disbanded the organization, executed its leaders, and had its militants tortured and sentenced to lengthy prison terms.

It would have been surprising had the Ikhwan not had a Syrian wing. Syrian *Shari'a* students studying in Egypt, had come into contact with the Brotherhood's dynamic organization and expanding influence. On their return to Syria, they set about emulating their Egyptian brethren. The Syrian chapter of the Brotherhood would be organized as a *jami'yah*, or religious and welfare society, following the example set by Western Protestant missionaries when they began their proselytizing work in the Middle East in the nineteenth century. In Turkey, a similar response by Muslims to the penetration of militant Christianity had, under the leadership of the activist wing of the Naqshbandi Sufis, taken a similar form. The members of these Islamic welfare societies tended to be come primarily from the newly emerging middle and lower-middle classes, quite unlike the political jam'iyah of the ruling nationalist elites.[61]

They shared with most of their Turkish forerunners a commitment to social and political activism and an abhorrence of withdrawal and religious quietism: "The social objectives of Islam—progress, justice and the general welfare of society—could not be achieved without consciousness, work and struggle," writes Amman Abd Allah in his account of the rise of the Ikhwan in Syria.[62]

With the suppression of the Egyptian Brotherhood, it was to the Syrian branch that fell the burden of defending the principles of the Islamic state. Its first leader was the charismatic Mustafa al-Siba'i, a native of Homs, graduate of al-Azhar University and close personal friend of Hasan al-Banna. Under his guidance the Brotherhood articulated an Islamic revolutionary ideology that posited itself, well before the emergence of Ruhollah Khomeini in Iran, as a "third way," as neither East nor West, neither Marxist nor capitalist. Al-Siba'i "had a remarkable ability to address the pressing issues of the time as Islamic issues with concrete Islamic solutions."[63] He spoke to people in terms familiar to them, drawn from the pages of the Qur'an and from daily life.

Syria in the mid-fifties was shaken by almost continuous social and political upheaval. The advent of Nasir in Egypt and his regime's dramatic shift toward the Soviet Union in the wake of the Suez crisis conveyed to the Arabs one powerful message: for the first time since the upsurge of their national movement during World War I, they could look elsewhere than to the West for a powerful protector.[64]

For all the rise of Arab nationalist and socialist forces like the newly emerged Baath Party, Islam remained a potent force in Syrian politics. As an indicator of its popularity, in a Damascus by-election to replace men convicted for involvement in a conspiracy to overthrow the parliamentary government that had replaced the Shiskakli dictatorship, Sheikh Mustafa al-Siba'i polled 47 percent of the votes.[65]

The elderly al-Siba'i's showing in Damascus was to be a high water mark for the Ikhwan in terms of electoral popularity. Shortly afterward, driven on by the impetuous younger generation who saw in union with Nasir's Egypt the sovereign remedy to Syria's ills, the two states concluded a marriage of principle that quickly came to look like a union of convenience for the Egyptian strongman. The Ikhwan, decimated and driven underground in Egypt, could look forward to little better in Syria.

Sheikh al-Siba'i's successor to the rank of *al-murshid al-amm*, the movement's General Supervisor, a man called Isam al-Attar, held that *jihad* in the form of armed struggle against the Baath regime would only bring greater suffering to the Syrian people and to the Brotherhood. But as repression increased, hotter heads began to prevail. They would emerge from the highly charged atmosphere of Hama, where rigorous interpretation of the Qur'an and a tradition of religious activism coexisted with a peasant revolutionary movement led by the charismatic Akram al-Hawrani.

Such was the religious and political climate in the city where Khaled al-Chami was born in 1942, into a traditional Islamic background: "I joined the Ikhwan in 1957. I found that the Brotherhood expressed my thoughts and feelings. We believed that to do good in the world, you must work within an organization."

As Syrian politics became increasingly radicalized, first under the short-lived United Arab Republic, then with the rapid ascent of the Baath Party, the leadership of the Ikhwan shifted away from the more cautious mindset of an al-Attar and toward men disinclined to compromise, men who saw no possible middle ground between what devout Muslims considered an anti-Islamic system of government and an ideal regime founded on the teachings and practices of the Prophet.

Within the ranks of the Brotherhood, dissent was not encouraged. In Egypt, such was his moral and organizational ascendancy that Hasan al-Banna demanded and received unswerving obedience, which the Brotherhood stressed as a virtue. "The concept of absolute obedience was know as *al-sama' wa'l-ta'a*, literally hearing and obeying. It began with the oath of loyalty taken by a member … and, in theory at least, continued through the person's life."[66] Discipline in the Syrian brotherhood, though less fixated on the personality of the supervisor, was no less strict. It was at once the organization's strength, the secret of its ferocious single-mindedness, and a source of vulnerability. Once a decision had been taken, once a course of action agreed upon, little or nothing could sway the Brotherhood from its path.

The same, in spades, could be said of the Baath Party, and particularly of the military wing that came to control it. But the Baath was finally to trump the Ikhwan. It would do so less by the sense of discipline and common commitment that makes political parties effective, for it had long forfeited any broad popular support, and more by a combination of Alawite exclusivism and a readiness to betray and kill both rivals and unwanted associates alike.

Sheikh Mustafa al-Siba'i had been a friend and protégé of Hasan al-Banna. The man who would direct the Ikhwan in its final conflict with the regime,

Marwan Hadid, who had taken part in the abortive revolt at Hama in 1964, and rose to influence in the Brotherhood in the early seventies, was a close friend of Saïd Qutb, the Egyptian ideologue of radical political Islam. Qutb held that a society fell into a *jahiliyah*—the state of ignorance and barbarism that characterized pre-Islamic Arabia—when it claimed that "the right to create values, to legislate rules of collective behavior, and to choose a way of life rests with men, without regard to what God has prescribed."[67] His position, which was to become perhaps the fundamental tenet of two generations of Islamic activism, turned Hasan al-Banna's teaching on its head: society would not change as observant Muslims produced Islamic life; it would only change when men transformed the society in which they lived.

Saïd Qutb was hanged in August, 1966, after being accused of heading an Ikhwan plot to overthrow Nasir. One decade later, the death of Marwan Hadid at the hands of Hafiz al-Asad was to set Syria on the pathway to tragedy. For Hadid had come to believe that only through violent conflict could the *jahiliyah* regime ruling in Damascus be defeated. Under his leadership, the Ikhwan set out to do just that. A policy of selective assassination of key figures in the military and security services was implemented, with devastating effect. But it was only the beginning of the long descent into hell.

"In the early seventies," says Mr. al-Chami, a note of resignation creeping into his voice, "when Marwan Hadid inaugurated a policy of force, our problems had become worse. I and others thought there was a problem with the style of the Ikhwan. Many of our members died for no good reason, in conflict with the regime."

Hadid's arrest only worsened a situation that was rapidly spiraling out of control. He immediately began a hunger strike to hasten his death, and died soon thereafter. Sources close to the Brotherhood assert that the Superintendent had been "murdered under brutal torture."[68]

Khalid al-Chami, at our meeting in Damascus in January 2002, filled in the missing details of the story: "When Marwan Hadid was captured, he staged a hunger strike. Hafiz al-Asad feared the outcome if he died. The Ikhwan had promised to avenge his death. Al-Asad understood what would be the outcome."

Whether under torture or by self-induced starvation, the death of Hadid on February 8, 1976, was the first shot fired in the Ikhwan's *jihad*, which it conceived as a fight to the finish against the al-Asad regime. Non-violent or peaceful means were no longer an alternative. The Brotherhood issued a chilling declaration: "We did not begin our *jihad* until the oppressors had begun to exterminate Islam."[69]

By 1976, the Baath regime could no longer be described as pan-Syrian, let alone pan-Arab. It became more easily identifiable as pan-Alawite and as such, its popular base and support had narrowed dangerously. As the Islamic Opposition gained strength, the government's attention was increasingly focused not on administration, but on suppressing revolt.[70] The Brotherhood, in drawing attention to the sectarian and minoritarian nature of the regime, sought to label it as non-Muslim, thereby illegitimate. "From an Islamic standpoint ... the religious beliefs and practices of the Nusairis [Alawite] set them off as a distinct religion."[71]

There was at the same time, explains Mr. al-Chami, a deep division within the Ikhwan ranks, one which would soon have a critical impact on the Hama uprising. "Syria was split in two: a 'northern wing' that included Hama and Aleppo, and a 'southern' wing made up of Homs and Damascus. The southern wing opposed the use of force, and preferred to negotiate. But in Hama the mentality was different; there they were more inclined to violence.

"Relations between the two sections were very bad. The Damascus wing was still headed by Sheikh al-Attar, who believed in the political path to power. But the Aleppo branch pointed to twenty years of failure, and wanted to combine politics with armed struggle. Damascus wanted to move cautiously; Aleppo, to speed up the political process with armed action. But a third section was growing. Their base was Hama. They were called the 'pioneers', and they believed that only armed conflict could succeed.

"At the time, I was a simple member of the Brotherhood. But because of my social situation, I was acting as a go-between for the Ikhwan and others, including sections of the Baath. You see, at the time, I was a businessman. I represented German and French construction equipment firms."

Mr. al-Chami saw his task as one of unification. "The second-in-command of the Hama section died, the brothers in Aleppo asked me to find a replacement. That was when my active involvement began. It was in September and October of 1979. The streets were erupting, but we were trying to calm the situation. There I was, attempting to reconcile the two branches; the government was convinced I was uniting the two against it."

The government had every reason to suspect the worst. The Brotherhood's campaign of low-level urban guerrilla warfare and selective assassination of the hated Baath Party's cadre had thrown the State onto the defensive. Instead of rallying to the besieged regime, citizens found ways of showing their support and approval of the opposition's campaign of violence and armed propaganda.

The Aleppo branch, says Mr. al-Chami, decided that a military wing of the organization was needed to carry the fight to the regime. He was handed the job. "I tried to contact higher-ranking officers, and to appeal to them for help to save the country. Our appeal was primarily a nationalist one, but we also made a strong religious argument: 'we are good Muslims.' There were very strong feelings against the Alawite ruling minority, particularly in the army and the security services."

As a man on the cutting edge, Mr. al-Chami was aware not only of his organization's strategy, but of the regime's plans to counter it. "Al-Asad and his closest advisors realized how strong the Ikhwan movement had become. They took the decision to strike first. The president called a high-level meeting, where two scenarios were discussed, one centered on Aleppo, the other on Hama. Finally he opted for Hama, and drew up a plan to provoke the Brotherhood. They would abuse women as a way of drawing young militants into the streets. There was definitely a plan."

One need not unquestioningly accept Mr. al-Chami's account to conclude that it is inconceivable that the Machiavellian Hafiz al-Asad did not possess a strategy, one which he would subsequently carry out with a ruthlessness that would leave the entire country gasping in horror. The regime's panic could be understood. It had more on its hands than a local fundamentalist uprising that could be isolated and repressed. Regional events seemed to feed into the conspiracy. In February, 1979, Ayatollah Ruhollah Khomeini had returned in sober triumph to Tehran after the flight of Shah Mohammad-Reza Pahlavi into exile. Iran's long smouldering Islamic Revolution had broken into a raging fire that had swept all before it.

Iran's Islamic revolutionaries had, during their years of struggle against the U.S.-backed monarchy, established contacts throughout the region. These contacts were particularly strong in Lebanon, where the charismatic Iranian-born Imam Musa al-Sadr had revitalized that country's Shi'a community, and where Iranian revolutionaries had trained alongside their Palestinian comrades-in-arms. Would the powerful example of an entire nation taking to the streets to dispose a detested ruler be repeated in Syria?

The leadership of the Ikhwan certainly hoped so. There can be little doubt that the ferment of Iran's Islamic Revolution had taken hold throughout the Middle East. It had become a source of fascination, pride and emulation for the multitudes whose faith may have been swayed by the chimera of Nasserism and Arab nationalism, but had never been altogether eclipsed.

When Saddam Hussein's forces crossed Iran's southwestern border on September 22, 1980, Hafiz al-Asad snatched the opportunity like a drowning man a lifebuoy. Breaking with the near-unanimity of the Arab dictatorships, he announced Syria's support for Imam Khomeini's singular revolution. The decision to back Iran, writes Patrick Seale, was perplexing but the Syrian president's motives could be analyzed and understood. "There were important strategic reasons for his move, but it was also rooted in his own background as a member of a community derived from Shi'ism and in the fellow feeling of a man of rural and minority origins for people, and especially the deprived Shi'a of Lebanon, who had themselves long been oppressed."[72]

But, suggests Seale, al-Asad's rage against the Sunnis, and particularly against the Muslim Brotherhood which had dared first to expose, then oppose him in the streets, may have been the more powerful motivating factor. The Syrian dictator's fury was well and truly reciprocated by the Ikhwan, nor was Iran spared. "The effective alliance of the Islamic Republic of Iran—the only state to have emerged in recent times from a revolutionary Islamic struggle— with the Nusairi-Baathist regime of Syria—a state engaged in the brutal suppression of a similar struggle—is highly incongruous," wrote Hamid Algar, an outstanding and outspoken Islamic scholar often supportive of Iran.[73]

Desperate for allies, the Iranian mollahs may have preferred the devil they knew. They may have suspected that Saudi Arabian financial support for the Ikhwan might translate, in the event of a takeover of Syria by a militant Sunni organization, into political support. Tehran, which later criticized the Brotherhood as providing aid and comfort for the Camp David process, may have thought it detected American meddling in the tragic events of Aleppo and Hama. Whatever the ultimate reasons, which will surely remain opaque, the leaders of the insurrection concluded that "like its counterpart in Iran, the Syrian Islamic Revolution has no supporters in the East or West."[74]

Facts on the ground have a momentum of their own. The Syrian Islamists may have been dismayed by Iran's failure to see in them a Sunni version of the overthrow of the shah. But the lines of battle had been too deeply drawn, the gulf of hatred had become a chasm. Iranian support or no, the regime seemed shaken. The showdown was approaching; the countdown had begun.

Hafiz al-Asad's policy of provocation was fully activated. In late September, 1981, the regime made its most daring move, one calculated to inflame traditional Muslim sensibilities. Militia groups, including squads of teenage girls in uniform known as the Daughters of the Revolution, backed by armed men, combed the streets of Syria's major cities, tearing the *hijab* from women's heads.[75] Two months later, the insurgents struck back. A huge bomb exploded in downtown Damascus, destroying the state security court and the military intelligence department and killing at least 500.

The choice of target made it clear to the regime that its opponents would not be deflected from their ultimate aim, the overthrow of the state apparatus.

It also showed intimate, perhaps even inside knowledge of the military and security establishment. Were that the case, the regime's days would have indeed been numbered.

Some members of the Syrian military could no longer accept the regime's violent behavior toward its citizens. They sent out feelers to the Ikhwan. The man responsible for linking these disenchanted officers with the revolutionaries was Khalid al-Chami. "Some high-ranking officers had begun to solicit support from us. One of them betrayed the secret. The government instructed him to continue, and to organize a meeting, which was recorded. Two army leaders, generals Lutfi and Halawi were arrested and tortured. They disclosed the role of a 'mechanical engineer' in bringing the two sides together. I was the mechanical engineer."

By late 1981, the apprehended insurrection could not be halted. The Ikhwan had plowed the ground of pious Muslim outrage at the secular excesses and corruption of the regime, it had sowed the seeds of revenge and fury. Now the crop would be reaped.

No longer did Hafiz al-Asad and his inner circle face a small though influential group of militant activists who were prepared to die for their beliefs. A broad Islamic Front had been set up, bringing together a much wider spectrum of the disenchanted. The Front formulated its appeal to the people not only in religious, but in political terms: "The worst calamity that befell our people was when the regime dispossessed them of their freedom, oppressively imposed its rule upon all sections of the society, and insisted on turning the people into a flock of sheep with no will of their own and no protection for their beliefs, ethics and resources."[76]

The Front's manifesto, couched in the constitutional principles of the "blessed jihad movement", promised Syria's citizens all that the Baath regime had systematically denied them: equality between the citizens; protection of the citizens; preservation of the dignity of the citizens; abolition of political prisons and detention centers; a system of mutual consultation (democracy); separation between the authorities; freedom to form political parties; direct election; freedom of thought and expression; freedom of trade unions; the rights of ethnic and religious minorities; an independent judicial authority.[77]

The Front's program was ambitious and sweeping. Given time, perhaps even a few more months of coalition building, it might have been decisive. But events were sweeping ahead at a pace the Islamists could not control, driven by Hafiz al-Asad's determination to provoke a confrontation while he could still maintain the initiative.

The month was December, 1981. Khalid al-Chami's mission had brought him from Hama to Damascus to meet the Ikhwan's now-compromised military sympathizers. "The authorities blockaded the city, and sent operatives out into the streets looking for me," he said. "I was trying to leave. It was impossible. So I telephoned a cousin and asked if I could stay at his house. I took a taxi through the back streets, got out and knocked on the door. It opened, and inside were the secret police agents waiting for me with their guns drawn."

Now in the hands of the regime's dreaded intelligence service, Mr. al-Chami faced interrogation. "We tried to follow a special organizing program," he explained. "That way, we kept secrets to a minimum. But when the police gave me a complete picture of our organization in Europe, I knew there was nothing I could do. 'You know them all,' I said. 'There are no foreigners involved. There is nothing I can add.'"

Mr. al-Chami's role as a go-between and a non-combatant may have spared him the excruciating, often mortal torment inflicted on Ikhwan fighters. He provided no details, and we asked no questions. Yet torture was and until recently, has been commonplace, even obligatory in the Syrian prison system. Those arrested with weapons or in combat situations could expect slow, agonizing death by impalement; they could expect their backs to be methodically broken, vertebra by vertebra, on a special chair devised by East German experts.[78] They could expect electroshock, or to see their wives or daughters raped in their presence.

Here, Mr. al-Chami's narrative deserted the broader tragedy of Hama and entered that of the Syrian penal gulag. "They threw me into a tiny cell, where I was held for three or four years for new investigations. Then they transferred me to Mezzeh Prison. In '91, they sent me to Palmyra, where I spent ten years, until August 2001."

Treatment, he said laconically, was "hard" at Palmyra.

I had earlier learned from other released political prisoners what "hard" meant. Following the 1980 massacre of inmates following the attempt on the life of Hafiz al-Asad, the authorities inflicted upon rank-and-file Ikhwan captives a living death. Week in week out, month in month out, for years, they were subjected to daily beatings. Regulations were draconian. In the presence of jailers, inmates were forced to bow their heads so as never to see their tormentors. Groups of prisoners, broken in body and in spirit, were told to write clemency petitions addressed to President Hafiz al-Asad in their own blood. These petitions were then ripped up in front of the men who had written them.

Higher-ranking cadre may have fared "better." Five of Khalid al-Chami's ten years at Palmyra were spent in solitary confinement, followed by a common cell. "For ten years, we had no contact with the outside world. Sometimes we saw scraps of newspaper. It was more than three years before we found out what happened in Hama. I was not surprised. I knew al-Asad's decision. I knew the Ikwan's reaction; I knew they would fight."

Fight they did. On December 8, 1981, Hama had come under full-scale occupation by the Syrian armed forces. One week later, Israel announced its formal annexation of the Jaulan—the Golan Heights—, territory captured from Syria during the June 1967 war. Preoccupied with the dire and immediate threat to his regime, al-Asad issued pro-forma protests and empty dire threats, and dispatched reinforcements not to the Jaulan, but to the Hama front. The move confirmed what many critics of the regime had long claimed: that Hafiz al-Asad's greater loyalty lay with his personal survival and that of his clansmen and fellow Alawites, and not with the territorial integrity of his country.

Several weeks after the arrest of Khalid al-Chami, which neutralized the threat of high-level defections from the Syrian army, the president gave his brother Rif'at a free hand in Hama. As the regime's inner circle shrank, through assassination and elimination of dissenters or potential rivals by purge or murder, Rif'at had become its shield. The Defense Companies, under his direct command and patronage, had become the best-armed, best-trained and best-paid units in the Syrian army. "To be Asad's brother ... was to be able to do almost anything one liked, and Rif'at was at times above the law," writes Patrick Seale, with perhaps a touch of understatement, for the only law in Syria was Hafiz al-Asad's whim.[79]

What the leadership of the Ikhwan and of the Islamic Front had learned from Khalid al-Chami, became apparent to all in early February: the regime's plan was to eradicate the city as a stronghold of Islamic tradition and identity.

"The people of Hamah rose in revolt. On February 2, 1982, the *ulama* proclaimed *jihad* against the regime ... and the call for liberation went forth from the minarets. Led by armed units of the Islamic Front, the citizens of Hamah swiftly gained control of the city and surrounding areas within a ten-mile radius. It took weeks of continued and pitiless slaughter to restore government control of Hamah, [during which] the regime resorted to long-distance bombardment with cannons and tanks, bombardment from helicopter gunships, and liberal use of the bulldozer ... "[80]

Ummar Abd-Allah's account of the savagery and intensity of combat at Hama was confirmed by Robert Fisk, the intrepid Irish Middle-East correspondent of the *Times* of London and later, *The Independent.* "I was, so far, the only Western eye-witness to the siege of Hama. It had been only the most cursory, the briefest of visits but it was enough to prove that the fighting was still going on, that it was on a huge scale—involving at least a division of troops—and that casualties must have been enormous. Something terrible was going on there."[81]

Patrick Seale's account, which reflects the official Syrian version, fills in the blanks: "By the morning of 3 February some seventy leading Baathists had been slaughtered and the triumphant guerrillas declared the city "liberated." [The local authorities] faced defeat by a full-scale urban insurrection such as had never before occurred under Asad's rule." Meanwhile, in Damascus, "there was a moment of something like panic when Hama rose. The regime itself shook. (…) Fear, loathing and a river of spilt blood ruled out any thought of a truce. Hama was a last-ditch battle which one side or the other had to win and which, one way or the other, would decide the fate of the country."[82]

For three weeks the battle raged. It was more a civil war than an ordinary military operation. Against the campaign of terror waged against the operatives of the regime and the Baath by the Ihkwan from its strongholds deep in the old city, the state mobilized the full arsenal of state terror. Civilians were slaughtered indiscriminately, acts of unspeakable cruelty were reported even—especially—after the government had regained control.

Hama, writes Hinnebusch, "was more than people bargained for: those who had joined the opposition less out of Islamic zeal than dislike of the regime, melted away, and people who had given succor to Ihkwan cadre now sought to distance themselves."[83]

For the religious opposition, the obliteration of Hama—both literally and figuratively—was a crushing blow. Why had the attempted revolution failed, especially when it believed itself to be expressing the frustrations of the majority against a tiny, usurpatory minority at the head of a brutal, unpopular regime? Why had the rest of the country not come to the aid of Hama? "Parts of Brigades 21 and 47 of the Syrian army mutinied and refused to fire on the people of Hamah, but in general the army held firm. There was nothing in the nature of a countrywide insurrection or a response of revolutionary proportions."[84]

In retrospect, it became clear that the Islamic Front did not enjoy sufficient support throughout the country to carry out a full-scale revolution. It also became clear that the Baath Party regime, though loathed by many, had proven itself tougher and more resilient than either its opponents, or casual observers, had expected. It is difficult to avoid the conclusion that Hafiz al-Asad had won his war against terrorism by becoming the greater terrorist.

But it is legitimate to ask whether the Ihkwan, carried away by a combination of righteous fury and illusions about its own strength, had been the author of its own demise. Khalid al-Chami will not say as much directly, but he confirms the judgement of many that the Ikhwan was heedless of critical opinion within and outside its ranks. "We did not pay enough attention to winning the support of other Islamic groups and of the sheikhs who influenced them. They saw themselves and their positions as important. The Ikhwan's mistake was to jump over these people, who then reacted negatively. Our movement was a political one, but it could not really deal with such matters. We should have handled them in a more sensitive way."

The decade-long split between the Ikhwan's Damascus branch and its militant Aleppo and Hama branches had, as events proved, never healed. Some Syrians claim today that had the Damascus section of the Brotherhood joined the battle, the al-Asad regime would have collapsed within weeks. Others suggest that the regime forestalled the threat by buying off the city's influential Sunni religious leadership with promises of lucrative monopoly export licenses.

Sheikh Ahmad Kuftaro, the Grand Mufti of Syria, had been approached well before the conflict, I learned from a reliable source. He had cautioned the hot-blooded Muslim Brothers to have a long, hard look at their tactics, and warned them against violence. His words of caution, said my source, were dismissed.

Then, too, came the question of leadership. Iran's Islamic revolutionaries could look to Imam Khomeini, a man of supreme charisma and stoic self-denial, who floated high above the melée, and whose instructions and injunctions seemed to his followers to fall just short of divine inspiration. The Syrian Brotherhood had no Khomeini, no Hasan al-Banna, no Saïd Qutb. Mustafa al-Siba'i and Marwan Hadid, respectively its founder and militant ideologue, were dead. The new leadership could claim doctrinal purity, but it could not move the country's pious Sunni masses.

In Iran, Shah Mohammad-Reza Pahlavi had proven himself a weak, vainglorious, hollow tyrant, a childish and pathetic brute tied to the apron-strings of his American keepers. His hardscrabble Syrian emulator, Hafiz al-Asad, was a schoolyard bully, a street-fighter, a hardened killer and a master of cynicism, the son of a mother who had schemed and clawed to promote her son, and taught him the vital importance of ferocity. Where the shah had collapsed, bringing his army and his state down about his head, al-Asad stood his ground. The shah may have believed his American sponsors' tall tales about a rapid restoration. Al-Asad had no sponsors, no protectors, nowhere to go. He would, and did, fight like a cornered rat.

Finally, for all its blatant corruption, favoritism and arrogance, the Baath regime had brought about a substantial improvement in the material conditions of the dirt-poor peasants who made up a majority of Syria's population. Once at the mercy of the large landowners of such traditional cities as Hama and Aleppo, the government had given them a path to social promotion and modest economic improvement. Many of the regime's most dedicated servants, and most ruthless defenders, were men of humble origin who owed everything to the Baath revolution and the Corrective Movement that consolidated power in the hands of Hafiz al-Asad. They might not have been prepared to die for it, as his palace guard had been, but they would kill for it.

One last unexamined hypothesis remains: that of a plot instigated by the regime's regional and international adversaries. A dissident journalist in Damascus, who asked me not to use his name, explained that Saudi Arabia and Jordan, who were providing the Brotherhood with financial support, believed the moment had come to topple Hafiz al-Asad, whom they would have replaced, had the uprising been successful, with the co-founder of the Baath Party, Salah al-Din Bitar. Bitar had been assassinated in Paris in June 1980: an indication of how much the regime feared him ... and perhaps knew of such a plan.

* * *

THE MEETING HAD BEEN LONG, detailed and, for Mr. al-Chami, exhausting. But nothing could obliterate the smile from his face, nor dim the undiluted delight of being able to speak freely, to tell his story, to certify that, after two decades of cruel punishment, he was still alive, that the world had not vanished, that a tiny fragment of that world might be interested in his story.

His release had come at ten o'clock on a December evening during Ramadan, on the streets of downtown Damascus, along with three co-detainees. "When they released us, I could remember nothing," he said, giggling irrepressibly, then breaking into nervous laughter. "I have no family, so I had nowhere to go, no one to turn to. So I went to a hotel and asked for a room. 'Your ID?' they asked. 'None' I answered. 'Your passport?' I had no passport. 'Don't send me back onto the streets,' I told the clerk, 'let me see the manager.' He came; I told him that twenty years before, I used to send customers to this hotel, well-paying customers, foreigners I was doing business with.' So they gave me a room.

"When I stepped into that room, you cannot imagine what I felt. When you're nearly sixty, your feelings are complex. I turned on the television, and looked for the channels I'd only heard about, the BBC, al-Jazira. For an hour I sat there watching. Then I took a bath, got dressed, and took the elevator downstairs. I paid 2,000 Syrian pounds [$40] to drink a cup of tea, take a bath and watch television. I walked out onto the street a free man. But where was I? Only one hundred meters from where I'd been arrested. There, I saw my friends waiting for me. No one had expected to see me alive."

Had not Hafiz al-Asad at Hama provided a model for dealing with terror? New York Times enquired. "But, the Ikhwan was not a terrorist organization," Mr. al-Chami replied. "The Americans are trying to confound all Islamic parties. Remember, at that time there was no way for us to explain or express ourselves. Today may be the same.

"It is dangerous to put all Muslims in the same bottle. It is wrong, and it is risky. Whoever reads history should know that it is hard to win a fight against religion. You will push others into a corner, and create an explosion. You cannot deal with it in such a way."

Despite his ordeal, Khalid al-Chami was impenitent. Though the Ikhwan failed in its attempt to seize power, he will not concede that its failure was due to any ideological or doctrinal weakness. The organization's general program is, he said, as relevant today as it was twenty years ago. However, the organization itself no longer exists in either visible or semi-visible form.

"The goal of any political party is to create a state. People are seeking a positive goal, one that can improve their lives. Today, we are looking for a party that would achieve this result. I am still supporting this idea. Religion is the perfect theoretical basis. The problem to be solved is this: how can religion serve life? But the problem is not in Islam."

Twenty years after being crushed beneath the wreckage of Hama, and tormented in the cruel cells of Palmyra, the Ihkwan al-Muslimin would, on the face of it, appear to have no future. According to Khalid al-Chami, perhaps 450 or 500 Islamists of his generation remain behind bars. The Brotherhood is illegal, and to speak its name in public is regarded as foolhardy.

And yet, on the streets of Aleppo, of Hama, of Homs and even Damascus, the overt signs of a revived Islamic identity are becoming more visible. What my Syrian informants told me only confirmed the evidence of my own eyes. Alongside the tiny, ineffectual pro-democracy movement which is restricted to a fringe of intellectuals and academics half-tolerated by the regime and perhaps encouraged by its bolder elements, exists a deeper, ill-defined, shadowy proto-movement that may still look to the Muslim Brothers as the only force capable of challenging the rule of the al-Asad family, or of supplanting it when it falls.

Such a movement would be clandestine, intensely secretive, determined and prepared to wait ... and would not swerve from violence if given no other outlet. The al-Asad regime faces a serious dilemma. President Bashar has yet to prove that he possesses his father's perspicacity, much less his ruthlessness and total control of the state and security apparatus. Where Hafiz al-Asad seized Syria by stealth and violence, his son has received the country as his inheritance, on a silver platter. Were a new Islamic movement, more hardened and determined than its predecessor, to appear and thrust for power, few believe he would be able to muster the will to suppress it.

Syria finds itself today in a double bind. No democratic reform can take place under the Hama rules. But these rules today govern the state, and form the bedrock of its stability. Remove them, and it would fall.

Invisibly, but palpably, an opposition is taking rudimentary form. Its ultimate contour—public, civil and peaceful, or underground, sectarian and violent—will be determined by the state's response not only to the liberal academics of the Damascus salons, but to men like Haitham al-Maleh, Ryad al-Turk, Khalid al-Chami, and to a voiceless, faceless generation of young people separated from its elders by a chasm of silence.

After invading and occupying Iraq, the United States now threatens Syria with "regime change," less for its violation of international order, for Damascus has always observed the rules with punctiliousness, more for its alleged support for "terrorism," which must here be understood as organizations determined to resist Israel's creeping dispossession of the Palestinians and its designs on Lebanon. In that event few Syrians, mindful of the Hama rules, would mourn the passing of the Baath regime. Fewer still would tolerate any governing system not created by the Syrians themselves.

4

'Ali and his Heirs

I IMAGINED I'D GOTTEN the Assassins out of my system years ago in Iran, when I visited the ruins of their original "eagle's nest" at Alamut overlooking the wild Rudbar valley in the mountains north of Tehran. But no sooner had I set foot in Syria than I heard once again the call of the shadowy minoritarian order that struck terror into the hearts of the cruel and the mighty.

Some, seeking to understand the phenomenon of "terrorism," called its practitioners the forerunners of contemporary Islamic reaction to the wider, state-organized terror of Israel against its captive Palestinian population, and to the Western military occupation of the Islamic heartland. Whatever the case, there could be little doubt that the men we today call the Assassins had been, for their day, the ultimate expression of militant religious politics. Now, in late December, 2000, I set out to renew an old acquaintance.

The day had begun in Hama. Dawn was breaking when my hired car swung onto the main Damascus road which we would follow until the turnoff for Lattakia. My first destination was to be the Krak des Chevaliers, the mighty Crusader castle that looms like a stone sentinel over the strategic passage through the coastal range along which traffic, merchandise, and in time of conflict, men and arms, move between sea and desert.

The Krak is a massive, brutish place, unambiguous in its functions of domination and control. No lesser an authority than T.E. Lawrence claimed the fortress to be the finest Medieval castle in the Middle East. It is the sort of place that would please a man like Lawrence, the tormented, self-mythologizing, self-aggrandizing and ultimately self-loathing adventurer whose final service to the men of the desert he professed to admire had been betrayal, a building in the image of the empire he served: cold, overbearing, brutal, vain.

Its walls are solid stone, several meters thick; its vast subterranean store-rooms capacious enough to sustain a garrison through the longest siege. Its fortified stables and barracks could accommodate thousands of armed men and their mounts. Never captured, never surrendered, the castle—linchpin of the dense network of castles erected by the Frankish invaders to perpetuate their reign over the lands of Islam—was ultimately abandoned for lack of defenders.

The Crusaders were as self-righteous as their modern-day British, French and now Zionist and American emulators. Their reign, measured against the history of the near Orient, was as ephemeral as it was violent. Their final demise, less at the hands of military might than from the arrogance of their own absolute domination, is as though engraved on the massive stone ramparts and towers that survive their passage.

What cannot be seen is the impact of the Assassins, whose strategic pinpricks so undermined the resolve of the occupying forces that when Salah al-Din at the head of an Islamic army appeared before Jerusalem in October 1187, the Crusader garrison capitulated. Not until Napoleon's expedition to Egypt in 1798 were Western armies to threaten the sacred city of the three Abrahamic faiths again.

At the Krak des Chevaliers, the weather had been fair, with puffy white clouds sailing across a pale blue winter sky. But as the car turned north toward Misyaf and its fortress along the winding road that followed the crest of the spur hills, tendrils of fog began to slither down the steep eastern flank of the coastal range.

It may once have been an eagle's nest, like its prototype at Alamut, but the Assassin citadel at Misyaf is remote and impregnable no longer. Today it clings limpet-like to a rocky hill that commands the eastern approaches to Syria's Coastal Mountain range, surrounded by a besieging force that offers no quarter. Where hostile armies led by illustrious commanders more than once failed to breach its defenses, a chaotically expanding town now holds the ancient fortress in a vise-grip of cinder-block and concrete, threatening to choke from it the last breath of life and submerge for evermore the curious tale its ruins tell.

By the time we arrived, in late morning, clouds had descended over the town and a chill drizzle had begun to fall. We stopped at a restaurant on the outskirts, gulped down a quick lunch of kebab, and called ahead to the office of the castle custodian, whose name I'd been given by an acquaintance in Damascus. Fifteen minutes later, I was making my way cautiously up the massive stone steps of the fortress.

"*Ahlan wa sahlan*," came the traditional Arab welcome as I stepped over the carved stone threshold. "We have been expecting you. I understand you are interested in this fortress."

A tiny, dented teapot atop a hot-plate; a bare light bulb swinging in the draft from the open door; a frayed map of Syria taped to the wall; a lonely telephone on a desk: of these sparse elements consisted the castle custodian's office, the dominion and sinecure of Abu-Rami, the stocky, billiard-ball bald man with the hoarse voice of an inveterate smoker who held out a hand in welcome.

I knew something of its builders, the Assassins, I allowed. Abu-Rami's eyes narrowed with interest.

"Ah."

"I've been to the Eagle's Nest, to Alamut, in Iran."

Abu-Rami glanced up at me from under raised eyebrows. He recognized that I was playing a strong hand.

"If you are interested, the tomb of Rashid al-Din Sinan Sheikh al-Jabal is not far from here," he volunteered. This Sinan, not to be confused with the later Ottoman mosque-builder, was the semi-mythical figure known and feared by the Crusaders as the "Old Man of the Mountain."

"Yes, the lieutenant of Hasan Sabbah," I added, indulging in some historical name-dropping of my own.

Hasan, in the middle of the eleventh century CE, had founded what we know today as the Order of the Assassins. A man of extraordinary spiritual and leadership qualities, he rapidly transformed a minority faction of Ismaili Shi'ism, itself a minority within a minority, into the world's most feared clandestine organization, and spearheaded the struggle to loosen the stranglehold on Iran of the Abbassid Caliphate and its Seljuq Turk masters.

Some have argued that he and his devoted followers, the men known as *fida'i*—combatants in the way of the faith—were the quintessential and original terrorists, precursors of Usama bin Laden's shadowy al-Qa'ida network, not to mention all those who dare oppose the long-term imperial strategy of the United States and Israel to reapportion the Middle East.

The comparison, though tempting, is ill-considered. The Assassins, when they struck, always did so in full public view, claiming credit for their acts and explaining their reasons. The order's stern discipline had prepared them for death as martyrs, and die they did, but not at their own hand.

"There is a man in Misyaf. He help you. I call him," said Abu-Rami. He picked up the handset, dialed, and spoke a few words in Arabic, from among which I could recognize a brief description of myself as an author from Canada. Fifteen minutes later an energetic young man burst into the caretaker's office, hand extended.

"Welcome in my city Misyaf," he said with a smile that was rarely to leave his face. "We have never left. History books say we are terrorists. But we were the original people here. What the Assassins were doing? Fighting for our land."

My sharp intake of breath must have been audible. I knew at that moment that I had come to the right place. Thus began my friendship with Muhammad al-Russeis, dentist, self-taught historian, Ismaili Muslim, the man who—as I would learn later—had discovered the secret hidden deep in the bowels of the citadel of the Assassins.

* * *

MY MEETING WITH DR. MUHAMMAD had lasted an hour at most. But it had been conclusive in the way that only random, chance encounters of the kind that bring us the women we love or the books that change our lives can be. Treading cautiously on the rain-slick pathways, we peered over ruined battlements, probed into dark, rubble-filled chambers, and clambered up the wobbling stone steps that led to the platform atop the fortress. Below us, on all sides of the citadel, lay the town of Misyaf, crouched beneath the drizzle, plumes of coal smoke wisping upward from sooty chimney pipes, donkeys braying, the occasional truck or automobile grinding its way along the cobblestone streets.

So close had the town drawn to the fortress that only a few meters separated it from the nearest buildings, hastily built overnight affairs.

Now, Dr. Muhammad explained, there were efforts afoot to rescue the Misyaf citadel from this kind of terminal encroachment, and to conserve it in a stable state. The initiative had come from the prosperous international Ismaili community. Its vehicle was the Agha Khan Trust for Culture, an organization that funds and provides expertise for the conservation, preservation and revitalization of Islamic monuments and settlements in places as far flung as Zanzibar, Pakistan and Samarkand, in Uzbekistan.

"Look there, see the old city wall?" he said, drawing my eyes to a line of stone slinking across the open, rocky field beneath the castle only to vanish in the welter of buildings. "We hope to free much of the space around it. To do that, we must relocate parts of the town outside the walls, and restore the old city center too."

In those few minutes, the citadel at Misyaf had come alive. An inert monument, a heap of romantic rubble no more, the fortress loomed as the centerpiece of an ambitious plan to preserve the past as part of a living urban environment. It was a plan, explained Dr. Muhammad, that had touched off controversy, and threatened to pit the inertia of the country's deeply entrenched bureaucracy against citizens struggling to participate—unheard of in a regime where power and representation were powerfully centralized and brutally monopolized—in the affairs of the city. Was the project an anomaly or a sign of the times, a harbinger of better things for a sorely-tried land, or an exception almost out of time and out of place? Only time itself would tell.

From the street far below the ramparts I heard a car horn honking. There stood my driver gesticulating, pointing at his watch. Dusk was gathering; he was anxious to return to Hama.

I took leave of Dr. Muhammad with a promise to return.

The questions, thoughts and dialogues of that rainy day were still fresh in my mind when, five months later, on a bright morning in May, I boarded an inter-city minibus for Misyaf at the Abbassayin terminal on the outskirts of Damascus.

As befits a poor country where a personal automobile is a distant dream for the huge majority of citizens, Syria's cities, towns and villages are served by frequent, inexpensive bus connections. Fairly well-maintained, so-called Pullman coaches offer express service. Few of the coaches are new. Most are Turkish hand-me-downs with cracked windshields, fraying upholstery and threadbare floor carpet. But they are marvels of comfort and efficiency compared with the bare-bones, no-frills rattletraps that link the smaller towns. These vehicles, which one hesitates to dignify with the term, depart from depots like Abbassayin, an open-air enclosure swarming with soldiers and militiamen on leave, Bedouin women with their bright hued robes, traditional religious families with infants in tow, students, and young men of no visible social appurtenance. The air is thick with diesel fumes and the nose-scorching smoke of chicken fat from the *shawarma* stands encrusted about the perimeter. Music screeches from dozens of competing loudspeakers; the ground is viscous with an ooze of crankcase oil and muck.

On these secondary lines travel buses that hark back to a bygone age, their battered, oft-patched bodies garishly painted, windshields decorated with tassels and calligraphed Qur'anic injunctions, crude bench seats bolted to the floor, low ceilings and soot-smeared windows that resist all attempts to prop either open or closed. On the semi-luxury main line coaches the no-smoking rule is rigidly enforced. These conveyances, however, are veritable *fumoirs* on wheels, where the air hangs thick and acrid with the stench of cheap Syrian tobacco. The Pullmans offer dismal Egyptian comedies on video cassette; their poor-man's counterparts deafen their passengers with the squalling worst that Arab pop music can secrete. Yet not a word of protest is uttered by the passengers. How could it? In Syria, protest can be far more dangerous to health than second-hand smoke, short-term deafness and/or cultural brutalization.

I now found myself seated aboard such a bus as it heaved and clattered noisily at idle, poised for departure. At the crack of ten o'clock the boy hawking roast melon-seeds, chewing gum and potato chips, who could not have been more than ten years old, leaped from the bus, the door creaked shut, and we careened out onto the Aleppo road.

Though apprehensive, I was not about to succumb to panic. From all I'd been able to determine, Syria lacked the gory bus crash tradition of its neighbor to the north. In Turkey, boarding a bus may be seen as tantamount to tempting fate. Shortly after I had left the country two years before, several tragic bus accidents had occurred. An investigation had revealed gross assembly deficiencies and non-standard materials in Turkish-manufactured Mercedes Benz coaches. The epidemic of deadly, fiery crashes had not been an illusion. The late-model vehicles had truly been travelling coffins. But old habits, once learned, die hard. It had become second nature for me to whisper the invocation pronounced by Muslims when embarking on a voyage or upon a venture: *Bismillah ur-rahman ur rahim.* "In the name of God the compassionate, the merciful." Once again, I found the comforting formula upon my lips.

At the city of Homs the bus veered off to the northwest. Behind us lay the highway with its long-haul tractor-trailers and its darting Korean and Taiwanese light trucks carrying loads of fruits and vegetables to market. Ahead stretched a narrow road that hugged the soft contours of the land, passed through small towns, skirted villages.

An hour later I caught sight of the citadel at Misyaf, silhouetted against the slanting afternoon sunlight. As we approached the coastal mountain range, the Jabal al-Nusayriyah, clouds had begun to gather. The day had turned dramatic. Would it have been on such a day, in 1176, that Salah al-Din approached the Assassin citadel, the sun glinting from his warriors' lances? For two months the standard-bearer of Islam besieged the castle, probing its defenses, waiting for a sign of weakness from its Ismaili garrison. None was forthcoming.

Then, one fine morning, so the legend goes, Salah awoke to find a dagger on his pillow.

The Assassins had penetrated his security perimeter. But they had chosen not to strike. The prince rapidly concluded a truce, lifted the siege and marched away. Another version of the tale, which I was later to hear on a visit to the headquarters of the Ismaili Council of Syria in the desert city of Salamiyah, held that Salah al-Din's most trusted bodyguards had themselves been "sleepers," secret members of the deadly confraternity who had insinuated themselves into his entourage. More conventional history relates that Salah raised the siege on receiving a promise of immunity against future attacks from the Old Man of the Mountain.[85] Whatever the reason, the fortress survived the most serious threat to its existence until its final capture by a marauding Mongol army more than a century later.

The bus shuddered to a stop in the main square of Misyaf. I swung down, bag slung over my shoulder, and struck off down the main thoroughfare toward the looming fortress. At its foot, I remembered, lay Dr. Muhammad's office. Combining my rudimentary Arabic with pointing to teeth, I found my way. I knocked on his door, and we greeted one another with the traditional embrace and soon we were sipping coffee in the waiting room of his dental surgery. It occupied a part of the house that had been commandeered by the French commanding officer during the tense years of the Mandate when revolt, rebellion and civil strife had wracked the mountainous hinterland, and punitive expeditions set out from this town to quell the insurgents.

That story, part of the tale of Syria's mysterious Alawites, would be for another day. My first task in Misyaf was to place myself under Dr. Muhammad's informed and expert guidance. We would not only be exploring the citadel and the town, but the history of the Order of the Assassins and of their Ismaili progenitors.

Refreshed and alert, we made our way up the steep steps to the main entrance of the citadel, where the fresh green grass of spring had now sprouted between the paving stones. In the caretaker's office Abu-Rami was waiting for us, teapot at the simmer. Today, in contrast to my first visit, the castle was humming with activity. An olive-skinned, black-eyed young woman dressed in khaki workshirt open at the collar, cargo pants and steel-toed construction boots, knocked at the open door and stepped in. Baida Husseyno would lead me on a stone by stone tour of the fortress, explained Dr. Muhammad, who was expecting several patients that afternoon.

Baida was also an Ismaili, an apprentice architect from Damascus. Instead of following her classmates who had emigrated to Canada, she had come here to execute the architectural drawings of the fortress. "I prefer to live and work in my country," she said with a smile. "But you never know what the future will bring … "

So far, Baida's future consisted of one very large chunk of the past. The citadel was built on six levels, she explained as we made our way upward along stone footpaths and over half-collapsed stairways. The bottom three were the remains of an early Byzantine fortification. Of this original structure nothing remains but a pair of crudely carved columns framing the main portal. The only surviving inscriptions are in Arabic.

Under the command of Rashid al-Din Sinan, the Ismailis took the fortress in 1140 from a local Arab prince. Sinan at once caused extensive additions to be made, including the towering superstructure at the summit of which we now found ourselves, breathing hard from the climb.

Directly below us, in a clearing next to a section of fallen wall, a work crew was sorting, cleaning and labelling stones.

"Look, up there," she added, pointing toward the mountainside that looms above the town. My eye followed her hand to a patch of white against the green of the forest. "That is his tomb. Maybe he is still watching us."

When seen surrounded by the encroaching city, the fortress appears a modest place. Once inside, its complexity becomes apparent. As we work our way downward, Baida guides me along the "long *suq*," the sixty meter passageway that rings the structure. Narrow beams of sunlight pierce the slit windows that punctuate its walls, from where the archers would have plied their bows against the besiegers drawn up below. Further down we climb, into the permanent penumbra. Here are the cisterns, and storerooms for grain which would have provided the garrison with supplies enough to withstand the most stubborn siege.

"How deep is it?" I ask, staring down into the utter darkness of a cistern.

"Listen!" she replies, and drops a stone. What seems like several seconds later, it impacts the water with an echoing, harmonious plop.

"There is a ladder. Do you want to see how deep?"

"I believe you."

Bending double, I followed her through a slit-like door. Suddenly we stepped back into the light. To our right was the entrance to Abu-Rami's office. We had returned to our starting point.

Baida and I shook hands at the main portal. I made my way down into the town to meet Dr. Muhammad. She, moving with lithe energy, disappeared upward into the labyrinth.

His last patient had departed; Dr. Muhammad was waiting. We left the dental surgery, and strolled through the narrow, winding lanes of the town to the house of his father, Abu-Ahmad. In the Arab cultural universe, men are identified as the father of their first-born son, in this case, Dr. Muhammad's elder brother. By the same token, I was soon to be called Abu-Antun, for my son Anthony. Beneath a bower of flowering vines, the entire al-Russeis family was drawn up to meet me. There would be no question of staying the night in the town's sole hotel. Abu-Ahmad's house would be my hotel and restaurant as long as I stayed in Misyaf. No derogation would be tolerated.

After relieving me of my travel bag and depositing it in the vestibule Abu-Ahmad, a wiry, bright-eyed, intensely alert man in his mid-sixties, showed me around the garden he had wrested from the rocky land with his own hands. There were medlar trees, already heavy with their glossy deep yellow fruit, budding pomegranates, orange, lemon, walnut and olive trees. Bees hummed industriously as they burrowed deep into flowers. In the dense foliage overhead birds chirped. "Come, follow me," he said, beckoning. "This rock is original old wall of city." Not only had the al-Russeis clan clung to the ancestral soil of Misyaf, they had made their house an organic outgrowth of the ancient ramparts.

From the terraced garden we climbed to the roof. There, in the late afternoon light, beneath fast-fleeting clouds, loomed the fortress, still dominating the town. For how long? The race was on, between the galloping demographics of a poor, young country, and the sharpened sensitivity to the need to preserve a unique historical and cultural monument. Who would be the winner? I was placing no bets.

Dinner that night was in the grand tradition of Arab hospitality: frugal yet abundant. Head bare and in full view of a male guest in the manner of Ismaili women, Abu-Ahmad's wife bustled about, assisted by her granddaughter. From the kitchen fragrant smells wafted into the sitting room which would soon see duty as a dining room. Atop a low table spread with newspaper in lieu of a tablecloth, appeared salads, zucchini and eggplant stuffed with rice served in a rich broth topped with yogurt sauce. Then came bread and olives, humus, and an immense platter of aromatic molded rice strewn with chunks of eggplant and roast lamb, and garnished with toasted pine nuts and almonds. Sleep that night was deep and untroubled.

The next morning, after a hearty breakfast of tea, bread, cheese, olives and apricot jam fragrant with summer, Dr. Muhammad and I set out for his office. As we strolled through the slowly awakening town, he told me the story of his struggle to protect the fortress from further encroachment.

"I grew up here, in the shadow of the citadel," he said. "So I felt a strong attachment to it. As a boy, I explored every part of it. When I came back to my city after graduation and opened my clinic, I was sad because of the misunderstanding about our community. Even there was some hostility. Each religious group was isolated.

"I wanted to live and work here. So I started to build good relations with people who did not care too much about religious affiliation. I tried to learn about their political and religious outlook. It took time, but I learned how to deal with others.

"All this time, my knowledge of our faith grew broader. The way I saw it, Ismailism is based on three principles: we do not know the whole truth, so we have no right to advise others; dialogue is the best for knowing other people and dealing with them because in dialogue there cannot be losers, only winners; we do not live alone, but in society, so we must improve our life together."

In the spring of 1999, a delegation of the Agha Khan Trust for Culture visited Misyaf, drawn by the town and its castle, which lay at the very heart of the Ismaili religious and secular heritage. They found in the young and eager Dr. Muhammad not just a pair of willing ears, but a man ready to make a leap into the unknown.

"They held a public meeting in the citadel. I attended, and afterwards I introduced myself to them. This was how it began."

A reasonably informed outsider might hypothesize that in a country with a recent history as fraught with upheaval as modern Syria, any news at all could be considered as bad news, perhaps even catastrophic news. A wiser strategy might be to keep one's head down and attract as little attention as possible. That which protruded, as recent events had shown, were likely to be lopped off, figuratively if no longer literally.

So, when the high-level delegation arrived in Misyaf that spring morning, it found a citizenry both skeptical and remote. Had the city been chosen for an injection of outside funds only because of its links with the glorious past of the Ismaili sect? And if it had, what would that mean to the Sunnis and Alawites who now dominated the population? Syria's veneer of modernity is a thin and fragile one; it conceals a profoundly traditional society where the lines between religious communities remain deeply engraved and obsessively maintained. In such societies, mistrust of change and initiative is deeply rooted.

All these, and more, were the obstacles the Misyaf conservation project would encounter. But, Dr. Muhammad told me, local hostility and suspicion had quickly given way to an attitude of watchful waiting. Criticism slowly abated. "When the project started hiring local people, they saw that qualifications, not religious affiliation, was the guiding principle."

As we walked beneath the parapet on our way to the dental surgery, we could hear, from high above, the ping of hammers against chisels and the scrape of shovels and trowels. The crew I had observed the day before was already at work, and Misyaf citizens made up the crew.

Not only did the AKTC plan to conserve the citadel, and not simply create some imagined modern version of its original form; it proposed to undo the indignities inflicted by twenty years of unregulated urban expansion. Starting with the castle, the long-term plan was to reactivate the historic core of the town, revitalize the *suq*, recycle old buildings as hotels, restaurants and cafés, transform streets into pedestrian zones. Later, in Dr. Muhammad's office, I examined the maps and diagrams detailing all that was to be done. Misyaf seem poised at a magical threshold, pregnant with possibility that sunny morning. Either that, or had I been carried off into the realm of the wishful by my host's persuasiveness and natural optimism.

It would not be a smooth and uneventful journey, he admitted. As the work advanced, jealousy had begun to show its viper's head. "Now the project is proceeding well, so some people are accusing me. They say I'm stealing antiquities. This is a serious matter in Syria. They say I am investing in the citadel for future profit. My answer is that you cannot serve two masters, money and God. I serve only God."

When we reached Dr. Muhammad's surgery a Toyota Hiace van driven by a heavy-set middle-aged man with a quick laugh named Hasan was idling in front of the gate. After a quick cup of instant coffee, we climbed in and headed east, down through the foothills, skirting Hama, then on to Salamiyah. Today's excursion would be both a trip into the past, and into the present of the Ismailis, the survivors of the once-mighty Fatimid Caliphate that in the tenth century CE had challenged the majority orthodox Sunni establishment for mastery of the world of Islam, and almost won.

* * *

FEW EVENTS HAVE HAD such momentous consequences for an entire civilization as the defeat, humiliation and death of the fourth caliph, 'Ali ibn-abi-Talib, cousin and son-in-law of the Prophet by marriage to his daughter Fatima. 'Ali by virtue of these connections concentrated in his person not only the legitimacy obtaining to Muhammad's four legatees, but the spiritual eminence accorded to the closest male relative of God's last Messenger.

Though his career had been for all intents and purposes a failure, 'Ali would continue, paradoxically, to exert an influence within the world of Islam second only to that of the Prophet himself.[86] Opposition to the Umayyad usurpers rapidly devolved to the large number of 'Ali's followers. His heritage and lineage was used cynically by the Abbassids who invoked him in their successful campaign to capture the caliphate, only to turn on his partisans.

By the second century of the Muslim Empire, the principle of dynastic succession and kingship founded by Mu'awiyah in Damascus had sunk deep roots. Power was wielded by a string of despots and madmen, enlightened reformers and pious recluses. Against them, in perpetual semi-clandestinity and incipient rebellion, was arrayed the *Ahl al-bayt*, the House of the Prophet, the descendants of 'Ali and Fatima, known as the Blessed Imams. They, unlike the Sunni caliphs, possessed the supreme prerogative of interpreting the law. Not only were they considered infallible, but also impeccable, divinely protected against sin and error.[87] They themselves, to paraphrase the Iranian philosopher Abdolkarim Soroush, were the proof of their own eminence.[88]

Our first stop along the road to Salamiyah was at Tell al-Dera, a dusty village at the feet of Qala'at al-Shmemis, an abandoned Arab fortress. There, in a small anteroom giving onto a shaded courtyard, we met Mahmud Aruh, a retired historian of 68 years, who had never left his village. The land across which we were travelling was Ismaili land, he assured us as we sipped our tea.

For Mr. Aruh, the arcana of Ismaili history were as commonplace as the beads on which devout Muslims tell the names of God. But for me, despite my relative familiarity with the genesis of Shi'ism, the particularities of the Ismaili breakaway remained arcane in the extreme. As Mr. Aruh talked on, with Dr. Muhammad translating, the sun had almost reached the meridian; locusts hummed in the acacia tree in the court. As a younger man—was it Mr. Aruh's son?—dressed in a warm-up suit and wearing rubber sandals carried a sloshing bucket of water across the courtyard, the falling drops threw up tiny puffs of dust.

At that moment, certain things seemed clear, if clarity can be defined as a positive quality when discussing a sect for which dissimulation and secrecy were long to remain paramount virtues. The mainstream of Shi'ism, known as the Twelvers, held that after the death of 'Ali, eleven of his descendants had inherited his qualities, qualifying them to wear his mantle. The last of these, the twelfth Imam Muhammad al-Muntazar ("the Expected One"), disappeared in 878, and is now believed to be in occultation until his imminent return as the Mahdi, the savior and redeemer who will usher in the millennium of universal justice.

The Ismailis shared the same line of succession until the sixth Imam, Ja'far al-Sadiq. At that point a crucial divergence occurred. Ja'far had designated his eldest son, Ismail, as his successor. The young man died prior to his father, in 760. After the death of the Imam, a majority of Shi'ites declared Musa al-Kazim, Ja'far's younger son by a concubine, to be the legitimate successor. For the minority, the succession had ended with Ismail, whom they considered the Seventh Imam and the hidden Mahdi.[89]

The Ismailis created a doctrine of the highest complexity and sophistication, based—not surprisingly—on a system in which the number seven held sacred significance. Fiercely minoritarian, they favored a system of initiation into the mysteries of their esoteric creed, in which appearances invariably concealed inner, deeper meanings.

The man who perfected the system, a certain Abdullah, the son of a Persian occultist, migrated in the eight century CE from al-Basra to Salamiyah, explained Mr. Aruh. From there his successors later dispatched secret emissaries to rally the legion of the dissatisfied who chafed under the corrupt and tyrannical rule of the Abbassid caliphs in Baghdad. The strategy was simple and brilliant: they would use religion as a vehicle for their esoteric doctrine, known as *batin*, to destroy the caliphate, and award Abdullah or his descendants with the throne. Abdullah died in around 875 CE. An Ismaili ruler took power in Tunis in 909, establishing the Fatimid dynasty that would soon extend its rule to Egypt and for a brief moment, to Baghdad itself.[90]

"During this period the secret organization called *al-Da'wa* was established in many places in the Islamic world," said Mr. Aruh. *Al-Da'wa* was a network of clandestine preachers, agitators and erudites who came within the proverbial eyelash of overturning Sunni domination. Its finest flowers had been Hasan Sabbah, the Iranian who honed the movement to the fine cutting edge of a dagger, and his Syrian heir, Rashid al-Din Sinan, Misyaf's most illustrious tenant and master. Coincidentally, the name is shared by the clandestine internal Shi'a resistance movement in Iraq under the Baath regime led by the family of the martyred Ayatollah Muhammad Baqir al-Sadr.

By now, my host's lists and relations of holy men, secret agents, enlightened ones and caliphal emissaries had become far too complex to keep track of, much less unravel. Having allowed myself to be distracted by the dappled quality of the light in Mr. Aruh's courtyard, I found my attention drifting, and his historical exposition fading like a distant radio signal.

What about the Assassins? I asked, rather abruptly. It was the verbal equivalent of a pinch to keep myself awake.

Mr. Aruh, who had been content to recite genealogical tables, dates and place names, snapped back into the present.

"But, they were people who were resisting against the seizing of their land. They were few, their enemies were many. Never they massacred civilian populations. They killed only military leaders. They had no armies, but highly trained commando forces.

"When Salah al-Din came to Misyaf he led an army of 40,000 men. There were only two or three thousand fighters in the castle. But they forced him to withdraw, and struck terror into the hearts of kings throughout the region."

"Is it true that they used hashish?"

"Bernard Lewis!" snorted Mr. Aruh, as if exorcising an evil spirit. The author of *What Went Wrong* is not a beloved figure among Arab intellectuals, of whatever stripe.

"Bernard Lewis promoted the legend of hashish eating, which he got from Marco Polo. But Polo's account was based entirely on hearsay."

The next stop on our whirlwind expedition was the spiritual capital of Syria's Ismailis. Salamiyah balances on the invisible but palpable threshold that leads from western Syria's last marginally cultivatable land into the desert that stretches all the way to the banks of the Euphrates and beyond. After a staggering midday meal at the home of a family friend, the soporific effects of which several cups of strong coffee were necessary to overcome, Dr. Muhammad led me along the sidewalks of the town, which seemed as drowsy at that hour as I felt.

As we turned a corner I noted a green dome, of the kind that usually indicates a shrine, looming above the low-lying houses. "It is the tomb of 'Ali Khan, do you wish to see it?" said Dr. Muhammad.

'Ali Khan! Images of the dapper, top-hatted playboy who once graced the glossy pages of *Life* magazine that my father accumulated in his suburban California garage, rushed into my mind. So, this was what had become of 'Ali Khan, the scion of the ruling Ismaili family passed over (wisely perhaps) for leadership of the community who had enjoyed a highly publicized affair, then marriage with the inimitable Lady from Shanghai, Rita Hayworth; the man who kept the company of luminaries like André Malraux, Baron Guy de Rothschild, Stavros Niarchos and Porfirio Rubirosa. All these bright lights of a bygone era had been waiting for him at a Swiss château when he died *en route* at the wheel of his Lancia cabriolet in May, 1960. The shrine was simple, respectful; the atmosphere, one of dustiness and a certain neglect. Among the photographs that hung from the walls, not one showed him in the company of the fiery Goddess of Love, nor of Gene Tierney who would later become his mistress. But the sardonic smile was there, and the cigar, as was the elegant insouciance and familiarity with wealth that had served him so well at the countless race-tracks and casinos, grand hotels and glittering restaurants through which he moved so light of foot. How far removed he lay now from the whirl and swish of the sweet life. The courtyard of the shrine was deserted. It was not a place where the devout thronged to pay homage.

"He is that man, indeed."

The confirmation came, in near impeccable English, from a bespectacled man named Mayhab Aizuqi. Mr. Aizuqi was a senior member of the Ismaili National Council of Syria whom we met in an office at the Salamiyah Ismaili school, just around the corner from the tomb. "'Ali Khan was not an Imam," he explains from behind a large wooden desk, with a schoolmasterly air. "He was a man of worldly affairs. He did good work for the community, but as son of the Imam. We here in Syria love and respect him very much. His role was to supervise Ismaili communities in Syria and Iran."

Mr. Aizuqi was understandably less interested in 'Ali Khan than in the past and present of the Order, and, to be truthful, so was I. Back, then, to the subject at hand.

It was here, in Salamiyah, he explained, that the mysterious Abdullah wrote the "Letters of the Brethren in Purity," a community manifesto combined with a document meant for ideological use. The times were treacherous, and the spies and hired killers of the Abassid regime sought him, to no avail.

"Few of his entourage could even identify him, so extreme was his concealment."

Conventional history identifies the Fatimid dynasty that ruled from Cairo as the greatest threat to the domination of the Sunni Abbassids. There had been no dispute in the world of Islam as to the genuineness of the Fatimid descent from the lineage of the Prophet until the beginning of the eleventh century, when al-Qadir, the caliph of Baghdad, issued a manifesto declaring that his rival al-Hakim—whom we will encounter again soon—was descended from a heretic.[91] That alone was evidence of a high level of mutual suspicion.

Not so, insisted Mr. Aizuqi: "The Fatimids never attempted to overthrow the Baghdad rulers. The underground movement that succeeded to govern Egypt, North Africa, Yemen and Syria never attacked Iraq or Iran. They wanted to leave the Abbassid regime in existence. Their aim was to show that there was another way of practicing Islam."

What is your view of Sinan, the Old Man of the Mountain? I asked.

"Ah, Sinan. He was a man of faith, a strong leader, the deputy of the Imam in Syria. Politically, he was shrewd, almost a copy of Hasan Sabbah. He rarely attacked, and only responded when attacked. But the Crusaders were invaders, and against them he took action."

The Assassins are said to have derived their name from the Arab word *hashishin*, hashish eaters, which they are alleged to have consumed before carrying out their daring operations, I ventured.

"Nonsense," said Mr. Aizuqi. "For difficult missions, only highly trained *fida'i* were chosen."

Though I was speaking to an official spokesman for a religious sect that had long practiced extreme forms of dissimulation, what I knew about the effects of hashish—from the literature, of course—tended to confirm his assertion. The *fida'i* may have been drugged to induct them into an earthly version of paradise, but when they struck with their poisoned daggers, absolute, single-minded dedication was their only narcotic.

There was a second reason to credit Mr. Aizuqi's claim. By now, close-hand exposure to Syria's Ismaili community, first at Misyaf and now in Salamiyah, made it clear that though they prided themselves on their heritage, the Ismailis no longer functioned as a clandestine sect. Quite the contrary.

"It is true, we practiced taqqiyah, or dissimulation, up until the fourth Islamic century," (llth CE) added Mr. Aizuqi. "But today, our faith is known and respected for its cooperation with non-Ismailis. We work to remove differences, and we preach and practice tolerance."

When Dr. Muhammad and I left the school building, the sun was setting over the low rooftops and dusty acacias of Salamiyah. Men and women were making their way toward the mosque located in one corner of the complex. There was no minaret; I had heard no call to prayer.

As the Toyota whirred westward toward Misyaf in the gathering dusk, I asked my friend about the secret of Misyaf. "When I tell you, it will be a secret no longer," he smiled. "But I will say it."

"I have discovered the workshop hidden inside the citadel where the Assassins made their daggers. I studied the research that had been done, and explored the fortress to compare what I knew with published studies. I found a gap. There are two places that are not mentioned. They are difficult to enter.

"The dagger workshop is at the bottom level, at the northeast corner near the great cistern. I found the entrance after many efforts. Nearby, I am convinced there is a secret passage to the outside, beyond the city wall."

It was dark now, and as our vehicle raced homeward, the headlights illuminated the silhouettes of animals darting across the road.

"Look, Abu-Antun!" exclaimed Hasan. "Jackals!"

My thoughts were too far distant, my senses lulled by the gentle vibration of the road. I never saw the fleeting shapes except as they tailed out of my field of vision and into the moonless dark.

* * *

DURING THE PEAK YEARS of the Fatimid caliphate in Cairo Misyaf and several other fortified towns of the Coastal Mountains of Syria had been Assassin strongholds. But with the defeat of the Order, the Ismailis had slowly withdrawn, leaving behind small communities stranded like seashells on a hostile shore. Dr. Muhammad confided that no more than one dozen Ismaili families still resided in the city beneath the citadel. Around it had grown up another community, even more hermetic and self-contained: that of the Alawites.

Before I left Damascus, I decided to ask Munir 'Ali for help. Sooner or later, all foreign journalists in Syria end up in Mr. 'Ali's office. No exception, I would lounge in one of the imitation leather armchairs sipping bittersweet coffee while my host fielded telephone calls or ripped incoming faxes from the machine directly behind my head. My project, to write a book on Syria and its connection with the iconoclast conflict, had piqued his curiosity.

Unlike what seemed to be a majority of civil servants in Syria, Mr. 'Ali took genuine interest, though it may have been skillfully feigned, in what his diverse visitors were up to. Tall and gangling, he projected a certain raffishness in his focused disorganization. More often than not, Munir—we had by then come to first name terms—was as good as his word.

So it was that when I mentioned my plan to visit the Alawite heartland, the Jabal al-Nusayriyah, he smiled broadly, and flicked from his sleeve a deposit of ash from his ever-present cigarette. Then he bent over the confusion of his desktop, jotted down a number on a slip of paper, and handed it to me: "Call this man. He may be able to help you."

The scrap of paper, firmly tucked into my address book, was to be my calling card, my passport to the land of the Alawites, the heterodox sect which in less than three generations had evolved from Syria's poorest, most down-trodden minority into a ruling caste whose members—like Munir 'Ali—now occupy the pinnacle of the state structure and many of the layers beneath. Like the Ismailis, they too were heirs of 'Ali. Unlike the Ismailis, for whom the past is now an open and proud book, the Alawites remain among the most hermetic and self-contained religious groups in the Muslim world. If indeed they belong to that world at all.

The name written on it was that of 'Ali Khalil, a sometime assistant and consultant to the Ministry, a man who contributed articles, translated documents and accompanied visiting dignitaries. He was, Munir 'Ali had told me, a man of wide and diverse knowledge.

"You are in Misyaf?" boomed the voice over the telephone. "You must come to my house immediately." Dr. Muhammad, from whose office I had made the call, jotted down the instructions in Arabic for the driver. Within one-half hour the taxi—Misyaf taxis were like the town, dilapidated and ancient—was sputtering up the mountain road. The town and the citadel dropped away beneath us. The foothills with their light green mantle of fresh-grown grass and darker olive trees spread out eastward, sloping into the lowlands around Hama. Several kilometers out of Misyaf, at a crossroads, stood a plump man with wavy, silver hair wearing a threadbare zipper jacket: it was 'Ali Khalil. With a hearty handshake he led me down a sloping path to his house, a half-finished reinforced concrete cottage perched on the slope.

The house was all but bare of furniture; there was no television set. As we made our way to the living room, where flies droned lazily in the sunlight that flooded in through the uncurtained windows, he introduced me to his post-adolescent children. "Two of them are attending university," he explained proudly, as if to say, 'we may be living in straightened circumstances, but it is so that our children may receive an education.'

After whispered instructions, the eldest son left the room. From what I assumed was the kitchen came the rattle of utensils against plates. Mrs. Khalil poked her head around the doorframe and greeted me with the traditional Arabic words of welcome, valid in all circumstances: "*ahlan wa sahlan.*" A meal, it seemed, was inevitable.

It was not long before the son returned, a bulging packet wrapped in a tea-towel under his arm, and with it, the smell of roasted chicken wafted through the house carried by the warm breeze. A platter heaped high with fried potatoes appeared, then came sliced tomato, cucumber, cheese, olives and bread which were to be washed down with *laban ayran*, a frothy beverage made from thinned yogurt. The chicken, purchased from the only roast-chicken outlet in Misyaf and served directly from its brown waxed-paper wrapping, brought up the rear. As we ate, I explained to my host what had brought me to his door. I hoped to learn more about the Alawites who had long endured in these rugged mountains.

"*Ahlan wa sahlan*," he said, "God willing, you will get the information. I know people who can tell you what you want to find." Mr. Khalil was himself an Alawite, among whom the name 'Ali was especially commonplace, and he knew that I knew it. But in the two days we spent together exploring the up-country villages, he never once spoke of his own beliefs. Was it discretion or the legendary Alawite reticence to speak of their faith; was it mistrust of an unexpected outside visitor (who nonetheless carried an introduction from a friend in medium-high places), or could it have been that his assistance was less a question of friendship than obligation?

The Alawite question had near-taboo status in Syria. A minority group that accounted for no more than twelve percent of the country's population had succeeded in capturing command of the military apparatus and of the state. Criticism of Alawite influence could not be spoken publically, only in whispers. Curiosity, especially if it became too pointed, could be dangerous. Heads had rolled before; they could roll again.

And yet, if I hoped to understand the country, its particularities and its history, I would need the broadest possible picture of the heirs of 'Ali, the heterodox Shi'a groups which have given it its unique social contours fully as much as the Sunni majority of the main towns, perhaps more so. Perhaps, too, my encounters with Dr. Muhammad and the Ismaili authorities had been deceptive, even unrepresentative in their ease and openness.

"There are two places I want to visit," I told Mr. Khalil.

Both were mausoleums. The first, to a man called Sheikh Salih al-'Ali, who fought the French during the early years of the Mandate. The second, that of the late President for Life, Hafiz al-Asad.

"I will take you."

* * *

THE VILLAGE OF AL-SHEIKH BADR, a hardscrabble settlement perched atop a ridge at the southern extremity of Syria's Jabal al-Nusayriyah, the tortuously pleated, craggy range that lies between Syria's arid interior and the Mediterranean, can be seen metaphorically as a storm-ravaged shoreline. Here, to this day, traces still remain of the great offense inflicted upon the Islamic Orient.

Like a tsunami stirred by a subterranean upheaval at a far distant epicenter—the assassination of Archduke Francis Ferdinand in Sarajevo—the shock waves of World War I flooded across upon the region. They swept away the political and administrative system that had created a common, though richly diverse, cultural, social and religious space that extended from the Balkans to the west of Istanbul, to Baghdad, Mecca, Cairo, and beyond. The effect was at once centrifugal and explosive, centripetal and implosive. A world had been blown apart, and had collapsed onto itself. The process of slow-motion demolition followed by breakup initiated by the forced integration of the Ottoman state into the European capitalist system was unleashed, in a burst of violent acceleration, upon the Arab interior. Not one corner of the heartland of Islam was to escape its levelling fury.

Though the spark that touched off hostilities had been struck in Bosnia— engulfed in the war of the Ottoman succession even today—it was to leave its deepest, most indelible imprint upon the Middle East. Today, the region still struggles, mostly without success, to understand and shake itself free of the heritage of treachery bequeathed by its putative imperial saviors, and perpetuated by the venality of their locally bought henchmen.

The Sykes-Picot accords, negotiated in 1916 behind closed doors in London and Paris, had portioned out the Ottoman domains between England and France, at the time the world's dominant powers. Two years earlier, during the first months of the cataclysm that was to give delayed birth to the monstrosity later known as the twentieth century, Great Britain had already grasped the strategic stakes. In a speech delivered in London on 9 November 1914, Prime Minister Herbert Henry Asquith predicted that the war had "rung the death knell of Ottoman dominion, not only in Europe, but in Asia."[92]

Well before victory over the Central Powers, of which the Ottomans were an ally, Britain and France had begun to jockey for position in the post-war Middle East. Sir Marc Sykes and François Georges Picot were charged by their respective governments with devising a scheme that would reconcile their conflicting claims in the region while taking into account not at all the aspirations or interests of those who lived there. Such a concern would have seemed quaint, beneath consideration. The circumstances of their meetings bordered on caricature: in the bordello-like plush pseudo-opulence of grand hotel rooms and in the muffled chambers of chancelleries, circumstances that entirely befitted their status as *courtesans de luxe*.

With a handful of minor rearrangements, several minor disputes, the odd misinterpretation, and a nominal access to independence, the map of the region today is that devised by these two Western European aristocrats. Syria, including Lebanon, was to be given to France, with the states known today as Iraq and Jordan going to Britain, along with Palestine. (Palestine was soon to be promised by the British government to the International Zionist

Organization as a national homeland for the Jews, and thus overrode the original accords.)

"The Sykes-Picot Agreement," writes David Fromkin in his encyclopedic yet rather patronizing overview of the impact of the war on the Middle East, "was approved by the British and French Cabinets at the beginning of February, 1916. But its terms and even its existence were kept secret; the very fact that the Allies had reached an agreement about the postwar Middle East was not revealed until almost two years later."[93]

When it was revealed, the revelation had come from the victorious Bolsheviks, who denounced the secret treaties condoned by Russia's former Tsarist masters.

It mattered not whatsoever that the Foreign Office and the Quai d'Orsay were appropriating and promising what was not theirs. Like their American legatees in Iraq, their sole concern was that the conclusion of the war would leave not the slightest opportunity for any other future. And in this somber regard, not only were they to prevail but to establish a benchmark for further Western intervention in the region. Sykes had earlier informed the British War Cabinet that Arabs "have no national spirit in our sense of the word, but they have got a sense of racial pride, which is good." They should therefore be content with a "confederation of Arabic-speaking states under the aegis of an Arabian prince."[94]

Sykes, however, was incapable of uttering publicly what he must have known and surely feigned to ignore: that the Arabs, and particularly the Syrians, were determined to establish a unified Arab state that would be fully independent, and not dependent on the self-interested generosity—as self-proclaimed—of European protectors.[95]

Both the British and the French paid fulsome lip-service to the ideal of independence they had invoked in order to mobilize the Arabs against their former Ottoman masters, but their secret and true objectives were entirely colonial and mercantile, cultural, ideological and geostrategic. Britain was determined to create and consolidate a pathway to its Indian possessions free of the apprehended threat from Russia. France hoped to turn its experience, and the *mission spéciale* that had been perfected at gunpoint in North Africa, to good effect in the Levant where it had already established itself as the "protector" of the Maronites of Lebanon. Underpinning the entire edifice was a stone and mortar foundation of innate, immutable and "self-evident" Western superiority.

Fast forward to 1918. General Allenby's forces had entered Damascus in late September, the Ottoman administration had vanished. On its march north through Palestine and into Syria, the British army, like the American forces in Afghanistan and Iraq, had claimed to be something other than a traditional conqueror, "for she was acting on behalf of an array of associated powers and causes … Among their banners was one designed Sir Mark Sykes for Hussein and the Arab cause." Its colors—black, white, green and red, the same colors in the same configuration as used today by all the Arab states of the region— would symbolize the past glory of Arab Moslem empires and suggest that Sharif Hussein, the Ottoman-appointed guardian of Islam's holy shrines, was their contemporary champion.[96]

With their capture of Damascus, Britain and France now faced a dilemma. Allenby's troops controlled the ancient city, not the French forces. Though strong voices were raised in London calling for renunciation, the Foreign Office stood by the agreement with France: "wherever in the Syrian provinces Britain established a military administration, France was entitled to have her officers exercise all civilian administration on behalf of the Allies."[97]

According to the terms of the Sykes-Picot deal, France was to be given direct control of the coastline. Inland Syria was to be independent—not independent in name only, as envisaged by the agreement—but substantively independent. The new country's ruler, it had been agreed in secret correspondence, would be a Hashemite.[98] That ruler would be Prince Faysal, the son of Hussein, the man who had earlier undertaken a mission to Istanbul to palliate the Sublime Porte which was planning to depose his father. From the Porte's point of view, the sherif had betrayed a trust not only by talking with the British about ridding Arabia of Ottoman rule, but by accepting British gold to do so. To attempt to persuade him to change sides, as they did, was entirely legitimate, just as it had been reasonable for Faysal to seek the best guarantees, and not blindly trust the Entente Powers.

Faysal's position was weak and would soon become weaker. He had not, as the British claimed, liberated Damascus. He and his small contingent of Arab cavalry had merely staged a ceremonial entry into the city several days after Allenby's arrival. For political reasons, it was necessary for London to pretend that the prince and his followers had played a substantial role in freeing Syria from Ottoman domination. Faysal, they claimed, "had therefore earned the right to serve as the ruler of a free Syria; and specifically that he should be free to reject French advice and advisers if he chose to do so."[99]

Through Faysal, Britain now exerted dominant influence in Syria. French troops had landed at Beirut, but not in sufficient strength to challenge what seemed a *fait accompli*. As the peace conference opened at Versailles, France and Britain were at loggerheads. Why not, argued United States President

Woodrow Wilson, send a commission to ascertain the true wishes of the inhabitants of the region?

The King-Crane Commission, a perfect Wilsonian model of futilitarian self-intoxication chaired by two American political hacks, pseudo-innocent precursors of their sinister successors who would act eighty years later as "honest brokers" between the Zionist settler state and the dispossessed Palestinians, traveled to Syria and Palestine to gather testimony in the summer of 1919. Not surprisingly, British officers were in a position to determine who should testify and who should not. Even less surprisingly, "the French were enraged by the British manipulation and organization of witnesses and testimony."[100] In the event, the Commission's hearings, deliberations and final report, which was never made public, were naught but eye-wash.

In the gilded, velvet-curtained conference rooms at Versailles, David Lloyd George and Georges Clémenceau were locked in a bitter struggle. For Britain, Sykes-Picot no longer reflected facts on the ground, to employ the terms later used by their Israeli acolytes. France was insisting not only on the spirit, but on the letter of the deal. Picot himself had hastened to Damascus immediately after its capture. The wealthy and influential *parti colonial* was in full cry in Paris. France was not to be denied.

In September 1919 Britain finally relented, less out of respect for France's claims than out of concern for anti-British upheavals in the Punjab and in Egypt. In November, British forces had begun to withdraw gradually from Syria, to be replaced by the French. That would leave the French and Faysal to settle all outstanding issues—and everything was outstanding—between themselves. The British had thus apparently honored their commitments both to France and to the Arabs The claim was as disingenuous as it was hypocritical. The British were to leave Faysal and the Arab administration that had nominally governed Syria for one year at the tender mercies of France.

No sooner had Britain withdrawn than Faysal faced the ineluctable. In January 1920, he reached an agreement with Clémenceau, the French Prime Minister, which recognized Syria's right to self-government and guaranteed its independence and territorial integrity. In return, writes Phillip Khoury in his monumental history of Syria under the French Mandate, Faysal agreed to accept outside assistance exclusively from France.[101]

The French fox, sharp of fang, was now amongst the Syrian chickens. That wily predator, by no lack of coincidence from the Burgundian city of Lyons, the seat of France's powerful colonial lobby and of the industrial interests that supported it, took the human form of General Henri Gouraud. A disciple of Maréchal Lyautey, the pacifier of Morocco, and a devout Catholic, Gouraud had been appointed in October 1919 as High Commissioner of the French Republic in Syria and Commander of the Army of the Levant.[102] Now he was to be given a free hand.

All the while, in Damascus, the nascent Syrian Arab nationalist regime, forgetting the extent of its political and financial indebtedness to Britain, began to behave as though it were a full-fledged national government. The Syrian General Congress had, in late January, voted to scrap the Clémenceau-Faysal agreement. Then, meeting again in early March 1920, it adopted a resolution proclaiming Syria to be completely independent within her "natural" boundaries, which included Lebanon and Palestine. Faysal was to rule as a constitutional monarch.[103] It also supported a proclamation attacking British claims to Mesopotamia. Whatever inclination London might have felt to restrain France soon evaporated.

In France, meanwhile, Clémenceau had been defeated. The new prime minister, Alexandre Millerand, was a firm believer in France's colonial mission. Adopting what might be termed a "Sharonist" policy toward Prince Faysal, Millerand was determined to undermine, then destroy him. There were, he might have argued, good reasons to do so. Not only was the young Syrian government's emerging policy entirely hostile to French domination, it threatened to touch off sympathetic resonance in France's North African colonies. The tactic chosen was to depict the Faysal government as being under the influence or control of extremists and to declare it irrelevant.

The strategic decision was made in April, 1920, and put into effect in July, when General Gouraud presented Faysal with an ultimatum to "demobilize his army, recognize the French Mandate and dismiss his extremist supporters or else he would be removed from Damascus. Even though Faysal reluctantly accepted the ultimatum, the French Army was already advancing. By July 25, Damascus had fallen into French hands."[104] Three days later the king fled his short-lived capital, never to return. As a consolation prize, the British installed Faysal on the throne of Iraq "where he ruled with some success until his death in 1933,"[105] success in this case being defined in terms of subservience to British colonial interests.

Readers will be forgiven for seeing, in the events of the early 1920s, a series of actions and behaviors powerfully evocative, if not predictive, of the events of 2002 and 2003. Statesmen come and go, the shape of empire is in constant flux, but its diamond-hard mechanisms, ambitions, and self-intoxications are forever.

Among the doomed King Faysal's "extremist supporters" was a man who was neither an extremist nor even a firm supporter. Sheikh Salih al-'Ali, a thirty-five-year-old landowner from the Jabal al-Nusayriyah made an unlikely rebel. His village, al-Sheikh Badr where I had travelled up from Misyaf in Hasan's Toyota with 'Ali Khalil in the front passenger's seat on that afternoon in early May, made an unlikely hotbed of rebellion. More unlikely still, what was to happen over the next several years in al-Sheikh Badr would have a decisive impact on the nature of the modern Syrian state, and upon the Baath Party that was to play a decisive role in fashioning that state.

By 1918, the French had begun to occupy the lands they claimed as theirs under the Sykes-Picot Agreement, beginning with the coastal areas of Syria and what is now Lebanon. As the retreating Ottomans abandoned their positions in the port city of Lattakia, French troops moved in, dismissed the national provisional government and prepared to take disciplinary action against the highlands which were described as being in a "state of complete anarchy"[106] at the time. By "anarchy" was meant "absence of French administration."

To his ancestral domain in al-Sheikh Badr, Salih al-'Ali summoned twelve of the regions' leading notables to discuss plans for unified resistance. The young chieftain brought to the meeting the natural authority of a man who had already acquired a reputation resisting the Ottomans. He and the clan leaders were, it seems, far less interested in the Arab nationalism radiating outward from Damascus than they were in safeguarding their mountain stronghold from outside influence. Because the Damascus government was weaker, they saw it as less of a threat than the French.[107]

This was the place where they met.

Amidst a patch of scraggly, wind-sculpted trees stood a green-roofed, double domed tomb, the only kind of religious structure one is likely to encounter in these rugged, densely populated mountains. Here, Salih al-'Ali was buried, his body entombed in a mausoleum that today is neglected, ill-maintained and ill-repaired. In the center of the chamber lay the catafalque, beneath a sheet of thick, dark-green baize crudely embroidered about the edges. The only light came from a dim bulb, augmented by the sunlight that filtered through the open door. Threadbare rugs covered the floor.

As 'Ali Khalil and I were putting on our shoes at the threshold, a man came toward us across the parking lot with a shambling walk and introduced himself: "I am Yusuf Abbas Salman, nephew of Salih al-'Ali," he said, "and I guard his shrine and his memory. You are most welcome."

Together we strolled toward Abbas Salman's house, which was located off to the side of the tomb building, separated from it by a ramshackle stone shed.

Chickens pecked in the dust, and swallows flitted busily overhead, darting under the eaves. We stepped inside, leaving our shoes on. The dwelling, like the shed, was built of stone, its split-stone shingle roof supported by rough-hewn beams. The floor was made of tamped earth. Inside, the air was thick with diffused smoke from the slow-burning embers in the fireplace.

"Sheikh Salih's family originally came from Egypt," said Mr. Salman. "They arrived in Syria with Ibrahim Pasha's expedition against the Ottomans. If you want to know about Sheikh Salih, my mother can tell you all about him. She's still alive. Wait a moment, I will go and call her."

Mr. Salman exited the dark room to fetch his mother. 'Ali Khalil and I waited in the penumbra, silent. Here I was at last, in the heart of Alawite country, the mysterious fog-shrouded, rugged mountains that have been the home and castle of this elusive sect for no one knows exactly how long.

Nor can anyone say with certainty when, or how, they came here. Today's inhabitants may be the descendants of the aboriginals who, for reasons known only by the adepts of the most opaque esoterica, might have adopted the secretive, some say heretical Alawite doctrine brought by itinerant divines. Unless they, like the Ismailis, had migrated to these inhospitable parts to protect their beliefs and their ways. Earlier that afternoon, as we made our way along the winding road to al-Sheikh Badr, 'Ali Khalil had explained that the Alawites who inhabited these inhospitable mountain crags were divided into clans that traced their origins back to the Fatimids.

"There seems little doubt," writes Patrick Seale, "that the Nusayris are a schismatic offshoot from mainstream Twelver Shi'ism whose history for the last thousand years has been one of stubborn survival in the face of invasion and repression."[108]

Seale and others call them Nusayris, after the putative founder of their sect, a certain Muhammad ibn-Nusayr, who flourished in the latter ninth century in southern Iraq. There, he proclaimed himself the "Bab"—door—of the tenth Shi'a Imam, and propounded a doctrine that considered 'Ali, the Prophet's son-in-law, as the incarnation of the Deity, hence the name "Alawite," from the Arabic 'Alawiyin.

This doctrine, say the scholars and erudites through whose books I leafed in an effort to discover the core of the Alawite belief system, is a highly syncretic one. In it, one encounters elements of Islam, Christianity, Zoroastrianism and pre-Islamic planetary worship in indeterminate proportions. "We are Muslims, of course," Alawite friends in Damascus had assured me as we shared the *iftar*, the Ramadan fast-breaking meal. They are heretics, argue the mainstream Sunnis, some of whom, following the censorious and straight-laced Ibn

Taymiyya, consider them more dangerous than Christians. They are masters of concealment, claim authors with a Zionist axe to grind, like Daniel Pipes: "Alawis have never been Muslims and are not now. [But they] have a long history of claiming Islam when this suits their needs, and ignoring it at other times."[109]

What was one to make of this? Abruptly, I was shaken out of my speculation by the arrival of a venerable woman wearing the white headscarf typical of Alawite uplanders. She carried a tray on which were a teapot and three cups. Greeting us, she poured tea, and sat down next to her son. Alert eyes shone from her deeply wrinkled face; her voice was tremulous, but she spoke with assurance, possibly the assurance of someone accustomed to repeating the message.

"He's not been dead that long," she said, shaking her head. "Only fifty-two years." That would have placed his death at mid-century.

"What kind of a man was he?" I asked.

"Ah, Sheikh Salih was a tall man, a manly figure. People like him are examples to be followed. Before the French came, he led a revolt against the Ottomans. He shot a policeman who entered his house. When the French came, he kept on fighting," she said, as 'Ali Khalil translated. "They came, and he fought them. I don't know why. I was a little girl at the time."

The catalyst for the Alawite revolt may have been a bitter, long-running dispute with the Ismailis, in which the French had attempted to broker a settlement. Their chances of success would have been minimal. Both sects were radical offshoots of Shi'ism, both revered the figure of the Prophet's son-in-law 'Ali, both chafed under the religious, economic and social domination of the Sunnis established in Syria's largest cities. Perhaps for that very reason, they were at daggers drawn. More prosaically, the dispute may have been over land and livestock.

Trying to stop a fight, especially when it's not your fight, can be far more dangerous than starting one. Their Ismaili adversaries temporarily forgotten, Sheikh's Salih al-'Ali's guerrilla fighters turned their attention to their would-be protectors, the forces of General Gouraud. Under his leadership the hyper-sensitive, combative Alawite tribesmen drove the tiny French garrison down from the rugged, roadless hills and back to Lattakia, on the coast. Never ones to overlook an affront, the French struck back.

"His followers warned him that the French were looking for him. He had only a shotgun. But he met the French in battle and defeated them with that gun. After driving them out, he moved on through the region, to Qadmus, Tartus and Banias. One of the battles took place right here, outside this house," Mr. Salman's mother said, reaching into the deep pocket of her cardigan and pulling out an ancient hand-grenade and a small collection of rifle shells. "Look, look at this."

"Three times the French destroyed this house. They even planted a bomb in the roof, but each time we rebuilt it."

"Sheikh Salih? He fought to defend our homeland. It was not a war of religion, but he was a religious man and our religion obliges us to defend ourselves against oppression."

In 1919, no national entity called Syria yet existed, except in the fervid imaginations of the nationalists whose rule in Damascus would be short-lived. And in the Jabal al-Nusayriyah, France's policy was to drive a wedge between the strongly regionalist, impoverished and historically isolated Alawites, and the powerful Sunnis who were seeking to establish a Syrian state.

Here Mr. Salman chimed in. "The French offered him the entire region to set up an Alawite state. But he refused to divide Syria."

By making the offer, France had tipped its hand. Gouraud, meanwhile, was playing a waiting game. As the months passed, the balance of power began to shift toward the Europeans. In June, 1920, the French called for a truce in their guerrilla combat against Sheikh Salih. Only a week earlier, General Yusuf al-Azma, commander of the infant Syrian army, had come calling to urge the Alawite notable to continue the resistance. Though the French had bought off a handful of the Sheikh's rivals, popular sentiment in the mountains was still behind the revolt.[110]

Two months after his visit to al-Sheikh Badr, General al-Azma's ragtag detachment was crushed at Maysaloun by an overwhelming French force. The death knell of Syrian independence had sounded. Deprived of support from Damascus, the revolt in the mountains sputtered on for almost two years before dying out.

"How was he defeated?" I asked.

"The French finally cut off his supply and escape routes and concentrated their troops. He was isolated, and finally defeated in 1922. Four years he fought against the invaders. He was never captured, even though they put a price of 100,000 francs on his head."

"I remember him, standing on the roof of this house," said the mother. "A French airplane was flying overhead; he shot it down. The parts can be seen in the village. In 1950, he died. He had come back to the village, and lived from the revenue of his property."

There was a problem with this account, I soon discovered. According to my best sources, Sheikh Salih did not die in 1950, but in 1926, four years after his defeat. In retrospect, it seemed doubtful that Mr. Salman's mother could have witnessed the events she described. At best, she would have been an infant when he launched his futile and heroic resistance. Difficult, too, to distinguish between what might have been the orally-transmitted memory of an isolated mountain people, and the official version propounded by the state, for which the Sheikh's uprising had been a nationalist, not a regionalist or a sectarian one.

In the real world, that which is inhabited less by stalwart ghosts than by skeletons in closets and exquisite corpses, the failure and collapse of the revolt opened the way for full occupation of the Jabal al-Nusayriyah. The French High Commission's campaign to isolate the Alawites from the nationalist forces in the Syrian interior could now begin.[111]

French policy in the Levant had, from the beginning, focused on the Maronite Christian minority of Mount Lebanon, of which Paris styled itself the protector. Now, in 1922, the policy of fragmenting the region's Muslim majority was extended to Syria. Separate mini-states were set up in the Jabal Druze, to the south east of Damascus, and in the Jabal al-Nusayriyah, where it became known as the "Territory of the Alawites." This rump entity continued to exist until 1936, when it was reintegrated into the French-controlled Syrian state.

The damage, however, had been done. The Alawites had, over the centuries, developed a fierce sense of their own distinctness. France's loving attention exacerbated matters. "The most extraordinary thing," writes Jacques Weurleusse, the French academic whose encyclopedic knowledge of the Alawites helped France devise and implement its colonial policy in Syria, "is that this subtle, refined religion of theologians became the mark of distinction of a population of mountain peasants who are among the poorest and most backward in all Syria."[112]

France's colonial policy would transform this backward peasant minority into the spearhead of its strategy of divide and rule, and in the process create the conditions for the rise of a political and military elite drawn from a group that represented no more than a small percentage of the population. For both French and Alawites, the strategy yielded substantial dividends. France recruited its *Troupes spéciales*—its special forces—from the minority whose social progress had been blocked by the majority Sunni establishment of the cities. Within less than fifty years this elite, in the name of pan-Arabism as propounded by the Baath Party, would take control of the Syrian state.

'Ali Khalil and I took our leave of Mr. Salman and his mother, and returned to our vehicle. The shadows were long on the ground now. Soon it would be time to return to Misyaf. As we rolled slowly down the long, curving drive that led from the shrine back to the main road, my guide spotted an elderly man wearing the traditional robe and white headcloth of an Alawite religious scholar. I asked Hasan to stop the van, we stepped down and walked over to meet him.

Here too chickens wandered, pecking and clucking, in the open space in front of the man's house, a humble, shambling cinder block and plaster dwelling surrounded by olive trees. Children peeked around the corner; a rusty motorbike leaned against the wall. He greeted us. Three chairs appeared. From the house a younger man arrived with cups of *maté*, the South American beverage made from the dried leaves of *Ilex paraguayensis* that had improbably become the convivial refreshment of choice in the Syrian highlands. *Maté*, which possesses the stimulative qualities of tea or coffee, found its way to the Levant in the trunks of returnees from the Syrian diaspora. As we sipped the grassy green infusion through silver-filigreed filter pipettes, the old man told his story.

His name was Sheikh Kamal, he was eighty-five years old, and yes, he remembered Sheikh Salih. "I was brought up in his house, under his protection. He was like a father to me," he said.

"When the French came, they wanted to find notables to endorse them. Sheikh Salih told them 'we won't replace Turkish rule with French.' The people asked him, 'how can we challenge the French?' 'We'll change acorns into bullets,' he said. And so the fight began.

"After he was defeated, the French began executing his commanders. He told them he would take revenge. For every man hanged, a Frenchman would die. The French commander called Paris for instructions; they told him to relieve the pressure. It was a kind of mutual non-aggression pact."

What was Sheikh Salih's opinion of the Alawite state the French wanted to establish? I asked.

"He would have nothing to do with it. 'We are all Syrians and Arabs,' he said, 'and we all drink the same water.'"

Usama bin Laden, the fearsome *mujahid* who had dared to defy two empires and helped to bring one down, came to mind. Al-Qa'ida martyrdom commandos had not yet impacted their captured airliners on the World Trade Center, but the elusive Saudi millionaire and his shadowy supporters had been linked with attacks on United States assets in several countries. "Terrorism" was already on the world empire's agenda, and on that balmy May afternoon in al-Sheikh Badr, its spectre already haunted the Middle East.

Sheikh Salih al-'Ali's career was, by today's definition, that of a "terrorist." He and his followers took up arms and engaged the military might of France; their stubborn resistance brought harm to French interests; they killed in defense of their land in a series of hit-and-run attacks described by the French as "cowardly;" France used aircraft, heavy machine guns and artillery against men armed with shotguns and primitive grenades, and against innocent populations who happened to be caught in the crossfire. Ultimately, Sheikh Salih was proclaimed wanted dead or alive by the war party in Paris, and by the French general staff.

He was a prickly kind of hero. As a member of the land-owning class, his motives were ambiguous; his nationalism may have been a flag of convenience, his Alawism a cover for his tribal or clan interests against those of the Ismailis whom his coreligionists fought for control of the land. Nothing about the life and death of Sheikh Salih seemed clear-cut, carved from the hard, quartz-like material from which monuments and heroes are constructed. But here, in al-Sheikh Badr, his legend—with modest assistance from the Baath/Alawite state and aided by fading memory—had taken root.

Here I was, sitting face to face with an Alawite religious scholar. The air was sweet with the scent of wood smoke and new grass; the *maté* mildly enervating; the twin green domes of the Sheikh Salih al-'Ali mausoleum were just visible through the silver green foliage of the olive trees. Would he reveal the secrets of Alawite belief? The hour seemed propitious.

"Sheikh Kamal," I asked the old man through Mr. Khalil, "tell me about 'Ali."

"Ya 'Ali," he said, by way of invocation. "O 'Ali! He was a great man. When Muhammad, peace be unto him, ascended to heaven he came upon a king surrounded by light. This was the image of 'Ali. And when the Prophet was sent a roasted fowl by Allah, and asked for the best of his people to share it with him, he saw the image of 'Ali.

"Once, Salman al-Farisi was sitting in his courtyard. 'Ali was eating dates on the roof. He threw Salman a date pit, which hit him on the head. 'Do you not respect my old age?' said Salman. 'Are you the elder?' asked 'Ali. Salman said: 'Once you were at an oasis in the desert, bathing, and a lion came and sat upon your clothes. A knight appeared and split the lion in two. Who was the knight, and what did you give him?' 'A bunch of flowers,' replied 'Ali. Then Salman gave him a bunch of flowers. 'Were these the ones?' he asked."

Sheikh Kamal would say no more, only smile beatifically when I urged him to expand. Admittedly it was absurd for me to imagine that, from a chance encounter with an aging sheikh in an obscure corner of the Jabal al-

Nusayriyah, I would be led by the hand into an arcane and complex world of belief that had remained hermetically sealed for centuries. Still, in the simple tales he told, Sheikh Kamal had confirmed by his own lips what the scholars I studied had been able to learn about the Alawites.

Unlike their orthodox Sunni countrymen, and even the mainstream Twelver Shi'ites who make up the population of Iran, and form a majority in Iraq and perhaps in Lebanon, the Alawites believe that Muhammad, 'Ali and Salman—a Persian and one of the first non-Arabs to profess Islam—form a holy trinity. This triad, in which 'Ali is divine essence, Muhammad figures as the "Name" of the divinity, while Salman is the "Bab," or gateway, is represented by celestial bodies: 'Ali, the moon, Muhammad, the sun, and Salman, the sky itself.[113] The system harked back—uncannily—to the gnostic Sabean doctrine that flourished until the twelfth century in the city of Harran, just south of Urfa in present-day Turkey, a place whose dust and desolation I had experienced at first hand several years before. Could the Alawites of Syria have been related, however distantly or remotely, through some curious filiation of ideas, to the sect that gave the world many of its finest astronomers? Few of the experts I later consulted were prepared to ridicule the idea but none could or would confirm it.

Few views in Syria can be more spectacular than the prospect eastward from the Jabal al-Nusayriyah. Almost one thousand meters directly below stretches the fertile al-Ghab depression with its crazy-quilt pattern of fields, rice-paddies and orchards, brought into being when the immense malarial marsh created by overflow from the slow-moving Orontes was drained by the al-Asad regime with financial assistance from the World Bank.

After bidding a last goodbye to Dr. Muhammad, and a final visit to the Assassin fortress, I had set out with 'Ali Khalil in Hasan's Toyota in mid-morning for a second excursion into Alawite country. After a long, wrackingly slow climb up the switchbacks that had looked as through they had been gouged out of the sheer eastern face of the massif, past dirt poor villages where children stared at us as we passed, we had reached the top.

Visibility was excellent that morning. Overnight, a spring rain had swept over Misyaf and the foothills; the air was pellucid. With binoculars we could have made out the ruins of Apamea, the ancient Roman city set high atop the bluffs that marked the eastern extremity of the valley, at least thirty kilometers distant.

For several kilometers the road followed the crest of the precipice, then veered westward. We wound down through cleft-like valleys, passing rock-strewn, terraced fields in which wheat, barley or oats might eke out a bare subsistence. Below us, a yellowish mist carried by warm air from the Mediterranean was creeping up through the rift-like gaps that ultimately open onto the sea.

"I will take you to meet a man who can tell you everything," 'Ali Khalil had promised as we returned from al-Sheikh Badr to Misyaf the previous afternoon. Now, as our van made its way down the narrow, winding road, plunging ever deeper into the mist as it writhed westward toward the coast, we began to encounter villages nestled in hollows, or clinging to hillsides where the valley narrowed. This was a Syria I had neither experienced nor expected. A landscape of ravines and convoluted canyons clotted with vegetation that closed in over the road.

Abruptly, at his instruction, we pulled to a stop by the roadside. Below us lay a tumbledown house surrounded by fallow terraced fields.

From the house emerged a portly man wearing the flowing, ankle-length robe popular among less westernized Syrians. He has been expecting us, 'Ali Khalil explains, with a proud edge in this voice, as though he had at last delivered me to the source for which I thirsted.

"I am Abdurrahim Selman," the man said, grandly as we moved toward him.

Mr. Selman's garment was blotched with grease spots, he was wearing tattered slippers, and his cheeks had a peculiar ruddiness. We sat down around a dusty table in the shade of a vine bower from which hung bunches of tiny, immature grapes. Slippers flopping, our host shambled off across the patio, disappeared briefly into the house, then emerged carrying a bottle by the neck.

"*Ahlan wa sahlan!* Here, have a shot of *arak*," he offered.

I demurred.

"No, no," he insisted, "it is rude to refuse. This is Syria."

In a country where more than three-quarters of the population is Muslim, to insist a guest drink alcohol might, on the contrary, have been considered rude. I didn't say as much, and smiled while lifting my head in the colloquial gesture of refusal common throughout the Balkans and the Middle East.

'Ali Khalil accepted, none too grudgingly. I threw what I hoped would be understood as a warning glance at Hasan the driver. For the briefest of instants I visualized the Hiace upside down at the bottom of a ravine, wheels spinning.

He took the hint and raised his hands, palms facing outward. Professional—
or religious—scruples had overcome temptation.

Mr. Selam unscrewed the bottle, which was already one-third empty, and
poured the viscous liquid, the Middle Eastern version of ouzo, into two
tumblers. Picking up the one closest to him, he knocked it back in a single
gulp, and wiped his mouth with the end of his sleeve.

Turning to me, he asked, out of the blue:

"*Mipos milas ellinika?*"

Wait a minute! That wasn't Arabic. It was Greek, modern spoken Greek. He
was asking if I spoke Modern Greek.

Over the years, experience had all but inured me to surprise, particularly
with regard to matters Hellenic. I'd heard of, though never met, Greek-
speaking Tibetans and of Cephalonian barbers amongst the Gauchos of
darkest Patagonia. Now, here, on the outskirts of a mountain village so tiny
that it appeared on none but the most detailed maps, I was sitting on a patio
with an *arak*-guzzling, Greek-speaking Syrian Alawite.

Hardly missing a beat, I replied in Greek that I did.

Mr. Selman, like me, had picked up the language of Kazantzakis in Greece.
There, as a younger man, he had gone looking for work only to end up in the
distinctly down-market seaside suburb of Loutsa, fifty kilometers from Athens.
The "mafia" had robbed him of everything he owned, so—I paraphrase—he
returned to his native village, older, wiser and poorer than when he left.

I could see, out of the corner of my eye, a look of alarm on 'Ali Khalil's face.
Had he been shunted aside? Where he had hoped to direct, and perhaps
control the conversation, had he suddenly become an uncomprehending
onlooker? Quickly I reassured him; his knowledge was essential to proper
understanding. I would speak in English, and he would translate.

It was just as well. Abdurrahim Selman in Greek reminded me of that rare
and vanishing species, the grizzled, venerable village polymath, the
pontificating school-master pedant, whom one used to encounter in tavernas
and coffee-houses in the provincial towns of Greece before mass tourism
struck. The men who, for a glass or two of wine or stronger, would unravel the
secrets of the universe. Like those depositories of hoary folk wisdom, New Age
gurus before the fact, he had devised a method for linking all phenomena,
worldly and otherworldly.

In the course of our encounter, as the bottle steadily emptied, he would
invoke the names of Plato, Jean-Paul Sartre and several lesser philosophical
luminaries to demonstrate that the beginning of all spiritual and intellectual

life, the beginning of all history could, in fact, be located in Syria. It was a method that seemed to be predicated on substantial doses of liquor, which would first function as an initiatory libation, then blunt the judgement of the listener until he came to believe in the slurred wisdom of his would-be spiritual guide. As in the cinema, the success of this method was predicated upon suspension of disbelief.

"The West has nothing to do with the two monotheistic religions which were created here," he asserted, through 'Ali Khalil. "The origins of Greek philosophy are here, in the East. The Greeks did nothing but give a form to the ideas that originated here."

Small wonder he'd been run out of Loutsa.

That was well and good, I told my guide. I might even agree. But hadn't he given his assurance that this man, Abdurahim Selman, would reveal the Alawite mysteries. Or at least lift a corner of the veil of concealment that lay heavily around them. 'Ali Khalil shifted uncomfortably on his seat, took a sip of *arak*, and rephrased his question to Mr. Selman, who brushed it aside as one would a bothersome insect.

"In the beginning, there was emptiness, then God and the seed of life … something like your Christian trinity," he explained. "Our faith comes from Judaism, Christianity and Alexander. Not your Western Alexander the Great. No, he came only yesterday! The Alawite trinity consists of … "

Of whom it consisted he was never to reveal.

"Knowledge," he digressed, after another slug of *arak*, "is for everyone."

That was certainly true, I said. "But how can we obtain the knowledge we seek if we do not have specific information?"

"The Alawites, they are the special people, they are the nearest relatives and companions of the Prophet," he said, his speech slurring. "They were 'Ali and his wife Fatima and Salman Farsi. Salman came from Persia. He lived for more than four hundred years, and it is said he had a third eye, a spiritual eye. It was he who anticipated the coming of Muhammad."

'Ali Khalil was becoming more discomfited by the moment. Nervously he glanced at his watch. "We must go now to al-Qardaha," he said. Hasan nodded in agreement. The bottle was empty, Mr. Abdurahim's head lolled to one side, his eyes fixed on his finger-smudged tumbler. Behind him, the fog billowed up from the sea, obscuring the stony hillside across the valley.

One hour later, the sun had taken on the appearance of a tarnished Syrian five lira coin dangling against an ocher-slate sky. The weather reminded me of a day several decades earlier, in the gritty southern Cretan port of Ierapetra. A hot wind had been blowing, carrying sand from the Libyan desert. The sky had been the same yellow-gray and the few raindrops that fell were muddy and opaque.

We had reached our ultimate destination, the birthplace of that quintessential modern Syrian icon which no one dared talk of smashing though I thought I had detected subterranean rumblings of the desire to do so: the late President for Life, Hafiz al-Asad, who came into the world here in October, 1930. al-Qardaha at that time, writes Patrick Seale, consisted of a hundred or so mud or rough stone houses at the end of a dirt track. There was no mosque or church, no shop, no café, no paved road, no village centre. It was in this forsaken place that al-Asad was born, "in a two-room flat-roofed house of undressed stone giving onto a front yard of beaten earth."[114]

Now he lies in state a few hundred meters from his birthplace, next to the remains of his eldest son Basel who died several years ago in what the authorities described as an automobile accident at the Damascus airport. Around the immense ceremonial structure that dominates the skyline lies modern al-Qardaha, a town of broad streets, prosperous villas and rank upon rank of multi-story apartment blocks, most of which were shuttered and seemed abandoned.

As we approached, 'Ali Khalil grew increasingly fidgety. The meeting at Mr. Abdurrahim's house had gone badly. He had made commitments upon which he had not been able to deliver. I had shown my impatience. Frustration had gotten the better of me—bad behavior for a guest in a culture which places a premium upon observance of the rules of civility and social etiquette. Now he was tight-lipped and sullen. Perhaps, too, there were other reasons. Were we, here in al-Qardaha, about to come uncomfortably close to a place in which one does not want to be seen as an idle visitor or, worse, in the company of an intrusive foreigner? (When they approach the sacred sites of the regime, all foreigners are by definition intrusive.) Did he, an Alawite, nourish a visceral but unavowable dislike for the ruling family? Unlikely but always possible. There was no such thing as an absolute identity of views between members of the minority religious sect and the ruling party. Not all had profited from his takeover, first of the Baath Party, then of the military, finally of the state. Many Alawites had opposed al-Asad and paid in blood or years in prison for their opposition; I had met some of the latter. Was he simply in a hurry to return to his house on the hillside overlooking Misyaf? I would never know.

al-Qardaha on that mid-afternoon was an eerie place, made all the more so by the cloying, swirling, dank mist. Its broad boulevards were absolutely empty, both of vehicle and pedestrian traffic. One thing set al-Qardaha apart from every other town in Syria I had yet visited: the high concentration of sleek late-model Benzes. But they were all parked in driveways or gleamed with not-so-subtle ostentation at curbside, as if waiting to whisk dignitaries and high party officials off to the Basel al-Asad airport at Lattakia, a facility built to serve the needs of the ruling dynasty and the rare international flight.

Leaving Hasan in the Hiace, we approached the shrine through a cavernous open-walled shed that was clearly intended for official functions. On one side, a reviewing stand; on the other, terraced platforms for the assembled Very Important Persons. Where, I wondered, would the common folk stand? A foolish thought. They would see the choreographed representation, the receiving line, the official delegations, the sleek, exquisitely made-up and coiffed women and sleeker automobiles, only on the interminable official television news bulletin in which the comings and goings of the dictator, his every breath and flutter of eyelid, were always and forever the lead story. The glitter of his gold buttons and the ballet of billed officer's hats too remote to touch but not to behold.

The shrine to the late president follows the octagonal form of the Alawite tombs that dot hillsides and villages throughout the region. But it also replicates the Dome of the Rock, the building that crowns the Haram al-Sharif in al-Qods (as the Arabs call Jerusalem). Though it would not have been beyond al-Asad megalomania to have instructed his architects to replicate Caliph Abd al-Malik's masterwork, the former can be demonstrated, the latter cannot.

Making our way around the perimeter of the monumental building we entered through the main portal. Beneath the great dome, surrounded by a sloping decorative apron of polished marble lay the tomb of the man who, from the rough stone of these mountains, sculpted modern Syria in his image. His tools: a fine blend of implacable cruelty, deft manipulation and the visceral instincts of the born politician. In the center, an opening in the floor reveals the raw stone of the Jabal al-Nusayriyah. At the Dome of the Rock in al-Qods, a gilded canopy shelters the stone from which the Prophet ascended to heaven. If the design of the shrine here at al-Qardaha was not a coincidence, and I did not think it was, who in this architectural allegory was the Prophet?

We had hardly stepped inside when we were intercepted by three young men from the security detail. They wore identical black suits over black shirts and black ties silk-screened with the image of the deceased, a sophisticated version of the paintings on black velvet that one sometimes sees on the far fringes of semi-rural North American gasoline stations.

These young men were as firm as they were affable: no photographs allowed—this they offered though I was manifestly not carrying a camera—, we must remain only in a limited area as renovation work was in progress. Dust and debris lay thick underfoot.

The building, which was not without a certain grace, might one day acquire the spiritual atmosphere that its designers surely intended. But today the tomb of Hafiz al-Asad breathed a mixture of ceremonial pomp and overstated, thus false, symbolism, overlaid with a fine patina of paranoia as pervasive as the dust that hung in the air.

In a country which rightly boasts of its hospitality, the al-Asad mausoleum is distant, cold, inhospitable, perhaps even a touch malevolent. The young security men feigned diffidence, but they hovered around us with anything but solicitude, as if their job was to hasten us on our way toward the exit. 'Ali Khalil said nothing, but his body language told me that he would rather be anywhere else. Feeling unwanted and unwelcome, we beat a hasty retreat.

The same curious combination of architectural grandiloquence and ersatz populism repeats itself perhaps two kilometers distant at the Naessa Mosque, an outsized, octagonal structure which the late president had caused to be built in memory of his eponymous mother, who lies buried here.

Above the courtyard that gives onto the mosque hangs a larger-than-life portrait of Hafiz al-Asad bending to kiss the hand of the beatifically smiling holy mother, from whose head radiate the beams of a sun-like halo. "Much younger than her husband, (she) was a strong-minded woman in her own right who came increasingly to be the dominant parent," writes Seale.[115]

The same halo effect can now be noticed on posthumous portraits of the president flanked by his two sons sometimes displayed in the *suqs* of Damascus and Aleppo. Was this an indication that within the innermost reaches of the Alawite religious community, the late dictator has been elevated to the status of "Bab," a position invested with great spiritual power, indeed with access to the Divinity? Did he and his sons—one dead, the other Syria's new president—now constitute a new holy triad? Well-informed sources in Damascus had whispered as much. How much was truth, that infinitely malleable commodity, and how much rumor, its cousin with the frayed cuffs? Impossible to say, impossible to know.

One thing seemed certain in retrospect: if these images were to be taken seriously, then the Alawites, through depiction of the sacred, were offering up evidence that, at the hidden core of their faith, lurked a doctrine of incarnation, of the Word made flesh. And were that so, the Alawites could not strictly speaking be considered Muslims at all.

Though it had all the attributes of a mosque, including the requisite *mihrab* and *minbar*, it was even more empty—and more ghostly in the thickening mist—than the mausoleum atop the hill. As were leaving, the azan rang out from the loudspeakers atop the minaret, but not a single worshipper appeared for prayer. Not a single automobile passed along the broad esplanade. Not one single pedestrian walked by. "Most people here work in Damascus," 'Ali Khalil explained in answer to my puzzlement as I climbed back into the van. "And besides, it's siesta time, they are all asleep."

His explanation was so unconvincing that he made no attempt to hide his disbelief. In the smaller towns and villages we'd passed through on our way here, shops were open and people thronged the streets. This was in fact the norm in a country where a great many people have large quantities of free time on their hands. In al-Qardaha, of this fog-shrouded afternoon, hardly a living soul was to be seen, with the exception of a motorcycle-mounted policeman waiting at an intersection for traffic—perhaps the phantom motorcade of Hafiz al-Asad—that could only be conjured up by the imagination.

No one I met could explain the ghost-town atmosphere of al-Qardaha. A friend in Damascus joked that perhaps the late President had come back to life as a vampire, and sucked the blood of the town's hapless inhabitants. But then, my informant mused wryly, he would hardly have stopped at the limits of his native village.

The mood in the van was morose. Hasan, who had driven more kilometers in three days than he usually did in a month, was anxious to avoid the mountain road to Misyaf after dark. 'Ali Khalil may have been dangerously exposed—in Syria, one never knew—by the visit. When I clambered down from the Hiace in the coastal town of Jableh to catch an express bus to Damascus, my guide's handshake was perfunctory, and the comfortable sum I slipped into his shirt pocket, against his theatrical but perfunctory gesture of refusal, could not redeem the day.

Raindrops thick with sand were spattering on the sidewalk. The dust of the Jableh bus terminal had turned to chocolate dark mud. As the bus pulled out I pressed my forehead obliquely to the window. At the other end of the terminal, I caught sight of Hasan's Hiace speeding eastward toward Misyaf, back to the land of the Alawites.

* * *

THE ALAWITES IN THEIR mountainous redoubt were not the only unsolicited beneficiaries of French colonial largesse. As France staked out its claim to a slice of the Levant, Syria's Druze population—largely unbeknownst to it—had also been selected for special minority status, and its traditional up-country homeland, the Jabal Druze (now officially known as the Jabal al-Arab), granted a kind of ersatz autonomy. This arrangement would only come to a formal end in 1936 when it, like the Jabal al-Nusayriyah, was officially incorporated into the French-controlled Syrian state.

The Druze, whose filiation with the Prophet's son-in-law makes it perhaps the most tenuous of the country's heterodox Shi'a sects, proved to be recalcitrant, even ungrateful. Unlike the Alawites, who thrived under French protection, the Druze wasted no time in rebelling. When they did, it was massive, near unanimous, violent and came within a hair's breadth of bringing down the Mandatory authority. The kind of outbreak that the new United States colonial authorities in Iraq may well meditate upon.

Five years to the month after French forces under General Gouraud had crushed the embryonic Syrian national army at Maysaloun, highlanders opened fire on a French observation aircraft circling the Jabal Druze. Three days later, an armed band commanded by a brilliant, charismatic local chieftain named Pasha Sultan al-Atrash ambushed a contingent of French and Algerian troops dispatched on a punitive expedition. Less than half the invading column survived. By nightfall, Sultan al-Atrash's ragtag forces had surrounded Suweida, the "capital" of the Druze region. By the last week of July, 1925, the Druze force had swollen to nearly 10,000 men.[116] France's policy lay in tatters. The Druze had declined to be divided from their Sunni neighbors, and they had given clear proof that they would not be treated as colonial pawns.

The Great Revolt had begun. It would continue for more than two years, and penetrate to the very heart of Damascus, before it was finally defeated by overwhelming French military superiority.

It was a hot Thursday afternoon in late May. A generous early summer light flooded Damascus. The first tiny, firm bittersweet apricots from al-Ghuta had made their appearance on pushcarts in the street corners. My guide and interpreter Salam and I boarded a bus at the downtown Baramke terminal for the two-hour run to Suweida, her home town.

Our excursion to Suweida would be, I hoped, less a systematic excavation than a random rummaging through the scattered shards of the recent and distant past. The Jabal Druze is exceptionally rich in such deposits. I hoped that they would reveal some of the connections between religious belief and the history of this strange and tormented land. "When we visit my family in Suweida, we will meet people who can tell you about the Druze religion," she told me. Salam, in sharp contrast to 'Ali Khalil, proved to be as good as her word.

Our bus, a clean, modern non-smoker, made good time. Soon we were climbing through the wheat and barley fields of the eastern Hawran. As we gained altitude, the air grew cooler, fresher. Villages scratched out a living from fields clogged with black basalt, the stone that provided, until the advent of concrete, the local building material. Here, as in Diyarbakir, further to the north in Turkey, everything was once black: houses, bridges, Roman temples, Byzantine churches, mosques. Whatever it might once have been, modern Suweida is more concrete gray than basalt black these days. But unlike most of the Syrian towns I'd visited, it radiates a curious, self-conscious prosperity. The secondary streets that branch out from the center are lined with massive villas boasting multiple balconies, elaborate gardens, and roofs topped with thickets of satellite dishes.

"Who can afford houses like this in Syria today?" I ask Salam.

"Families who came back to Suweida after years in Venezuela," she laughs. "No Syrian can make such a house. Unless he has, how do you say it? Connections, it is okay? Yes, connections with the government."

The house where Salam's parents lived, a modest two-floor concrete structure surrounded by fig, cherry and apricot trees, was no pseudo-Venezuelan villa but its walls seemed to emit accumulated human warmth. After the timeless, touching rituals of Arab hospitality—tiny gold-rimmed cups full of strong, cardamon-scented coffee followed by a dining table laden with savory and sweet dishes followed by a platter of spiced rice and chicken as its centerpiece—Salam and I set out to meet a nearby neighbor. He would be expecting us, said Salam's father Saïd, a proudly self-confessed Communist who, though he pretended to mock religion, maintained close contact with the town's sheikhs. In fact, he himself had arranged the appointment for us at his daughter's request.

We met Jamal Zahar al-Din, a teacher of Arabic and initiate into the mysteries of the Druze faith, in the anteroom of his residence, just down the street from Seyyid Saïd's. This was the space reserved for receiving visitors with some formality while protecting the private precincts of the home. While the

Alawites I had encountered were secretive, elusive and even evasive about their beliefs, the Druze sheikhs I met in Suweida seemed quite the opposite, but where the Alawite women were visible in their homes, those of the Druze in traditional households were not.

"All things have appearance and essence," said Mr. al-Din. "The Druze belief is the essence of Islam, as the kernel is the fruit of the nut."

As he spoke, there came a gentle tapping at the inner door. He got up, opened it slightly, and turned back toward us carrying a small tray bearing sweets and cups of coffee.

Unlike the complex and hidden belief system of the Alawites, whose origins are surrounded in a mystery wrapped in conjecture, the roots of the Druze doctrine are firmly etched in time and place. The time: the pinnacle of the power and reach of the Ismaili Shi'a Fatimid caliphs, who in the closing years of the tenth century CE, were mounting a mortal challenge to the Abassids of Baghdad for leadership of the *Dar al-Islam*. The place: Cairo.

The Fatimids, ostensible heirs of 'Ali who claimed descent from his wife, the Prophet's daughter Fatima, had promised simplicity as an alternative to the pomp of the Abassid court. As had the Abassids when they overthrew the Umayyads, only to exceed their wildest excesses. A few short years passed before Cairo, the capital city they founded in 973, surpassed all but imperial Baghdad in the beauty of its palaces which had been set out by royal astronomers in alignment with the heavenly bodies. Caliph al-Aziz, under whose enlightened reign the city prospered, was distinguished for his tolerance of non-Muslims, and accorded to Christians and Jews unprecedented privileges. To him was born by a Christian of Byzantine origin a daughter, Sitt al-Mulk, who would for several months reign as uncrowned ruler of the Fatimid state. This she accomplished upon the death of her younger brother, whom she may have had murdered.[107] It is upon this younger brother that turns the tale.

Struck down by a calamitous accident at the height of his power and prestige, al-Aziz was succeeded by his eleven year-old son abu-'Ali Mansur al-Hakim. "No one ever suspected," writes the Moroccan Islamic scholar and feminist Fatima Mernissi, "that with this child, with his look of surprise and his brow bound with precious stones, madness and horror would enter the city."[108]

As he grew to troubled maturity, al-Hakim began to terrorize the citizens of Cairo with his capricious moods and impulsive behavior. Twelve years his beautiful sister's junior, he saw illegitimate suitors and worse, lovers, wherever he turned. A spiral of jealousy, perfidy, murder and impenetrable mystery gripped the land. No one was safe from the young caliph's murderous rages or his constantly shifting impulses.

For reasons unexplained by the chroniclers, he declared Cairo forbidden to dogs, and had them killed. He would make strange public appearances, on horseback, riding on a donkey, floating down the Nile in a boat, borne in a litter atop the heads of his lackeys. Obsessed with astrology (already a doctrinal concern for the Ismailis), and plagued by insomnia, he ordered the city lit up by night so that his retinue could enjoy the sight of streets teeming with activity. Then he began to wander those same streets, hair disheveled and without the royal turban, clad in a coarse wool tunic (as the Iranian Saffavid ruler Shah Abbas the Great was to do six centuries later in Isfahan and as the emperor Nero had done in Rome). Gradually, all things related to pleasure— first among them being women—began to haunt the caliph. Women were banished from public view, "and did not set foot in the street for seven years and seven months, until the death of al-Hakim," wrote a contemporary scribe.[119]

Al-Hakim reversed the munificent policy of his father, and persecuted both Jews and Christians. Perhaps his most monstrous deed was the demolition in 1009 of the Church of the Holy Sepulchre in Jerusalem, an act which may have precipitated the Crusades. But the extreme point of the sixth Fatimid caliph's bizarre and enigmatic career came when he declared himself the incarnation of the Deity.

As an Ismaili Imam and spiritual heir of 'Ali, al-Hakim by his very nature "held a position in his community corresponding to the cosmic intellect."[120] The distance travelled was both short and very great. It is unclear whether, in proclaiming himself tantamount to God, al-Hakim had been manipulated by one of his soothsayers, a Persian called Hamza ibn-'Ali, or whether the the caliph himself was the manipulator. What is known is that a Turk named al-Darazi early on joined the al-Hakim cult, and with astonishing success propagated the doctrine of his Godhead until his death in 1019, two years before the disappearance of the mad caliph. It is from Darazi that the Druze sect derives its name.

Al-Hakim's pretensions were, for Islam, monstrous. God, for Muslims, is One, whose unity—known as *tawhid*—is absolute and whose identity cannot be shared. In them, we can discern the same temptations that the earliest Islamic authorities had detected in their Christian counterparts, then in the throes of the struggle against sacred depiction. But the caliph's stature, and his identification with the lineage of the Holy Imams, made open criticism a delicate matter. As for the motives of those who promulgated his Godhead we can only speculate. His Turkish and Persian acolytes may have been the occult power behind the throne, manipulating an otherwise mad caliph to their own advantage. They may also have seen in his eyes a flickering of what they interpreted as divine presence.

The facts are these. One year after an attempt to set Cairo ablaze because the Cairenes had lampooned his claims to divinity, al-Hakim vanished while on a night-time excursion on the city's outskirts. According to ibn al-Athir, a search party discovered his donkey and followed its hoofprints to the caliph's clothes, which had been cut to shreds. "There was no longer any doubt about who had killed him."[121]

All Arab historians but one, writes Fatima Mernissi, agree that Sitt al-Mulk, his sister, had him murdered. Surely, few in Cairo could be found to oppose her succession, as was proven by the calm with which the city's normally disputatious and fractious citizens apparently awaited a resolution of the issue.

But it is here that our tale diverges. The life and death of al-Hakim plunged the Fatimid caliphate into discredit in the eyes of many Muslims. But the followers of his two heralds, Hamza and Darazi, had contrived to migrate out of Egypt. The caliph, they intimated, was the One and Unique embodiment of the highest cosmic principle. He had not been murdered; he had gone into concealment.[122] By paths unknown though by no means untrodden, those followers made their way to that traditional place of refuge, the mountains of Syria—what is today territory controlled by Lebanon, Syria and the rogue state of Israel—where they settled, and established their own distinctive system of law and tribal solidarity.[123]

The Hawran, with Suweida at its heart, was home to one of the largest, most compact of these Druze communities. And our host, Mr. al-Din, was manifestly more than a simple teacher of Arabic in that community.

"The Druze sect began in 1017 of your calendar," he told me through Salam. "God had prepared a small group of men whose leader was master Hamza ibn-'Ali, to receive the message. They taught the way to discover the new reality. Eventually, the believers learned to communicate by telepathy."

"Each of the Fatimid caliphs were wise men; they were men who made ready the arrival of the new religion. The Imams had a spiritual, not a political nature, one of love and confidence. It was much more sincere than any political consideration."

This meant, he explained, that their thoughts were so deep that people were not always prepared for the message of which they were the bearers. Would that explain the extreme and extraordinary case of al-Hakim? I wondered aloud.

"Al-Hakim was the true master. Hamza ibn-'Ali was like his 'translator'," he said, nodding at Salam with a smile. "Hakim used his political position as caliph to promote the true religion among the people. Then he disappeared. His mission had ended. At the end of days, when the world becomes nothing but love, he will return. But no one can say when that day will come."

Dusk had fallen. As we left Mr. al-Din's house, the coolness of the evening had begun to creep up from the ground. Overhead, the first stars gleamed implacable, cold, indifferent, in the clear upland air over the Hawran, their movements tracing the esoteric reality which alone shaped earthly events,[124] if we are to believe the Ismaili Shi'a of al-Hakim's day. And perhaps his contemporary Druze followers as well.

Like her father, Salam was not a believer.

"How can he say such a thing?!" she had interjected to me, *sotto voce*, at one point during our talk with Mr. al-Din.

The barrier that divides translation from editorial comment was proving porous. Salam was alert and serious; to a fault, perhaps. She was signaling to me that for her, as a woman, the esoteric reality of the Druze elders cut no ice.

"Our job is to hear what he has to say, not to prove him wrong," I reminded her, not for the first time.

Tight-lipped, she nodded. I liked Salam's reaction. Indignation kept bubbling up into the vacuum created by incredulity. This woman did not intend to wear the horse-blinders of professional discipline.

Her father had arranged a second meeting. Several hundred meters along the road, we stopped in front of a much larger building. It looked like a cross between an apartment house and an institution. After ringing at a street level door, we were shown down a corridor, and up a flight of stairs to a spacious, elegantly furnished reception room. At the far end of the room Mahmud Janbih awaited us.

Mr. Janbih, a sturdily-built man whom I estimated to be in his mid-seventies, was dressed in the traditional Druze garb of white headscarf and long, belted black coat. "Yes, I am a sheikh," he said. "I am also a geographer, a graduate of the University of Damascus, and I lived ten years in Venezuela."

Like the Alawites, the Druze exist in the extreme ultraviolet zone of the Islamic spectrum, as far from the vital center of mainstream Sunni beliefs as are the infrared-dwelling pure-minded Salafi revivalists and their distant cousins, the followers of Usama bin Laden, who hark back to an idealized vision of Prophetic Medina stripped of all the accretions of tradition. Were they, in fact, Muslims? One must, of course, be cautious about framing the question in these terms, especially in Syria where questions of religious identity can easily spill over into the dangerous realm of the political.

Feeling my way cautiously, I ask Mr. Janbih if the Druze acknowledge the five pillars of Islamic belief. "We believe in them," he says, "but we do not perform them in the usual way. We fast in repentance of sins. But we believe that the Ka'aba [the structure housing the black stone which Muslims circumambulate during the annual pilgrimage] is an 'ethnic' symbol, an idol. Why then should we worship it? We do believe it was built by Abraham, but to walk around it is not acceptable for us."

Other fundamental articles of Islam seem also unacceptable to this compact, tight-knit minority. The Druze may proclaim themselves to be Muslims of the Shi'a persuasion, but they do not read the Qur'an. *Dixit* Mr. Janbih. "We read only from the *Hikme*, the holy book of the Druze belief."

The *Hikme*, which means "wisdom" in Arabic, is a compendium of letters written by Hamza during the reign of al-Hakim, an interpretation of the Qur'an. "You will not see it on this bookshelf," he says, pointing over his shoulder to the glass-fronted bookcase behind him. "The *Hikme* is forbidden to all non-believers. Because there are differences of interpretation, we feel that outsiders might reject our beliefs and ideas."

Forty years after its founding, the new religion closed its doors forever, locking away as well the mystery of al-Hakim. Now, says Mr. Janbih, no one can enter, and no one can leave. "Belief can be transmitted only through blood ties. If your father is Druze, you are Druze also."

With its narrowly prescribed system of transmission, its powerful esoteric overtones and its emphasis on a life of stern personal and public morality—the Druze neither smoke nor consume alcohol, allow a man only one spouse, forbid remarriage after divorce and insist that the truth must be spoken at all times among coreligionists—the mountain strongholds developed a keen sense of solidarity. This heritage, combined with a willingness to fight to defend the group and the faith, have given their communities a well-deserved reputation for reluctance to be pushed around, not to say for warlike proclivities.

Rarely had this quality been more evident than in the third decade of the twentieth century, when Druze discontent boiled over into open revolt. France had attempted to set Syria's rural areas against the nationalist towns, to isolate the country's compact regional minorities from the mainstream of Syrian-Arab political culture, and to play one elite against another.[125] In the Jabal Druze, the new French system of constitutional office-holding, built upon putatively democratic procedures imported from republican France, was a dagger pointed directly at the tradition of family hierarchy and group cohesion that had taken form in the early eighteenth century.[126]

The Salih al-'Ali uprising in the Jabal al-Nusayriyah had been a minor skirmish in comparison with what was soon to follow. In 1919, a revolt led by Ibrahim Hananu, the revolutionary firebrand, had broken out in the countryside around Aleppo. Three years later, unrest flared in the Jabal Druze, a harbinger of what was soon to come. Sultan al-Atrash, who was bitterly opposed to any form of French mandatory rule in Syria, had contacted and been given the backing of nationalist circles in Damascus.[127]

French Mandate Syria was by then seething with unrest. When Lord Balfour, author of the infamous declaration that promised to the International Zionist Movement what was not Britain's to promise—the land of Palestine— as a homeland for the Jews, visited Damascus in April, 1925, he was greeted by huge, hostile demonstrations that rapidly turned violent. Escorted by French troops and aircraft, Balfour beat a hasty retreat to Beirut.

Disenchantment, then anger over France's supposedly anti-feudal reforms and its autocratic administrative methods, spread through the Hawran highlands. In towns and villages, the followers of Sultan al-Atrash began their preparations for armed confrontation, hermetically sealed off from prying French eyes, beyond earshot of France's most diligent spies. The walls of silence were impenetrable. When General Sarrail had arrested several of the Druze chieftains who had come to Damascus to discuss their grievances, the point of no return had been reached.[128]

Discussion of grievances was of little interest to the French authorities. Their Syrian wards were to listen attentively and carry out instructions. Failure to do so could be dangerous to health. The policy had been perfected by General Lyautey, the pacifier of Morocco, who had described his system as "the economic and moral penetration of a people, not by subjection to our forces or even to our liberties, but by a close association, in which we administer them in peace by their own organs of government and according to their customs and laws."[129] Of course, Lyautey's ultimate recourse in the event of a people's reluctance to be thus administered was not enlightened French *raison*, but the violent repression of *raison d'état*. In this respect, he can be seen as a model, however schematic, for the imperial methods that the United States would later attempt to employ in conquered Afghanistan and Iraq and would eventually apply to Syria.

Repulsed by draconian French defensive measures, the People's Party, Syria's main nationalist organization, and the Druze leadership under Sultan al-Atrash established a provisional government in the Jabal Druze in early September. Its principle goals were Syrian unity and independence, from the Mediterranean to the far reaches of the interior.[130] Within less than two months, much of the country was in full revolt and France's policy, founded on Lyautey's principles of paternalistic pandering, subversion and deceit, was facing its most serious challenge.

Given its traditionalist leadership, the Great Revolt could hardly qualify as a revolutionary movement. It was no more revolutionary, in social terms, than the movement led by Mustafa Kemal in neighboring Turkey. But it did reveal "new broadly-based alliances linking together different elites like the Druze and the Damascenes, both urban and rural forces, and different social classes and religious communities."[131]

Friday morning in Suweida dawned warm and clear. The birds and insects were already hard at work in the fruit trees when Salam and I, fortified by a copious breakfast of tea, olives and cheese, set out by hired car for the village of al-Kraya, birthplace of Sultan al-Atrash, ten kilometers south.

Hardly a mountain, more a molehill, the Jabal Druze rises slowly from the basalt-strewn Hawran lowlands, without sharp peaks or precipices. Already, in late May, the air was dry, the sun biting and spring's short-lived greenery yellowed. When we pulled into al-Kraya, the village seemed deserted. In the middle of what may once have been intended as a parking lot but was now a dusty field, loomed a half-finished, semi-monumental concrete structure.

"That is the memorial to Sultan al-Atrash," volunteered the driver. "But they are not finishing it so fast."

"Buildings take a long time in Syria," chimed in Salam in perfect deadpan. By then I'd had accumulated enough experience with the country to understand that there could be only one secular shrine, only one icon, only one hero, he whose mausoleum I had visited in al-Qardaha and whose image was everywhere visible, perhaps by now even on the inside of my retinas. This lesser shrine, to a lesser hero, would probably never be completed, she seemed to be saying.

As we pulled up in front of a basalt house built in the traditional style, a man emerged from a smaller, adjacent dwelling.

"*Ahlan wa sahlan,*" he welcomed us, hand over heart. "I am the caretaker here. What can I do to help you?"

The man who led Syria's infant independence movement in its greatest uprising against French rule was the son of a wealthy family, explains the caretaker. He was also a simple man who willed that he be buried in a simple grave. Marked by an upright gravestone, it lies in a corner of the parking lot, ostensibly awaiting transfer to the monstrous unfinished concrete building.

These words are engraved in Arabic on the marker:

"We must protect our independence as Arabs and guard the land irrigated by the blood of our martyrs. Without the support of my comrades, I could have done nothing. May God forgive my sins."

The caretaker led us into the coolness of the basalt house, where we sat down on the *madaf'a*, the traditional stone bench ringing the large room where the resident dignitary would receive his guests and display for them the munificence of his hospitality. Every day, visitors and supplicants for favor flocked to meet him, to sip from a tiny cup of dark, bittersweet coffee, to partake of the food that would surely be served. So sacred is the obligation to protect one's guests that some date the beginning of the Great Revolt to al-Atrash's refusal in 1922 to surrender a fugitive from French justice. The man, a certain al-Hanjra, was ultimately captured, explains our host. That, for the chief, had been the ultimate insult.

Portraits of the thick-browed, square-shouldered Pasha Sultan al-Atrash as an aging warrior, and as a Druze sheikh, peer down from the rough walls. "During the revolt, his house was bombed and destroyed by the French while he was in exile, in Jordan," says the caretaker. "He returned to Syria in 1936, and lived in a tent in the village right in front of this house, which was built by the villagers."

France had offered to the al-Atrash clan the entire Jabal Druze as an autonomous entity. The British later proposed to create an independent Druze state to be allied with the Jewish state, to be a buffer between Israel and the Arab lands, our host explains. "He refused: 'I am a Arab first, and second a Druze. We are fighting to expel the French from all Syria, not just the Druze lands.'"

This sounded like the tale of Sheikh Salih al-'Ali I had heard several weeks before on my excursion to the Jabal al-Nusayriyah. The foursquare folk hero, man of the people, imbued with all the dynamism and energy of the national cause. But where the Alawite rebel's brave resistance to the French had found little support amongst his own people, and not at all among the elite, the movement led by Pasha Sultan al-Atrash was an entirely different matter.

The lion-hearted Druze chief was as good as his word. The insurrection against French rule spread like a blaze in tinder-dry forest, springing up in new, unexpected places, drawing cruel and predictable response from the imperial authorities. In Hama, the nationalist movement staged an uprising that threatened to overwhelm the city. French reinforcements from Aleppo and Damascus were rushed there, and bombarded the commercial district, totally destroying two *suqs* and more than 100 shops. The events in Hama sent shock waves across the country. It was now clear for all to see that the guerrilla combatants outside the walls had joined forces with the more traditional nationalists inside the cities.[132]

This radical alliance soon made its presence felt in the capital. On October 18, the insurgent fighters made their way into Damascus, linking up with the nationalist forces there. The French command dispatched tanks throughout the city, particularly into the teeming *suqs*, the throbbing heart of the Revolt. "Then, at 6 p.m., without warning the European residents scattered throughout the old city, the French used artillery and airplanes to shell the southern area of Damascus."[133]

For two days the French assault on the city continued unabated. The death toll was high, the devastation enormous. To this day, the sunlight that filters through the holes in the arched roofs of the Suq al-Hamidiyeh bears witness to the intensity of the artillery barrage. *L'Humanité*, the Communist newspaper that alone in France condemned the crime, published figures from the Damascus municipality of 1,416 dead. The French, writes Phillip Khoury, blamed the destruction of the city as much on rebel looting and pillaging as they did on their own shelling. "The evidence, however, clearly indicts the French."[134]

Among those French residents who presumably "had not been warned" (to write such shocking words implies that for Khoury only Europeans, and not the entire civilian population, warranted a warning) was a young French woman:

"The War Council convened on a permanent basis at the Serail, and yet it seems that men were being shot without judgement at the citadel. The uprising may break out at any moment in the city, and in the rebel villages where the repression is acute ... It was in this climate of extreme tension that the [rebel] attack on the Azem Palace on October 18 touched off disorders among the population of Damascus, which was soon joined by groups who had entered the city from al-Ghuta. (...)

"Faced by a city which they now considered for the most part as rebel territory, the French forces 'in a state of legitimate defense' decided to use artillery to restore order. That evening, for a part of the night, and for two full days more, Damascus was bombarded."[135]

For several months, a near-stalemate prevailed. Rebel forces still occupied al-Ghuta and the settlement of al-Midan just beyond the walls, to the southeast. Rather than face casualties themselves at the hands of insurgent snipers or in ambushes, the French sent into combat poorly trained, badly disciplined irregular recruits from the tiny Circassian, Kurdish and Armenian minorities. French strategy now was to isolate Damascus, using bulldozers to open the ring roads that still disfigure the city, and let the rebels exhaust themselves.

In mid-July, 1926, the French launched what was to be their final offensive. The intensive aerial and artillery bombardment sapped nationalist morale, while the French command, employing tactics later refined by the Zionist state against the Palestinians, "relishing its victory and intransigent in its belief that the rebels were nothing more than professional brigands, would settle for nothing less than unconditional surrender."[136]

In November 1926, the revolt was near collapse. The French, however, postponed their final campaign until the winter months had passed. By June of the following year Sultan al-Atrash and several hundred of his elite fighters slipped across the border to safety in Transjordan. The flame of the Great Revolt had, for nearly two years, flared bright. Now it flickered and died.

Like the tomb of Salih al-'Ali in the Jabal al-Nusayriyah, the grave of Pasha Sultan al-Atrash seemed, by its state of neglect and dusty disrepair, to provide indirect evidence of the regime's obsession with its own pedigree. And of its haughty disregard for those forebears who by the nature of their deeds and by their character make poor candidates for the Procrustean bed of state ideology. Though official historiography has inscribed both Salih al-'Ali's resistance to the French and Sultan al-Atrash's Great Revolt in the sacred annals of the national cause, the two men are eclipsed by the domineering figure of Hafiz al-Asad. Yet their careers, their weaknesses, success and failure, suggest that without them, he would have been nothing.

Would his precursors have seen in him the fulfillment of their aspirations? That is an altogether different question.

Sultan al-Atrash died an old man on March 26, 1982. His dream of an independent Syria had been realized. The Druze minority enjoyed respectability, if not decisive influence in the Syrian Arab Republic for which his efforts and sacrifices had laid the foundations. But would the old rebel have countenanced the brutal repression that was beginning even as he died, as the elite troops of the al-Asad regime crushed the revolt of the Muslim

Brotherhood in the city of Hama with a methodical savagery far exceeding even that of the French against the Great Revolt?

Five kilometers north along the Suweida road, on the outskirts of a village even tinier and dustier than al-Kraya, at a word from Salam, the taxi veered off the main highway and up a steep gravel drive, then pulled to a stop in front of a tiny, mud-brick cottage. It was nearly noonday now. In the distance, the Golan Heights loomed against the southwestern horizon, shimmering in the heat haze. A pomegranate bush in full crimson flower blazed crazily at the foot of the path that led to the house.

In the shade of the tiled canopy that overhung the entrance an elderly man was awaiting us, dressed in the now familiar long, belted black coat and white headscarf of a Druze sheikh. "I am Saïd 'Ali al-Henawi," he said in halting but comprehensible French, extending his hand. "I am eighty-five years old, and I am a graduate of the French *lycée*."

For an atheist, Salam's father had done his job well. Sheikh al-Henawi was surely one of the few survivors of that bygone era when Sultan al-Atrash incarnated both the legendary stubbornness and singularity of the Druze, and the widespread Arab thirst for independence from imperial rule. What the Sheikh told me resonated with actuality.

"It was persecution by the French that led to the Great Revolt," he said, grey eyes looking straight into mine. "The French commander [a certain captain Normand] for the Jabal Druze was an evil, repressive man. A delegation was dispatched to Damascus with complaints. But it was dismissed.

"Sultan al-Atrash took a national position, but our religious beliefs played a role for sure. Because the Druze believe in reincarnation they do not fear death. This was their ultimate weapon. But it was not a fight for our religion; we are a tiny minority. We could not win. We were not fanatics; the French were the fanatics."

Through the open front door, I could see the faded photographs of Hafiz al-Asad and his son Bashar on the wall. It was unlikely that I would hear a discouraging word about the ruling dynasty, and it would have been impolitic to ask. But I did ask Sheikh al-Henawi about the customs that had preserved the impenetrable solidarity of the Druze community over the centuries.

"In the past, we were as one," he said, laying his first finger atop the second. "In mutual assistance and in hospitality. Every member could rely on the community for support to build homes, tend the fields and bring in the crops. We stood together in hardship and in good times."

A wistful expression traversed his face like a cloud shadow. Today, he continued, materialism is intruding on Druze community life. Part of Syria's ruling ideology is based on slavish admiration of Western technical progress, but Sheikh al-Henawi seemed less than convinced that it was a good idea, more concerned about the negative imports from the West.

"Now there is immoral behavior, selfishness, the curse of individualism. We see things around us that go against our moral standards. What they call freedom in the West is closer to the behavior of animals."

I had not come to argue with our elderly host. Even if I had, I would not have disagreed. My short stay in Suweida, at the heart of the Druze community, suggested that the Western model of "development"—which in its latest update would be applied by Americans to the citizens of Iraq—had little to offer to this curious yet coherent form of traditional social and spiritual wisdom. Triumphalist globalization, which combined both metaphorically and concretely the tactics of a Lyautey with those of the Israeli army's armored bulldozers, would likely encounter here—as it would elsewhere in the Arab and Islamic world—a reaction similar to that experienced by the French in the Jabal Druze more than seventy-five years ago.

The sun was low in the sky by the time Salam and I returned to Suweida. As we'd left the town that morning, she had pointed out to me a roadside shrine just outside the old city gates hewed, like everything else before the age of concrete, from basalt. There we returned at day's end.

It was Friday. The courtyard of the shrine which, with its small cell-like rooms opening onto the porticoed corridor that reminded me of a Christian monastery or a Sufi lodge, was thick with gamboling children. Around the fountain, families had spread their rugs and set up portable gas burners on which they were brewing *maté*. Small piles of the cracked shells of roasted pumpkin seeds—that quintessential time passer—filled plates and had begun to accumulate on the foot-worn paving stones of the court.

"We call this place Ain al-Zaman," said a smiling, stocky paterfamilias who had lived several years in southern Ontario. "That means, 'eye of time.' People found a tomb here. When they opened it, a bright light came from inside. Right away they closed it, because they understood. It was a holy grave."

In the sepulchral chamber, men and women lined up with no apparent division of sexes to kiss the shrine and light candles. Others were chatting affably in corners or lounging on knitted rugs around the fountain in the center of the courtyard. The graves of mortals, no matter how glorious and accomplished, seemed to reflect the ebbing of memory that would eventually consign them to oblivion. But this humble wayside shrine had about it the feel of timelessness.

It was impossible to determine whether it was due to the enveloping warmth of dusk in Suweida, to the soporific yet gently stimulating effect of the *maté*, or to the soft small talk of those who had come here less as pilgrims or suppliants and more in search of community. For reasons about which I did not care to speculate, the location of these living sacred spaces often obeyed a logic at long remove from the rationalism that makes it impossible for us to see the world with the eye of time. Trapped in our orthodoxy, blinkered by images, we could see only the present.

Salam tugged gently but firmly at my shirtsleeve. The last bus for Damascus would be leaving in twenty minutes she mimed, and pointed at her watch. We parted with a handshake at the Suweida depot which consisted of a stretch of sidewalk outside the transport company office.

As the coach rumbled down through the foothills of Jabal Druze and onto the flat lands of the Hawran, the lights of Jabal Qassiun began to sparkle against the darkening horizon. When the bus stopped in Jeramana, almost all its passengers got off, leaving me and a handful of conscripts to disembark in the whirl of Baramke terminal.

5

He Who Must Vanish

S OME IMAGES ARE BEST KEPT well hidden in the heart.

In a corner of a graveyard on the outskirts of Damascus stands a flat-roofed cinder block hut, its metal door secured by a padlock. In the light of an overcast December day filtering through the barred window I can make out the inscriptions scribbled in Farsi upon the inside walls. My gaze, on its downward path into the penumbra, comes to rest upon a low, rectangular grave strewn with flowers long dessicated.

At the foot of the grave, etched in Arabic numerals, I can distinguish the birth and death dates of its occupant, and above them, a name.

The dates, transposed from the Islamic solar calendar in use in Iran, are 1933–1977.

The name, Ali Shariati.

The same Shariati—mercurial, brilliant, intense—who, in the decade before the social, political and religious upheaval that overturned Shah Mohammad-Reza Pahlavi's Peacock Throne, brought the youth of Iran to a combative reading of Islam. The man whose fiery sermons and public lectures filled the Husseynieh-e Ershâd, the auditorium in North Tehran that today perpetuates his memory and heritage. The religious thinker and social scientist who single-handedly rehabilitated and actualized the ancient and thoroughly modern principle of martyrdom and, as he did, brought hope where there had been only despair, and the triumph of what Ayatollah Ruhollah Khomeini, never one for understatement, called "blood over the sword."

Ali Shariati's life and work had a seminal impact upon my own education about Iran and my understanding of Islam. My visit to his tomb in Damascus was an act of devotion to a secular but profoundly religious saint. No image of Dr. Shariati hung from the wall; no icon. If there had been one, it would have been the portrait of the philosopher displayed in some Tehran bookshops: that of the elegantly dressed man with the air of a European intellectual whose gaze seems to bore from beneath prominent eyebrows straight into the onlooker's soul.

The stark simplicity of his tomb could not have been at greater remove from the immense mausoleum erected over the grave of Imam Khomeini on the outskirts of Behesht-e Zahra cemetery to the south of Tehran. In its poverty, it made a fitting monument to a man who bequeathed no system of infallibility, who saw himself as the living expression of no institution, whose passage through history was as fleeting as it promises to be lasting, fraught with ambiguity yet firmly rooted in the fecund soil of Shi'a Islam.

The concrete block hut also marked, as though it were an invisible esoteric indicator, the starting point of a story: that of the virtual yet portentous encounter between Shariati, murdered in exile, and a fellow Iranian who was then pursuing a sacred mission in Lebanon. Hidden, humble, unassuming, it embodied the concealed and complex web of historical, cultural, religious and political connections that link three countries: Iran, Lebanon and Syria.

Once I had realized the existence of this web, it was easy to understand why imperial strategy for reshaping and controlling the Middle East depends, ultimately, on its destruction. One of the aims of the Sykes-Picot accords had been to separate its constituent elements; one of the strategic goals of their American and Israeli successors will be to isolate, then subvert and destroy each of them.

A dusty laneway separates the Damascus graveyard where Shariati lies from one of the city's strangest and grandest shrines. Here tradition places the final resting place of a figure doubly revered in Islam: Zaynab, granddaughter of the Prophet. Many, perhaps most of the people who throng to her shrine and file past her tomb, touching or kissing the silver-filigree lattice-work that surrounds it, come to venerate her as the sister of Imam Hussein. Around his willing sacrifice the Shi'a cult of martyrdom, the uttering of a ringing "No" to the injustice of the tyrant Yazid, was later to coalesce. From dawn well into evening, the shrine is thronged with pilgrims from the timeless depths of the Iranian hinterland.

These Iranians, women in black chadors and men with stubble beards, are a fixture in the down-market hotels wedged in between the city center and the Hijaz railway station. Twice a week they fly in by Iran Air from Tehran—a flight I knew well—expostulating reverentially when the aircraft takes off, when it lands, and at propitious moments during the flight. As they wait at the airport, they squat on carpets and brew tea on portable burners. Theirs is a life unregulated by the clock, an existence in which time belongs to the continuum of prayer, dawn and dusk, and the recurring holy days of the Islamic lunar calendar as it creeps backwards across the solar year.

They are joined by busloads of Lebanese Shi'ites come to visit Syria's sacred places, by religious students, by Sunni Damascenes there to enjoy the peaceful atmosphere, by children darting back and forth, chasing balls or playing tag while their parents sip tea under the turquoise tiled portico. The polished, marble-clad courtyard surface reflects the golden Persian dome that seems from a distance to float above the sanctuary.

I had come here one afternoon via microbus from one of the city's suburban terminals, where fleets of white, oft-scratched and much dented beetle-like vehicles roar off toward their destination as soon as all seats are filled. "Zaynab! Zaynab!" rasped the driver from his lowered window, as veiled ladies laden with bulging plastic bags rushed for the last places and heaved themselves aboard with a rustle of coarse fabric. Then, as the door slid shut the bus swung out into the traffic that swirls about the terminal. Inside, around me, passengers clutched the handles with a white-knuckled grip, staring straight ahead. It was as if they preferred ignorance to the familiar and perpetual spectacle of oncoming disaster averted at the last possible second. Smugly inured to the worst that Tehran traffic can generate, I was not about to panic. My travels in the Middle East had inoculated me with the vaccine of acquiescence, not to say fatalism. *Insh'Allah*—God willing—we would arrive safely. Twenty minutes later, through the ragged fronds of the palms that line the street, the golden dome loomed ahead and to our left, aglow as though illuminated by an inner source. Terminus. The door slid open. I clambered out.

The shrine, my destination, has given its name to an entire satellite town, complete with a thriving *suq*, five- and six-story apartment blocks, clothing and furniture stores, open-air fruit and vegetable stalls, not to mention the sidewalk *felefel* and *shawarma* stands, juice bars and sweetshops that agglutinate around high-traffic destinations like the this one. As I entered the graveyard, I inquired about the whereabouts of the tomb in the best Arabic I could muster. "Straight and to your right," the gatekeeper shot back in Farsi.

Minutes later, I am standing alone in front of the tiny, anonymous mausoleum.

For Ali Shariati Seyyida Zaynab—Lady Zaynab—was the emblematic figure in whose name women would rally to the cause of Islam.

It was the afternoon of Ashura, the tenth day of the month of Muharram, AH 61 (October 10, 680). The place: Karbala in the Iraqi desert where today stands a great shrine. There, Hussein, the second son of 'Ali, at the head of a tiny band of his followers and their families, refused the ultimatum of Yazid's military commander, 'Umar, son of a distinguished general, Sa'd ibn-abi-Waqqas, with an army of 4,000 men. "The grandson of the Prophet fell dead with many wounds and his head was sent to Yazid in Damascus."[137]

To her fell the horror and the honor of transporting the severed head of her brother to the caliph. With it she carried a message: "The mission of the message begins this afternoon," wrote Shariati. "This mission is upon the delicate shoulders of a woman—Zaynab—a woman who alongside her, manliness has learned manliness."[138]

Nine days after his murder on June 19, 1977 in London by agents of SAVAK, imperial Iran's secret police, the force that had been established at the behest of the CIA following the 1953 coup d'état and trained by Mossad, Shariati's body was transported here to Damascus where it was interred near the tomb of the great lady of Islam. Burial in Iran had been forbidden, and only through a powerful intercession that had come at the insistence of a fellow combatant was authorization granted for him to be laid to rest in a corner of the graveyard in the shadow of Zaynab's shrine.

That intercession had come from the highest level of the Syrian state, from President Hafiz al-Asad himself. His was not a name ordinarily associated with pious works if such did not concern the promotion of his Alawite clansmen, the granting of favors to compliant sheikhs or the reputation and enrichment of his family. But al-Asad had received an extraordinary petition, a proposition he could under no circumstances refuse, for to its drafter he owed his religious legitimacy and thus, his political career.

It had been delivered by emissaries of a charismatic Iran-born Shi'a clergyman. Years before, a distinguished *mullah* named Imam Musa al-Sadr had migrated from Iran to Lebanon where, in less than two decades, he had breathed new life and vitality into that country's downtrodden Shi'a community. As he did, his stature as an eminent authority in religious matters had rapidly transcended local concerns. The Damascus authorities, from the president on down, began to take notice.

Al-Asad owed his friend Musa al-Sadr a favor. When Syria's new constitution was promulgated in 1973, protests erupted because it omitted to specify that the president of the republic must be a Muslim. The oversight, if indeed it was an oversight, was quickly corrected. But it gave rise to a graver question: could an Alawite—in the event, Hafiz al-Asad—be considered a

Muslim? To resolve the issue, al-Asad appealed to the highest-ranking Shi'a cleric he knew, Musa al-Sadr, who had by then acquired the honorific title of Imam. The Imam issued a *fatwa* confirming that "the Alawis were indeed a community of Shi'i Islam."[139]

The virtual encounter between the two men—the murdered Shariati and the eminent spiritual and political leader Musa al-Sadr—was rich in symbolic impact. Though they had never met in life, the two men were contemporaries and held remarkably similar views on the role of religion in politics. Both were to enjoy after death a prestige and influence that few among the living could aspire to. Where Shariati bequeathed to posterity a rich corpus of work, and a legacy of lectures and sermons preserved on tape and widely listened to in Iran today, Musa al-Sadr had chosen the landscape and social fabric of Lebanon as the slate upon which he would inscribe his testament. Both still bear the indelible traces of his passage. As much as the violent civil war which wracked Lebanon had altered the human configuration of the land, Imam Musa had transfigured it more.

Shariati met his death before the climactic events of February 1979 brought Ayatollah Ruhollah Khomeini to power in Iran, wrecked the shah's pretensions to restoration of the ancient imperial monarchy, and inflicted stinging humiliation on the United States, the country's imperial tutor. The young men and women who fought on the barricades of revolutionary Tehran, and who later captured the U.S. Embassy, were his spiritual children. Though a layman, Ali Shariati was the son of a religious family, and wielded the emotionally charged traditions and symbols of Shi'ism with a fluency that lent them sudden relevance and reverberation.

Musa al-Sadr, whose intervention had brought Dr. Shariati to Damascus in death and who spoke the funeral prayers at this graveside, was at the height of his influence in the Middle East. He was a man to whom the leaders of the Arab world, and the Iranian revolutionaries, attended. The Imam—so he was called by his devoted Lebanese followers, evoking the double resonance of the term, as both congregational leader and, for the Shi'a, a descendant of the Holy Family, the direct descendants of the lineage of 'Ali—had conferred Islamic legitimacy on Hafiz al-Asad. He had also enraged the Shah for condemning Iran's close relations with Israel, an alliance that bore the unmistakable signature of Henry Kissinger.

Lebanon's once scorned Shi'a community had emerged as an independent force in that bleeding country. Where the conflict-ridden Lebanese factions spoke war, Imam al-Sadr spoke peace. Where Israelis, Maronites and Palestinians sought to divide the country into tiny principalities locked in mortal conflict, he insisted on the unity of a Lebanon that was "too big to swallow, too small to divide."[140]

At his initiative, the organization known as Amal was founded. From Amal in turn would emerge *Hizbullah*, the force that would finally defeat the Israeli army on the battlefield.[141] It was an accomplishment that exposed the inability of Arab nationalism to defend itself against the small but powerful intruder, and the vitality of Islam as a rallying cry. Small wonder it quickly won the designation of "terrorist," which might be taken as meritorious mention for opposition to Israel.

Though he was a Shi'a clergyman educated in the holy city of Qom who had attained high hierarchical rank, Musa al-Sadr had about him an openness and an easy grace that endeared him to simple folk. His dignified carriage and elegance opened doors among the religious and political elites of the region. Not unexpectedly, his exceptional popularity and public impact also made him suspect in the eyes of the powerful. Even a fool, and certainly the man on the street, could understand the threat he posed to their illegitimate rule, to their shameless demagoguery. Always outspoken, he had dared to criticize the Libyan leader, Colonel Muammar Qaddafi, blaming his support of ultra-radical Palestinian factions for the agony of southern Lebanon.[142] Qaddafi was not a man to forget a slight. But he was not the only one to be given offense by Musa al-Sadr. At the memorial service in late June, 1977 at Shariati's graveside, the Imam had denounced the Shah's complicity in his murder. The Iranian monarch, stung by the sound of truth, had responded by stripping him of his citizenship.[143] Less than fifteen months later, on a trip to Libya, he was to vanish without a trace.

* * *

MY JOURNEY INTO THE SHI'A MOVEMENT in Lebanon had begun several months earlier in Tehran. There, in a North Tehran villa, a mutual friend had introduced me to Fatima Navab-Safavi, the daughter of an Iranian revolutionary icon. Navab-Safavi was the *nom de guerre* of Seyyed Mojtaba Mirlauhi, the founder and leader of the Fedayin-e Islam. His organization favored mortal violence against those it saw as obstacles to a return to strict Islamic principles.[144] The group carried out several highly charged political assassinations. Navab-Safavi himself was finally arrested and hanged following the 1953 CIA-sponsored coup that overthrew the reformist Mossadegh government, even though he had opposed Mossadegh as a westernizer. A huge portrait of him is still visible on the side of an apartment building adjoining the expressway that leads from Azadi Square to Tehran's northern suburbs.

The morning was cloudy, and a chill, damp wind was blowing from the snowy slopes of the Alborz mountains that tower above the Iranian capital. As I waited for Fatima to arrive, I looked from the balcony window of the villa down into the deserted garden, where a forest of spindly pines choked amid tangled undergrowth. White-bellied Tehran crows cawed in the branches. The villa, a requisitioned property that seemed as neglected as the garden, housed a foundation nominally devoted to women's issues, of the sort established for the regime's loyal servants.

When Fatima Navab-Safavi bustled in, carrying a breath of fresh mountain air in her billowing chador, it became clear that there was nothing of the time-server about her. She radiated a kinetic, infectious energy. When I explained to her that I had come to seek her assistance in meeting people in Lebanon, her glossy black eyes lit up.

Glasses of scalding tea soon appeared, and none too soon at that, for the ancient villa was dank and drafty. "So, you want to go to Lebanon, eh? Well, I will send you to meet the right people. You may tell them I sent you. It will be enough."

For the next two hours, we pored over scrapbooks of photographs showing her and her comrades-in-arms training for guerrilla combat alongside the fighters of Amal, the Shi'ite resistance movement. Like many of her generation, Fatima Navab-Safavi had looked to revolutionary Palestine and to its Lebanese allies for the front-line, live-ammunition training that they would soon need in their fight against the Shah. Most of them were students, some leftists, some Islamists. Among their number were many like the young man Robert Fisk recalls meeting on the outskirts of a Shi'a village one stifling morning in 1977:

"He grinned brightly at us: 'I am from the opposition in Iran. I have come here to learn how to fight. We understand a common cause with our Palestinian brothers. With their help, we can learn to destroy the shah.'"[145]

Had Fatima Navab-Safavi been asked, she would undoubtedly have given the same answer. Was her presence in the Tehran villa not living proof?

Several of the Iranians who trained and fought alongside the Palestinians in Lebanon were more than simple volunteers. One, Dr. Mustafa Chamran, was a professor of mathematics at the University of California who abandoned a brilliant academic career to join Musa al-Sadr,[146] and later, to become Islamic Iran's first minister of defense before perishing in mysterious circumstances which some claimed were anything but accidental.

Western and Israeli terror-mongers have long branded the Iranians who traveled to Lebanon after the 1979 Islamic Revolution as the instigators and paymasters of Hizbullah. But the connections between Iran and Lebanon far antedated the handful of revolutionaries who trained alongside the PLO, who lent their support to Imam al-Sadr, and later established themselves at Ba'albak, at the northern extremity of the Biqa' valley. In fact, Shi'ism in Lebanon claimed a spiritual pedigree—and an Arab genealogy—that stretched back to the era of the Prophet. It was to Lebanon, the southwesternmost corner of the *Bilad al-Sham* that Shi'a Iran owed its religious *bona fides*, and not the reverse.

When I arrived in Beirut, in the winter of 2001, the name of Fatima Navab-Safavi not only caused doors to swing open, it brought broad smiles to the faces of veterans of the Lebanese resistance movement, and led me with what seemed like the mechanical ineluctability of fate, to the life of the man who was destined to disappear, to Imam Musa al-Sadr.

Though my lodgings in Beirut were in Hamra, the international sector of West Beirut that borders on the American University, I spent as little time there as possible. The Beirut that interested me was not the overblown downtown reconstruction project designed to restore the city to its pre-war stature as the crown jewel of the "Switzerland of the Middle East," not the Corniche with its joggers, sunbathers and fishermen, its private clubs and glossy apartment complexes, its bumper-to-bumper traffic of Mercedes Benzes and BMWs, but the densely-populated warrens that lay to the south and east, places like Ouzai and Haret Hreik and Bir Hasan.

In these tenement neighborhoods with their choking traffic, their winter dampness and sweltering summer heat, I would find the clergymen, the theoreticians and the practitioners of violence and resistance who would lead me into the convoluted history of Lebanon's Shi'a movement. Along these streets I could test, almost touch, the temper of the times. Everywhere hung posters, some small, some huge, icons whose presence conveyed a message at once religious, social and political, at once dangerously timely and timeless.

The dark-browed, grim-lipped image of Imam Khomeini shared a lamp-standard with that of Seyyed Hasan Nasrullah, the dynamic young cleric who today leads Hizbullah. Farther along, portraits of martyrs in the liberation struggle vied for position with photographs of Ali Khamene'i, Iran's Mr. Supreme Guide. But all are outnumbered by depictions of a smiling face with quizzically raised eyebrows and a turban worn ever so slightly askew: that of

Imam Musa al-Sadr. More than twenty years after his disappearance, his presence hovered over the city, evoking all the more poignantly his inexplicable absence.

In the heart of Bir Hasan, amidst tumble-down dwellings at the end of a blind alley, stands the Imam al-Sadr Center for Research and Studies, housed in a vocational school run by those who have continued his charitable work among the dispossessed. I'd been sent on the recommendation of a friend of Fatima. There, in groundfloor offices at the rear of the building, I met a soft-spoken, scholarly man named Ahmad Issa, a full-time program coordinator at the Center. After several minutes of conversation and a cup of Arabic coffee, a tall, broad-shouldered, slightly stooped man with prominent cheek-bones and what seemed like a constant smile, strolled through the door and walked over, hand extended. His face reminded me of someone I knew.

"I am Sadreddin al-Sadr. You are welcome to Beirut and to our Center."

I was writing a book about Syria, I explained. A book that would also touch on the story of the Lebanese resistance movement. "I am aware," I told Mr. al-Sadr, "of your late father's contribution to this movement."

Still smiling, but with unmistakable firmness in his voice, Mr. al-Sadr replied: "But, Mr. Reed, my father is not dead."

Silence.

"He is alive," he said, looking me in the eye.

At that instant, it became clear that I must attempt to tell the story of the man whose presence had laid bare the treachery and double-dealing of virtually all of the political forces locked in mortal conflict in this tiny corner of historic Syria called Lebanon. The man who—so that the delicate web of war, treachery, civil strife, injustice and clashing interests that plague the region, and at the center of which Lebanon lies could be preserved—would have to vanish.

* * *

THE SOCIAL, HUMAN AND RELIGIOUS complexity of Lebanon defeats the most detailed map. Such a map may well account for the names of towns, villages, mountains, wadis and rivers, but it cannot convey the extreme diversity of the landscape, neither its welcoming intimacy nor its forbidding remoteness, neither the richness of its hidden valleys nor the harshness of its exposed, rocky plateaux from which generation upon generation of hard-bitten men and women have coaxed, prayed and cursed a living, drawn their subsistence from olives, cheese and cracked wheat, from hope and fortitude.

The same complexity also defies the very idea of census. Lebanon's last official head count took place in 1932, under French colonial auspices. Nearly three-quarters of a century later, it represents a generally accepted fiction ossified into patent falsehood from which hangs the legitimacy of the Lebanese state, the oft-discredited but stubbornly surviving arbitrator of factional power-sharing arrangements. Its primary beneficiary is the Maronite Christian minority to which France assigned the country as a putative majority; its great victim, the Shi'a, who are today generally understood to constitute the largest of the country's confessional communities, if not a narrow though clear majority.

My journey through this landscape and along the sinuous and fatal path trod by Musa al-Sadr began on a winter morning in the hilltop village called Tul. Winter in Lebanon can range from cool and rainy along the Mediterranean, to chilling in the rocky uplands. The sun shone wanly in a pale blue sky, but the wind sweeping down from the looming snow-clad peaks of Jabal al-Sheikh, known as Mount Hermon, was bitter.

I had left Beirut earlier that morning in the company of my interpreter and guide, Cilina Nasser, who was then working as a freelance journalist in the cut-throat Beirut news market. Cilina, whom I had met through the vagaries of my quest for Musa al-Sadr, had a keen yet critical eye for the grievances of the community—as the daughter of Shi'a parents she would have absorbed it all— and to the abuses committed in its name. No one in Lebanon had clean hands, she insisted. It was her determination to show the multiple sides of the story that convinced me both of her sincerity and her humanity.

Our destination was the largest building in the town, the Lycée Bilal Fahs, flagship of the educational network run by the Amal Movement in South Lebanon. The school, atop a windswept hilltop, is named for the first member of the Amal Movement to carry out a martyrdom-seeking operation, for which he was bestowed in death the title "bridegroom of the south."

Khalil Hamdan, the director of the institution awaits us in his office, beneath portraits of Imam Musa al-Sadr and Nabih Berrih, the current leader of Amal and speaker of the Lebanese parliament. No photographs of Iranian religious leaders are to be seen, nor could they be. Amal has long abandoned the franchise to its more militant competitor Hizbullah. Still, its original links with Iran remain a source of pride.

"Imam Musa first visited Lebanon in 1955," says Mr. Hamdan "That was when he met *Hujjat al-Islam* Seyyed Abdel-Hussein Sharaf al-Din, the spiritual leader of the Lebanese Shi'ites, who was eighty-two years old at the time. The al-Sadr and Sharaf al-Din families were related. Both had originated in Lebanon. The Shi'a had been migrating out of Lebanon since Ottoman times, due to oppression by the Sunnis. Imam al-Sadr's grandfather was one of them."

Sharaf al-Din was more than a high-ranking alim. He had a reputation as an energetic reformer, as a scholar and as an eloquent spokesman on behalf of his community, who stood at the forefront of the nationalist movement advocating the cause of Syrian unity.[147] The close ties that developed between the two men, the elder Sharaf al-Din and the younger Musa al-Sadr, embodied symbolically the age-old ties between Iran and the Jabal Amil, the Shi'a heartland of south Lebanon.

Sunni theologians had long treated Shi'ism as a schismatic monolith, a non-Arab, non-Islamic and marginal phenomenon that delegitimized by its insistence on the succession of infallible Holy Imams God's message as transmitted through the Sunna of the Prophet. The Shi'ites of Lebanon, not to be outdone, traced their religious roots back to Abu-Dharr al-Ghifari, a Companion of lowly origin of Muhammad. Abu-Dharr had been an outspoken critic of the third caliph, 'Uthman, and had criticized Mu'awiyah's extravagant spending on his palace in Damascus, thus earning the opprobrium of the man who would soon establish the Umayyad dynasty.[148] When the caliph sent him into exile for his trouble, none other than 'Ali insisted on escorting him out of Medina.[149] Abu-Dharr, after some wandering, finally established himself in the Jabal Amil where he preached the precepts of what would become Shi'a Islam among the Christian population and, over time, converted them.

Fast forward nearly 900 years from the earliest years of the Islamic era, to the beginning of the sixteenth century, CE. When Shah Ismaïl, the founder of the Saffavid Dynasty in Iran, captured Tabriz and proclaimed Twelver Shi'ism the religion of his newly established state, he found only one classic theological text in that city. "Teachers and jurists were needed to fill this lack of religious and scholarly infrastructure. Jabal Amil provided one ideal source from which they could be drawn."[150] Four hundred fifty years later, Musa al-Sadr, in returning to Lebanon, was to repay Iran's religious debt.

The man who would breathe new life into Lebanon's Shi'a community was born in Qom, the holy city on the edge of the desert, notorious for its summer heat, its brackish water and Iran's highest per-capita concentration of mollahs. There he completed the traditional religious curriculum before enrolling at the University of Tehran's Faculty of Law and Political Economy, becoming the first "black turban," worn by members of the *Ahl al-Bayt*, the House of the

Prophet, to graduate from a secular institution. "It was only upon the urging of his father, who feared for the preservation of Iran's Shi'i institutions" writes Augustus Richard Norton, a scholar specializing in the history of the Lebanese Shi'a, "that he discarded his secular ambitions and pursued an education in Islamic jurisprudence."[151]

Mr. Hamdan swings around on his swivel chair, reaches up to the bookcase behind his desk, removes a gilt-bound volume and leafs through it. "Sharaf al-Din died in 1957. In his will, he specified that Musa al-Sadr was to be his replacement. An invitation was sent by the community," he reads, and Cilina translates. "All the leading religious figures of Lebanon saw him as a personality of promise. 'This man will not limit himself to the region of Tyre alone,' they said. 'His influence will extend to the whole Islamic world.'"

If the country's religious leaders indeed saw in Musa al-Sadr such qualities, they could not have been unaware of the excellent recommendations that accompanied him. His religious mentors in Qom, Ayatollahs Bourjerdi and Khomeini, gave him ringing endorsement. So, some say, did the Shah.[152] Seen from the high ground of hindsight the claim, if true, is revealing. Even under the staunchly pro-Western and obligingly pro-Israeli Pahlavi regime, Iran would have regarded Lebanon as part of its sphere of influence, and the Shah clearly believed it prudent to mollify and even to cultivate the potentially fractious mollahs who had the ear of the Lebanese population.

Whatever the coalition of religious and political forces that brought him to Lebanon, Musa al-Sadr's impact on the Shi'a community was a dramatic one, says Mr. Hamdan.

"You must bear in mind that the situation of the Shi'a was tragic. They were in a state of rebellion, even before the establishment of Lebanon. Members of the community fought against the French Mandate, and opposed the separation of Lebanon from Syria. Sharaf al-Din was critical of the policy of the Lebanese state, which centralized all political activity in Mount Lebanon.

"This policy reflected the Maronites' loyalty to the West. For them, France was a 'loving mother.' The Muslims looked eastward. The Christians portrayed themselves as alone and isolated in the Middle East, but the Muslims were neglected."

For an Iranian, whatever his original roots in the land, to step into the quagmire of Lebanon demanded extreme fortitude and considerable daring, not to say foolhardiness, in equal measure. By all accounts, Musa al-Sadr possessed these qualities in abundance. He also, says Mr. Hamdan, held "the religious conviction that serving humanity was the highest form of worship."

"The Shi'ites have been here for as long as Lebanon itself," Musa al-Sadr himself proclaimed shortly after his arrival in Lebanon, in 1959. "They took part, with others, in building its very plains and mountains, guarding its south, east and north, and lived through good times and bad. They irrigated its soil with their blood and raised in its skies the banners of its majesty by leading most of its revolutions."[153]

When Musa al-Sadr came, he identified three problems, explains Mr. Hamdan. These were indigence, government neglect of the South, and Israeli aggression against Lebanon. Where his predecessors had deplored, prayed and wrung their hands, he swung immediately into action. "To fight indigence, he established institutions to keep beggars off the streets, trade schools for the youth, women's centers to teach domestic skills. He encouraged the people to fight against Israeli violations of Lebanon's border. 'We can either be victims or martyrs,' he said. 'No one will stand with us if we do not stand up on our own.'"

Not surprisingly for a man who had sat at the feet of Ruhollah Khomeini in Qom, Musa al-Sadr had a keen awareness of the power of religious symbolism and imagery. Not in a narrow sense, insists Mr. Hamdan, "but in a broad, open way, acceptable to all. He was the first Muslim religious figure in Lebanon to enter a church. At the same time, he merged politics with religion."

"For him, all religions reject oppression. He took his examples from the Bible and from the Qur'an. For him, the oppressor and the oppressed were accomplices. One commits oppression, the other accepts it."

The advent and rise of a man like Musa al-Sadr, and with him, of Lebanon's most downtrodden community, had an almost prophetic quality. The dominant ideologies of the time, from Arab nationalism to communism, had failed to improve the lot of this poorest of all constituencies. From the swamp of political marginality, social alienation and the fear of loss of national identity at the hands of Westernization, emerged a man unlike any other, possessed of a singular capacity for combining the spiritual with the temporal.[154]

Neither "spiritual" nor "temporal" were terms that could suffer an abstract definition in the Lebanon of the sixties and seventies. In this tiny land, with its patchwork patterns of ethnic and religious minorities, the heavy hand of the dominant political forces of the Arab world, the constant threat of Israeli incursion along with its corollary, the destabilizing presence of hundreds of thousands of Palestinian refugees and resistance fighters, forgave no error, pardoned no oversight.

With a sure-handed grasp of Lebanese reality Musa al-Sadr, before turning his attention to the social and political obstacles the Shi'ites faced, set about building bridges to the country's two dominant Christian sects, the Maronites and the Greek Orthodox.

Nothing better illustrated the daring and brilliance of his manner than one of his first visits to Tyre. I heard the story from Hajj-Afif Aoun, one of his first lay followers, whom I met one spring morning several months after my winter trip to Tul, in a village on the outskirts of Lebanon's southernmost city. Once more, Cilina accompanied me.

"Here in Tyre, there was a popular ice-cream shop run by a Christian. Some people had advised the Muslims to boycott his business, saying it was *haram*, forbidden to Muslims. One Friday, after prayers at the mosque, Imam Musa walked to this shop, entered, sat down at a table and ordered a bowl of ice-cream.

"The shopkeeper came over and whispered, 'But, Imam, I'm a Christian.' 'Your food is *hallal* [permitted] for me, and mine is *hallal* for you,' said the Imam."

His dramatic opening to Lebanon's Christians was soon to produce an unexpected benefit. In October 1964 Ayatollah Khomeini was arrested by the Shah's police after having denounced legislation giving American military personnel in Iran extraterritorial status (which they now enjoy, along with immunity from war crimes, in almost all countries except Iran), Musa al-Sadr hurried to the office of the Vatican's representative in Lebanon. There he used his influence to request that the Pope intervene to pressure the Shah to release his former teacher, who was promptly exiled to Turkey.[155]

Bridge-building as a method for reconciling communities divided by decades, or centuries, of enmity and mistrust could, however, only go so far. Not only did Musa al-Sadr's good intentions outrun his practical capabilities, they soon came up against the festering, purulent abscess that has poisoned the Middle East since 1917: the disastrous sequel of the Balfour Declaration that culminated in 1948 with the expulsion of the Palestinians and the creation of a racialist settler state on their stolen lands, all with the sanction of the "International Community."

Feeding off the legitimate grievances of the dispossessed, betrayed by the craven collapse of their Arab "defenders," the Palestinians created the nucleus of a government in exile. Lebanon, where their cause found vocal and powerful defenders among the country's influential leftist factions, was to become the grudging host. An explosive situation was exacerbated by the events of

September 1970—"Black September"—when the Kingdom of Jordan militarily crushed the growing power and assertiveness of the Palestinians.

In Syria, Hafiz al-Asad, who was then defense minister, dispatched an armored brigade to support the Palestinian units who were fighting for their lives against superior Jordanian forces. But after Jordan attacked the brigade with the full political support of the United States and Israel, the Syrian armor turned tail and retreated to Damascus, leaving the Palestinians at the mercy of King Hussein.

If Black September dealt a blow to Palestinian hopes of capturing the Jordanian state, it had an even more devastating impact on Lebanon, which became the designated rear area of resistance against Israel. Rapidly, a *de facto* state within a state arose in the poor and downtrodden south. It seemed to matter little to the resistance authorities that the very lands on which they had established "Fatahland" were those belonging to the Shi'ites.

Imam Musa warned the Palestine Liberation Organization, led now by the dynamic and resourceful thirty-five-year-old Yasir Arafat, that it was not in its interests to allow such a situation to arise in southern Lebanon. "He is reported to have stated that 'the PLO is a factor of anarchy in the South … ' In private, he challenged the revolutionary *bona fides* of the Palestinians. He argued that they lacked a sense of martyrdom … "[156]

The Lebanese government was unable to protect its citizens when heavily armed fida'iyin retreated to Lebanon after Black September, and the presence of large numbers of Palestinian fighters made Israeli incursions in the South a certainty. Musa al-Sadr drew his conclusions. He would mobilize the Shi'a for armed struggle. Polite representation, lobbying, fence-mending and bridge-building had brought him and his constituents far, but not far enough. In February 1974, at the little town of Bidnayil, in the Biqa' valley, he declared:

> We do not want to clash with the regime, with those who neglect us. Today, we shout out loud the wrongs against us, that cloud of injustice that has followed us since the beginning of our history. Starting from today we will no longer complain or cry; our name is not *mitwali* [a name for the Shi'a that had taken on derogatory connotations]; our name is 'men of refusal' 'men of vengeance,' 'men who revolt against all tyranny,' even though this costs us our blood and our lives.[157]

His words had been intended as a warning. The warning was, for the most part, ignored by the authorities to whom it was addressed. But it touched a raw nerve among the Shi'a of Lebanon. One of the thousands to hear it and to understand its near-revelatory power was Hasan Trad, of Ma'rakeh.

One half-hour by automobile from Tul, Ma'rakeh is a pleasant, hilltop town of 15,000 souls midway between the inland city of Nabatiyeh and Tyre, on the coast. There, in the *hussaynieh*, the public prayer hall used for celebrations of the martyrdom of Imam Hussein, Mr. Trad, a gaunt, rangy man with sunken eyes, was waiting for us.

"I joined Amal when it was established, in 1975," he said, as we sipped tea in the threadbare office upstairs from the meeting hall beneath the photographs of three martyrs killed when an explosion ripped through the building in 1985, three years after the Israeli invasion of Lebanon. "I was eighteen at the time. What impressed me was the Amal charter. It underlined the need for human freedom and a sincere belief in God. Imam Musa had the qualities I admired most. He was civilized, loyal to humanity and to God.

"All those things drew me to the movement, and particularly his personality. I first saw him at a mass rally in Tyre, and later, at a lecture he gave at the al-Zahra' school there. After the lecture, I wanted to kiss his hand, but he refused to allow me, and hugged me instead," he said, eyes sparkling.

"Imam Musa al-Sadr believed that Israel's long-term strategy was to settle the Palestinians permanently in Lebanon, then divide the country and establish a Palestinian Authority on Lebanese territory. The leftist groups at that time wanted a 'socialist' regime, and the Christians wanted a pro-West state for themselves."

Musa al-Sadr's response to the continued neglect of the Shi'a, and to the looming threat from Israel's regional strategy, could not be limited to the political arena. This was, after all, Lebanon. A country where, beneath the cloying orange-blossom scent, the *dolce far niente* and the pseudo-Western veneer lurked then and lurks today a sense of the brooding, the violent and the sinister which none have evoked better than Robert Fisk in his epic chronicle of the Lebanese civil war, *Pity the Nation*.

This, Imam Musa al-Sadr must have early and instinctively understood, was the reality against which he must ultimately fight, not only with the elegance and persuasive powers of the trained religious scholar, but with the iron principles of the man of God and the tactical deviousness of the instinctive politician.

On March 17, 1974, some 100,000 Shi'ites—and others—massed in the streets of the ancient city of Ba'albak near the spring of Ras al-'Ain to hear Musa al-Sadr speak. On that day, he called for the creation of the *Harakat al-Mahrumin*—"Movement of the Disinherited"—that would challenge the Beirut government over its inaction. The movement, born as an expression of the aspirations of the Shi'a community and as a reflection of the hopes of the

Lebanese underclass, set out to prevent the total destruction of southern Lebanon. "What does the government expect, what does it expect except rage and revolution?" he thundered,[158] continuing:

> Arms are the adornment of men and we support the carrying of arms. We will fight the autocratic tyrants. We will not stand on the persecuted. We will not keep silent on injustice, conspiracy, bribery and the theft of people's money. We want the South to be an impregnable area. We want the South to be a rock where Israel's dreams and designs will be shattered and a nucleus for the liberation of the Holy Land.[159]

Sixteen months later, in July, what Musa al-Sadr had alluded to became public knowledge. A military wing of the *Harakat al-Mahrumin* had been established under his auspices. The decision had been taken in late December, 1974, at the Beirut headquarters of the Shi'a Supreme Council under the presidency of the Imam himself. Also present was Mustafa Chamran.[160]

It was agreed that the armed body would be Lebanese in scope, not Palestinian or Arab. The militia, called *Afwaj al-Muqawama al-Lubnaniya*— Lebanese Resistance Detachments—better known by its acronym Amal (which in Arabic also means "hope"), was initially trained by Fatah and played a minor role in the fighting of 1975 and 1976.[161]

Mr. Trad confirmed this account: "I began training as soon as Amal was announced, in 1975," he said. "I called some friends who thought like me and invited them to my house. My best friend Khalil Jradi,"—he turned and pointed to one of the portraits on the wall, that of a sad-eyed, bearded young man, the kind of face one sees on posters throughout towns and villages in the South—"also called his friends."

"In 1975, our trainers were from the PLO. Advanced officer training took place in Syria, at an army camp near Damascus. Once I met Mustafa Chamran there, and Sadreddin, Imam Musa's son."

Did that not give Syria control over Amal? I asked.

"Imam Musa once said: 'No one can define my role. Only God, my country, and humanity.' For all that, Amal and Syria had a common strategy. Syria saw Amal as a necessity, and we needed Syria. The Imam used to say that Syria was Amal's lungs, and he was right. To the south there was Israel, to the west, the Mediterranean. Civil war was raging. Imam Musa believed in the unity of Lebanon, which Syria saw as being in its interests."

The creation of armed Shi'a fighting detachments throughout the south provided the spark that was to ignite the tinderbox. In towns and villages, resentment of the Palestinians was growing. "Imam Musa supported the Palestinian cause, but he told Yasir Arafat to keep the resistance directed at ending the occupation of Palestine, and not to tamper with Lebanese internal affairs. Arafat did not agree, and the situation became tense. They wanted to set up a state of their own. They even planned to build an airport not far from here, at Ansar village."

Even as the first Amal units entered combat against Operation Litani, the Israeli invasion of March 1978 designed, as usual, to "root out terrorists," Musa al-Sadr's position was becoming untenable. "Whatever he may have been, despite his occasional histrionics, the imam was hardly a man of war. (...) His weapons were words and symbols, and as a result his political efforts were short-circuited by the din of war. He seemed to be eclipsed by the violence that engulfed Lebanon."[162]

Imam Musa's star was indeed waning in the late 1970s, argues Peter Theroux, whose account of his life combines verifiable information with wild speculation and unattributed quotes. According to Theroux, his dedication to promoting and protecting the Shi'a of Lebanon led him to "hold seemingly contradictory or at best ambiguous positions. Against the extreme Israeli-allied right in Lebanon he sought alliance with the Syrians, Palestinians and Sunni Muslims as well as with the Arab powers at large; to the Arab nationalist forces that rallied to his cause, he presented his Lebanese face. When the Syrians incongruously linked up with their former enemies in the Christian Phalange in order to preserve the status-quo in Lebanon and keep it under their control, Sadr threw in his lot with them."[163]

Not all commentators see things that way. If Imam Musa allied with the Syrians, writes Majed Halawi, it was because of his grave apprehensions, and his open opposition to a restructuration of Lebanon along lines proposed by Libya's volatile leader, Muammar Qaddafi. In the growing Islamic revolutionary movement in Iran, his policies of openness and cross-confessional dialogue had put him at odds with the "fundamentalist radicals" who were attempting to monopolize access to the undisputed leader, Ayatollah Khomeini, and enjoyed strong ties with both Libya and the PLO. Several Arab states with sizeable populations of "disinherited" Shi'a within their borders—not to mention Iraq where the Shi'a formed a repressed majority—were growing restive at al-Sadr's success in revitalizing and mobilizing the Shi'a of Lebanon: they feared "contagion." And in Tripoli, the Libyan dictator had raised the issue of Musa al-Sadr's Iranian origins, by implication questioning the Arab credentials of the Lebanese Shi'a and of their movement, and with it, the legitimacy of Lebanese Shi'ism as an organic outgrowth and integral part of Arab Islamic culture.[164]

Either he had become superfluous, as "irrelevant" as would Yasir Arafat in the eyes of Ariel Sharon and George W. Bush decades later, or he had emerged as the focus, the personalization of Lebanese opposition to converging though outwardly conflicting strategies drawn up in places as diverse as Tripoli, Tel Aviv, Riyadh, Neuphle-le-Château, the Paris suburb where Khomeini's followers were plotting their next move against the faltering shah, or perhaps even Washington.

The extent of the Imam's alleged irrelevance could be measured in Israel's efforts to recruit his reputation to their cause. The zionist state's 1978 blitzkrieg offensive into South Lebanon had been a brilliant military success. Capitalizing on the unpopularity of the PLO, Israel had brought its powerful propaganda machine to bear with full force on the Shi'a population. Here, the results were less than brilliant.

"Two days after the invasion," relates Hasan Trad, "the Israeli occupation forces began to taunt us. They distributed leaflets in Arabic that said, 'we are against Khomeini but for Imam Musa Sadr,' then they claimed 'we are against the PLO but for Imam Musa Sadr.' They even attempted to set up a kind of 'national guard' against the Palestinians. But because the Imam had always been against Israel, and Amal's followers were well trained, only a handful went along with the Israelis."

The *fida'iyin* had been callous, arrogant and shortsighted in their dealings with the local population. But the mighty Israeli army and intelligence services would predictably prove to be even more so. General Rafael Eytan set the tone: "We will continue to take action where we want, when we want and how we want. Our own self-interest is supreme and will guide us in our actions not to allow terrorists (i.e., the *fida'iyin*) to return to the border fence."[165]

Eytan's declaration may have reassured public opinion in Occupied Palestine; it would have pleased his paymasters in Washington who, twenty years later, would address conquered Iraq in precisely the same terms. But both in tone and content it utterly failed to impress the Shi'a of south Lebanon.

Within weeks, resistance against the Israeli occupiers got underway, taking at first the form of civil disobedience. "We began to patrol the streets unarmed. When Israeli intelligence entered the town and stopped the patrols for questioning, our men all identified themselves with the name of 'Musa al-Sadr.'"

Two months later, armed operations began, to end in 1985 when the Israeli forces evacuated the occupied lands to retreat into the buffer zone along the border which they and their South Lebanese collaborators were to occupy until final defeat by Hizbullah and its allies in 2000.

Operation Litani had been launched in March. Five months later, on August 25, 1978, the man whose name the first Amal resistance forces had chosen for themselves, boarded a flight from Beirut to Tripoli, at the invitation of the Libyan strongman. Six days later, on August 31, he had vanished without a trace.

* * *

NABATIYEH, IN SOUTH LEBANON, is famous—some would even say notorious—for its fierce attachment to its Shi'a cultural and religious heritage. It was in Nabatiyeh, on October 16 1983, that an Israeli army convoy on its way north in yet another of the Zionist state's offensives against "terrorism" drove into a throng of thousands of worshippers celebrating Ashura, the anniversary of the martyrdom of Imam Hussein. In Nabatiyeh, celebration of Ashura is peculiar in its intensity. Following Iran's Islamic Revolution, the religious authorities there gradually convinced the most fervent celebrants that shedding their own blood was unnecessary and even un-Islamic. But in Lebanon, and particularly in Nabatiyeh, drawing on a tradition of oppression and minoritarization, the Shi'a community plunged into the commemoration with spectacular literality. Men transfixed with grief not only struck their backs with scourges made of chain with more than symbolic intensity, they lacerated their scalps with sharpened knives, causing blood to flow down their faces. Wrote Robert Fisk of the event: "The Israelis were stoned, their trucks overturned and burned. The soldiers, facing a frenzied crowd, some pointing knives at them, opened fire. They killed two of the worshippers and wounded another seven ... "[166] Within a week, the Israeli forces operating in southern Lebanon had come under a sustained guerrilla attack that was not to abate until their final defeat in May, 2000.

I'd driven down to Nabatiyeh with Cilina in the spring of 2001, on a daylong excursion into the newly-liberated territories, and into the past of an organization that the U.S.-Israel axis would dearly love to eliminate, not only from its actual influence as a political and military force in Lebanon and in the Middle East, but from recent history itself, as with the gigantic gum rubber eraser it loves so well. Cilina knew this ground intimately, and had arranged for me to meet people in several villages in the former so-called "Security Zone" from which Israel had been expelled. Best of all, her natural journalist's curiosity supplemented my own, often substituting detailed queries for my more general questions. Through her eyes and ears, as well as through my own, I quickly formed an idea of the grittiness and opacity that lay beneath the heroic claims, and for the heroic acts that lay hidden behind the crude ritual accusations of "terrorism."

It is difficult, if not impossible, to locate or identify the exact moment of genesis of Hizbullah, the "Party of God" that supplanted Amal as the spearhead of Shi'a resistance to Israel. But in south Lebanon today, and in the Biqa' Valley, the "Resistance" as it is popularly known, wields a prestige—and a religious, social, political and moral authority—that stamp it, rightfully or not, as heir to Imam Musa al-Sadr's historic initiative to arm his coreligionists in defense of their rights, a decision he had proclaimed at the historic rally in Ba'albak in March, 1974.

Some argue that Hizbullah could only have arisen and flourished in the absence of Musa al-Sadr.

Shortly after his disappearance, Iranian clergymen such as Ali Akbar Mohtashemi, who became Islamic Iran's first ambassador to Lebanon (Mr. Mohtashemi was not without enemies: his forearm had been blown off by a letter bomb during his tenure in Beirut), and Lebanese Shi'ites anxious to link themselves to the rapidly growing prestige of the Iranian revolution, had begun to discuss ways of radicalizing their movement.[167] By the time Nabih Berrih took over leadership of Amal, in 1980, a strongly religious, pro-Iranian tendency was causing deep rifts in the organization, exacerbated by Iranian efforts to influence their Lebanese coreligionists and to export their revolution to a country where, they reckoned, it might have a chance of success. There could be no mistaking the force of the tremor that had brought down the Shah's regime. The after-shocks would be felt, spreading out in concentric circles, among the downtrodden and voiceless throughout the Muslim world. The Iranian revolutionaries would do their utmost to take advantage of it.

The new organization's founders, including its current secretary general Seyyed Hasan Nasrullah, were all members of Amal who had taken issue with its decision to join the Lebanese government. Its first incarnation, known as Islamic Amal, was founded in March 1982 by a schoolteacher from Ba'albak named Hussein Musawi. That was the month during which Hafiz al-Asad had crushed the uprising of the Muslim Brotherhood in Hama.

It had also come three months before the Israeli invasion of Lebanon, code-named "Peace for Galilee," would begin. This was the operation that claimed to "root out Palestinian terrorism" and, by ricochet, provided the conditions that led to the emergence of Hizbullah, the force that finally defeated Israel in the rocky hills of the south.

The appearance of Hizbullah fighters stiffened Palestinian resistance to the Israeli onslaught, and gave shape to what Robert Fisk, in his riveting account of combat on the beach at Khaldeh, south of Beirut, calls a "remarkable phenomenon:"

(...) The Shia militiamen were running on foot into the Israeli gunfire to launch grenades at the Israeli armour, actually moving to within 20 feet of the tanks to open fire at them.

Some of the Shia fighters had torn off pieces of their shirts and wrapped them around their heads as bands of martyrdom as the Iranian revolutionary guards had begun doing a year before when they staged their first mass attacks against the Iraqis in the Gulf War a thousand miles to the east. When they set on fire one Israeli armoured vehicle they were emboldened to advance further. None of us, I think, realized the critical importance of the events of Khaldeh that night. The Lebanese Shia were learning the principles of martyrdom and putting them into practice. Never before had we seen these men wear headbands like this; we thought it was another militia affectation but it was not. It was the beginning of a legend which also contained a strong element of truth. The Shia were now the Lebanese resistance, nationalist no doubt but also inspired by their religion.[168]

In the summer of 1982, as Israeli forces surged northward, a 1,000-strong detachment of Iranian Revolutionary Guards took up quarters in the barren hills around Ba'albak. This was Hussein Musawi's home ground, where firebrand Shi'a clerics inspired by Iran had gained the upper hand, by dint of incendiary preaching, hard work, judicious disbursement of funds and, when all else failed, intimidation, over the religiously oriented laymen who formed the cadre of Amal. Hizbullah was anything but a unified organization then. Rather, it was a coalition of smaller groups who had resolved not to rule out the use of violence in pursuit of their aims, and above all, of the creation of an Islamic Republic in Lebanon. The Iranian contingent was not to see action; it did provide training and ideological instruction for the growing numbers of young volunteers who flocked to the Hizbullah banner. Having learned the arts of guerrilla combat alongside the PLO in Lebanon prior to the Islamic Revolution, the Iranians were now paying back their debt of hospitality and gratitude. The Lebanese responded.

"Free downtrodden men," rang an early Hizbullah proclamation. "We are the sons of Hizb Allah's nation in Lebanon. We ... consider ourself a part of the Islamic nation of the world, which is facing the most tyrannical arrogant assault from both the East and the West ... (...) We, the sons of Hizb Allah's nation, whose vanguard God has given victory in Iran and which has established the nucleus of the world's central Islamic state, abide by the orders of a single wise and just command currently embodied in the supreme Ayatollah Ruhollah al-Musavi al-Khomeini, the rightly guided Imam who combines all the qualities of the total imam, who has detonated the Muslims' revolution, and who is bringing about the glorious Islamic renaissance."[169]

Along the road to the creation of an Islamic state in Lebanon, something happened. Or rather, did not happen. In spite of the Israeli invasion, and an almost continuous succession of crises, the Lebanese state held firm. It did not collapse. While the Shi'a certainly made up the largest of the country's identifiable confessional groups, they lacked the demographic and religious legitimacy to set up a state on their own. What had begun as a religious movement with narrow doctrinal aims gradually began to evolve into a political organization that was both religious and national in scope. The necessity for resistance to Israel's seizure of more than ten percent of Lebanese territory provided an overriding justification.

Nabatiyeh, with its rich tradition of religious intensity, rapidly became a center of resistance to the occupation. Many of the neighboring villages which, under Amal leadership, had begun to crawl free from the stifling embrace of the PLO, quickly joined the fight. As the struggle ground on, with its daily toll of death, injury, insult and humiliation, the relative moderation of Amal gave way to the confrontational, combative style of Hizbullah, the men who wore the headbands of martyrdom, who could no longer be described as death-defying, but as death-welcoming.

In a nondescript apartment block on a hillside overlooking the city center, Ahmad Obeid leans over a map, his forefinger tracing the border line that separates south Lebanon from Occupied Palestine, as he calls Israel. Behind him, on the walls of the room, are photographs of Abbas Musawi, the Hizbullah Secretary General killed in February 1992 along with his wife and infant son in an Israeli air attack, and a large mural depicting Islamic combatants charging an enemy position under the stern but benevolent gaze of Imam Khomeini and his successor, Ali Khamene'i.

A rangy man with a distant look in his brown eyes, Mr. Obeid had spent nine years in an Israeli prison. He had been visiting the house of a close relative, Sheikh Abd al-Karim Obeid, well north of the occupied zone, when an Israeli commando attacked. "They drugged me and carried me away," says Mr. Obeid. "I woke up in jail. Sheikh Obeid resisted his attackers. Blood was discovered on the floor, which proved that he put up a struggle." The blood,

Hizbullah would later claim, was not that of the Sheikh, but of one of his abductors.

(Abd al-Karim Obeid remains in Israeli custody today, a forgotten hostage in the eyes of an "international community" that has eyes only for Americans, Europeans and Israelis on the finely calibrated scale of whiteness against which human worth is measured.)

After a cup of coffee—even fearsome Hizbullah, in Natabiyeh as in Beirut, proved punctiliously observant of the rules of Middle-Eastern hospitality— Mr. Obeid wedged himself into the back seat of Cilina's Toyota, and we headed south. No map can begin to convey the multifold irregularity of the terrain, its forbidding rocky grandeur, its deep valleys and cliffs. The dotted lines, dots and altitude gradients we had examined a few hours earlier now took on a complexity utterly unmitigated by the intimacy of scale.

"The resistance began in 1982, and spread out from Nabatiyeh," he explains. "Our first operations took place along the dividing line between Lebanese territory and the occupied zone. We used abandoned houses and caves. Classic guerrilla tactics."

Those classic guerrilla tactics, when combined with the willingness to die, proved devastatingly effective. So effective that they were eventually to demoralize, then defeat, a militarily superior adversary.

From the summit of the Château Beaufort, a twelfth century Crusader fortress, the bright ribbon of the Litani glistens far below, at the bottom of the gorge, and from the radio mast atop the castle's highest battle tower the yellow banner of Hizbullah snaps in the morning breeze. Three eagles float on the updraft. On the eastern horizon looms the snowy peak of Jabal al-Sheikh where the Jordan River rises. In the middle distance, a truck winds its way slowly up the road to Marjayun, its laboring motor audible here, several kilometers distant.

"See that truck," says Mr. Obeid, pointing. "That is where we carried out one of our best operations in 1992 against the collaborators."

He was talking about the South Lebanon Army, the force commanded by Antoine Lahd that acted as Israel's collaborationist proxy in the occupied "Security Zone."[170]

"It was designed as a martyrdom operation, but the Hizbullah fighter survived. Three roadside bombs were planted, and when the SLA convoy drove by, they were exploded. The first one, at the head of the convoy, to stop it. The second, at the end, to block a retreat. The third one in the middle. When all the vehicles were stopped and their crews climbed out, our fighter opened up with his machine gun. They were taken by surprise. There was no return fire, no resistance. At least seven of the enemy were killed.

"Only a few hours later, the attack was broadcast on al-Manar TV [the popular Hizbullah television station in Beirut]. Look down there," he says, leaning over the parapet, an almost sheer drop to the river lying vertiginously far below us. "A few dozen meters down is a cave. The film crew [from Hizbullah's war media group, which had been set up in the 1980s] scaled the cliff from the bottom of the gorge the night before, and waited. When the convoy appeared, they started filming. Right under the nose of the Israelis!"

A few hundred meters from the castle ramparts lay the twisted structural steel and concrete rubble of the Israeli observation post. It had been bombed into oblivion by American-made F-16s, after being overrun by Hizbullah fighters during the chaotic retreat. Obliterated were sophisticated computers, databases, monitoring devices, weapons and food supplies. Cans with labels in Hebrew still littered the wreckage. Before the air raid, says Mr. Obeid, Hizbullah fighters had captured a Merkava tank, the pride of the Israeli army, boasting advanced technology that was off limits even to the United States. They also copied the contents of the hard discs. "Now we know all the secrets of that tank, and all about the people who worked for the Israelis."

Today, only the wind disturbs the stillness; the wind, the fluttering of the Hizbullah flag, and the distant growl of vehicles laboring up the Marjayun grade. The Hizbullah detachment that mans the fortress is nowhere to be seen. Throughout South Lebanon, few armed militiamen are visible. Those that are stand on guard in rather relaxed fashion at security check-points and keep watch over the border fence. Appearance are, no doubt, deceiving. There may be as many as 5,000 heavily armed combat-trained fighters posted throughout the region, and 10,000 reservists at the ready. "They are there," says Mr. Obeid, cracking a rare smile. "But you cannot see them."

The two places perhaps most emblematic of the victorious resistance cling to rocky hilltops. One is the proud castle that Israeli air force bombs and rockets could not destroy. The other, al-Khiam Prison, the house of infamy where Israeli-trained torturers wracked the bodies of thousands of Lebanese men and women whose crime was resistance or refusal to collaborate.

In the 1990s, Israeli authorities attempted to distance themselves from the horrors perpetrated at al-Khiam. Later, they were forced to admit that the torturers had been trained by Israeli intelligence operatives. Latter-day apologists for the SLA and its masters, including *New Yorker* reporter Jeffrey

Goldberg, refer to the abundantly documented abuse of prisoners at al-Khiam as "alleged."[171]

Al-Khiam was more than a prison. Not only was it the key to Israel's strategy for controlling South Lebanon; it created, in the heart of traditional Shi'a lands, bitter proof of the lengths to which the occupiers were prepared to go to protect their rule, and to break the population's will to resist. One is tempted to say that the Israelis invented nothing. Al-Khiam village had been, during the French Mandate, the site of a penal colony. Only a few minor modifications were necessary to update it. Such is the utility of prisons, that they outlast the regimes that originally create them.

Striding ahead of us, Mr. Obeid greets one of the gate-keepers with an embrace, then introduces him. His name is also Ahmad. He is a "graduate" of al-Khiam who spent nine years confined here, in the blazing heat of summer and the chill of winter. "Because of all those years in darkness, I cannot bear the light," says Ahmad, as he leads us through the somber corridors, flashlight in hand. He shows us through a low-linteled door into what had been a prisoners' barracks. Detainees—they were the fortunate ones—slept on crude wooden shelves that remind one of those seen in photographs of Nazi extermination camps, ten to a room less than three meters square. The only source of light and ventilation, a ragged hole in the ceiling.

The walls of another corridor are lined with the doors to isolation cells, tiny chambers with concrete floors, where prisoners were held in total darkness, some of them for years. "Many became mad," explains Ahmad in a blank, emotionless voice. "Go in," he tells me. I step through the door, head bowed, my shoulders scraping the ceiling. The door steel door clangs shut. I am alone. The blackness is absolute. I turn and immediately collide with a dripping stone wall. Worse than the isolation cells was the punishment cell, a box measuring sixty by sixty centimeters wide, and ninety centimeters high. Here those who refused to talk were held for days, bent double, unable to move.

Shaken, I backtrack through the corridor, climb a short staircase, and step squinting into the light of an empty room. "This is where they tortured us," says Ahmad. "They used electric shocks, they beat us with electrical wire, they covered our heads with dirty bags." Outside the room, in an equally empty courtyard, Ahmad pointed to an electricity pylon. From it prisoners were hung naked, unable to touch the ground, exposed to the sun or the cold rain.

More than 3,000 passed through al-Khiam. In the end, it remains little more than a cruel memory, and a monument to futility. The mechanisms of betrayal, expulsion, torture and murder conceived and approved at the highest levels of the Zionist State had not only failed. The masterminds who conceived al-Khiam as policy stand revealed through it. Their signature is everywhere, indelible.

As I shake hands with Ahmad, he points to a crudely lettered sign in English above the main entrance to the prison. It reads: "Free men's detention center."

One half hour south of al-Khiam lies the frontier that separates free Lebanon from Occupied Palestine. We pull up at the outskirts of Kfar Kila, the Lebanese village that lies almost atop the fortified fence. On the Israeli side, heavy construction machinery rumbles to and fro, hoisting reinforced concrete panels into place to strengthen the border wall. Ahmad looks across the border, where the Israeli settlement of Metulla basks in the mild winter sunlight. There, surrounded by fruit orchards, houses with red-tile roofs march in orderly ranks up and down the gentle hillsides, reminding me of a Southern California real-estate development. All seems somnolent, calm, contented. Overhead hovers a radar balloon, part of the complex communications monitoring and security apparatus that runs the length of the frontier and is designed to detect, intercept and destroy any interloper.

Here, on the Lebanese side, most of the buildings close to the border have either been left unfinished or are in ruins. Olive groves have been reduced to heaps of uprooted logs and massive splinters, fields abandoned, now overtaken with weeds. Like fields throughout the South, they were mined by the fleeing Israelis. At a seedy café several hundred meters from the border we order a snack. Only *shish-tauk* is available, hurriedly grilled over a charcoal brazier on the porch.

There is no sign of a Hizbullah military presence. Yet the section of the border where the fence is being strengthened was the scene, in October 2000, several months after the Israeli defeat, of the capture of three IDF soldiers by the Resistance forces. Also involved was a colonel, an army reservist, who was arrested in what was described by Sheikh Hasan Nasrullah as a complex sting operation in which the Resistance lured him to Beirut after the officer's attempt to meet a Hizbullah official outside of Lebanon. They are still being held, offered in exchange for all Lebanese captives in Israeli prisons, an unspecified number of Palestinians and other Arabs, as well as the surrender of maps pinpointing the location of land mines in the south, Mr. Obeid says.

I could go no farther. At last I had reached the boundary, the ultimate flash point, the line of high and constant friction where a revived, armed and confident Shi'a Islam now confronts, across a heavily fortified border, the expansionist and aggressive Zionist state.

The atmosphere was eerily quiet. From the terrace of the café we watched as United Nations patrol vehicles rolled slowly down the roadway that parallels the border. Further along, a white Mercedes-Benz pulled up and two men got out, surveyed the fence, returned to their car and drove away. "They are Hizbullah," said Mr. Obeid.

The *shish tauk* was greasy and full of gristle, the canned soft-drink tepid and cloying sweet. A high, diaphanous cloud had drifted across the sun, the breeze turned cool. Our guide was anxious to return to Nabatiyeh. The three of us climbed back into Cilina's Toyota and we began our long drive over the few short kilometers that separated what might become, in the wrong circumstances, a free-fire zone, from the teeming streets of the Beirut suburbs.

Hizbullah today represents a respected and respectable segment of the Lebanese political spectrum. Its parliamentary deputation of twelve, in a 128-seat house, enjoys a reputation for integrity in a country where a deputy's vote is seen as another item of merchandise for sale, purchase or exchange. From its tumultuous beginnings in the early eighties, which may well have included involvement in the massive bombings of the U.S. Marine and French army barracks in Beirut in October 1983 and the kidnapping of Western hostages—which some claim were carried out on orders from Iran—it acquired the symbolic capital that made it a force to be reckoned with, in a region where that which is reckoned with above all is force.

Sheikh Hasan Nasrullah presides over the organization with the benediction of Iran's Supreme Guide Ali Khamene'i, but also in close consultation with the moderate President Mohammad Khatami, ensuring it of religious capital and equally vital financial support. But perhaps most important, Hizbullah has, since the early nineties, abandoned the perspective of an Islamic Republic as part of its political program, though it may hold to the long-term ideal. In doing so, it has integrated itself into the tightly woven fabric of Lebanese social institutions, and worked to compensate the glaring lack of these institutions among the poor. Writes Joseph Alaghal, author of a study of the resistance: "Hizbullah's social network of effective and well-functioning welfare system helps it gain more and more legitimacy and popularity at the expense of the Lebanese state and its institutions."[172]

The rise of a democratically-inclined reform movement in Iran has had an effect on Hizbullah's shift away from a narrowly sectarian religious approach to a community-based, national one. Though it remains close to Tehran, the organization maintains a broad decisional autonomy. In fact, it must. More,

Hizbullah's leadership now takes positions on such issues as cultural dialogue and democracy that would locate it, in Iran, among the strongest critics of the clerical regime.

Though Amal, the movement founded by Imam Musa al-Sadr, still exists, and under Nabih Berri, now Parliamentary Speaker, has become part of the Lebanese power structure, its heritage and presence act as a moral constraint on its more militant coreligionists. Middle-class members of Amal have joined Hizbullah, bringing with them their more moderate, nationalist outlook.

Perhaps it was not a paradox that, although Imam's Musa al-Sadr's mysterious disappearance may have opened the door to the radicalization of religious politics in Lebanon, Hizbullah has, over time, come to look more and more like the *Harakat al-Mahrumin*—the Movement of the Oppressed he founded on that blustery March day in 1974 at Ba'albak.

What he had proclaimed then comes to mind as a prophecy two decades later: "We will not keep silent on injustice, conspiracy, bribery and the theft of people's money. We want the South to be an impregnable area. We want the South to be a rock where Israel's dreams and designs will be shattered and a nucleus for the liberation of the Holy Land."[173]

* * *

WHEN LIBYAN ARAB AIRLINES Flight 225 from Beirut touched down at Tripoli, Imam Musa al-Sadr, his close friend and adviser Sheikh Muhammad Shahadih Ya'qub and journalist 'Abbas Badreddine were met at the airport by the head of Libya's Foreign Relations Bureau. The meeting with Colonel Qaddafi for which they had been invited to the Libyan capital had been postponed, they were brusquely informed. It was to be postponed once again, before finally being rescheduled for September 1. However else they differ, accounts of the meeting concur on one thing: it began on a note of tension, and ended in acrimony, death and tragedy. The official agenda had consisted of one item, "the dangerous situation in Lebanon." In fact, its purpose was to induce Imam Musa al-Sadr to drop his opposition to the armed Palestinian resistance in South Lebanon, and in particular to the strained relations between the Shi'a movement and the *fida'i* factions backed by Qaddafi. Al-Sadr reportedly expressed his reluctance in strong words of a kind to which the dictator was unaccustomed; Qaddafi flew into one of his legendary rages, and ordered the three men shot. The sentence was carried out and their bodies were then dispatched to a farm project run by a relative of the colonel near the coastal city of Sidra.[174]

But wait.

Knowledgeable observers were quick to note that if Muammar Qaddafi had wished to eliminate the stubborn and recalcitrant Imam, the task could have just as easily been accomplished in Lebanon, which possesses an unimpeachable reputation as a haven for gunmen prepared to kill for a price. It was a convincing argument, one I was to hear repeatedly.

The disappearance of Imam Musa al-Sadr may have been an accident, a quirk of fate like the many that have punctuated the recent—and not so recent—history of the Middle East. Or it may have been a plot involving one or possibly several participants, all with vital strategic and tactical interests at stake. Opaque clouds of conspiracy soon began to gather around the disappearance.

One version had Qaddafi accusing Imam al-Sadr of misappropriating for his personal use a one million dollar stipend intended for political purposes, and ordering him killed or imprisoned as a result of this malfeasance. To the charge, the Imam's supporters countered that they would agree to their leader's arrest and even execution if the slightest wrong-doing could be proven against him.

His disappearance had, some said, been caused by Iran's SAVAK, smarting still from Imam Musa's biting criticism of the Shah at Ali Shariati's funeral the previous year in Damascus. No, said another Iranian faction. Though the Islamic Revolution had not yet triumphed, Musa al-Sadr was a potentially dangerous rival to Ayatollah Khomeini himself. In Iranian revolutionary circles it was being whispered knowingly that two Imams were one too many.

Speculation did not end there. The Imam had, almost overnight, transformed Lebanon's Shi'a community from an aggregate of isolated and downtrodden paupers led by a handful of corrupt notables and well-meaning but ineffectual clerics into a dynamic, focused political force. The example might prove contagious, the rulers of Arab countries with substantial Shi'a minorities, or simply those nervous about the reliability of their Muslim subjects, may well have reasoned.

Meanwhile, in Beirut, concern was mounting among Imam Musa's associates on the Supreme Shi'a Council. Several days after his last telephone call, his lieutenant Sheikh Muhammad Mahdi Shamseddine called the Libyan Embassy. To no avail. The Council then approached PLO Chairman Arafat and Syrian President Hafiz al-Asad. Neither had any information. Or if they did, they were not disclosing it. Finally, a direct appeal by Lebanese Prime Minister Selim al-Hoss to the Libyan Ambassador drew a response: Imam Musa al-Sadr and his two companions had departed Libya on the night of September 31 on Alitalia Flight AZ 881 for Rome.[175]

Three men had indeed checked in at the Rome Holiday Inn on September 1, and booked two rooms for one week paying cash in advance. Ten minutes later, a man who claimed to be Imam Musa al-Sadr exited the hotel with his two companions, walked out onto the street and vanished. The visitors left behind two large suitcases, and briefcases containing personal documents and passports. On September 21, the hotel manager notified the Lebanese Embassy of his guests' absence.

The Rome gambit was soon exposed as an elaborate *mise-en-scène*. The three Lebanese had never left Tripoli, never arrived in Italy.

At the insistence of the Lebanese government, an investigation was launched. Reports submitted to Prime Minister Hoss from his own intelligence services and from Rome's police prefecture reached identical conclusions: "three impostors had travelled to Rome carrying the effects and falsified papers of Imam Musa al-Sadr and his companions."[176]

The Shi'a Supreme Council immediately endorsed the findings of the Lebanese and Italian intelligence experts, and petitioned Libya to release the Imam. But in one of the enigmatic and inexplicable twists that have come to surround the story of Musa al-Sadr, the file containing the Imam's date-book and passport vanished in turn from the public prosecutor's offices in Rome a few weeks after the end of the inquiry, never to be found.[177]

Meanwhile, a wave of protest swept the Middle East. On December 21 1978, at the first summit of the Steadfastness and Cooperation Front held at the Damascus Sheraton to protest the Camp David agreements of September, a motorcade of more than 300,000 Lebanese Shi'ites demonstrated with banners asking "Where is the Imam, O Arabs?"[178]

And when Ayatollah Ruhollah Khomeini returned to Iran in early February of 1979, he warned the Libyan leader that "any delay in solving the matter quickly and satisfactorily will have extremely adverse effects." Yet two years later he was to caution the al-Sadr family and several high Lebanese Shi'a dignitaries at a ceremony in Qom that "Imam Sadr has been detained for two years. We must remember that his ancestor Imam Musa al-Kazem was detained for seven years … "[179] Chill comfort indeed.

With his disappearance, Imam Musa had entered into a political labyrinth, a hall of mirrors reflecting distorted images receding endlessly into darkness, an echo chamber where conflicting versions and wild rumors reverberated from the walls. I had expected, when I encountered his family in Beirut, to find insight, if not into the unsolved puzzle of his disappearance, at least into the nature and character of the man who must vanish. What I found was a struggle between consternation and frustration at the indifference of the established political order on the one hand, and the brimming optimism born of hope—and perhaps supported by evidence too delicate to be revealed—on the other.

* * *

THE 2001 EDITION of the annual Beirut Book Fair was held in a complex of tents pitched on the weed patch known as Martyrs' Square, at the heart of the capital's ambitious but empty downtown reconstruction project. Here publishers from throughout the Arab world and the Middle East take advantage of Lebanon's relatively liberal social and intellectual environment to display titles that would earn them the displeasure of the mighty, censorship, a jail term or perhaps even death in any number of neighboring countries. High ranking delegations from Qatar, Saudi Arabia, Syria, Yemen, Egypt and Iran swept through the crowded stalls, trailed by television cameras. Knots of Shi'a clergymen, Sunni and Druze sheikhs and smooth-faced young men—PR flacks and plainclothesmen—chattering into mobile telephones rubbed shoulders with sleek young women in high-heeled shoes and miniskirts and Islamist ladies dressed in *hijab* in a part of the city where to do so is to make a political statement.

Adjacent to the pavilion used for public events was a makeshift café, a drafty, echoing place that combined the worst of the Western fast-food ethos, down to the flimsy plastic cutlery, styrofoam cups and dishwater coffee, with the smoke-filled, semi-conspiratorial atmosphere of the traditional Middle-Eastern coffee house.

Sadreddine al-Sadr, the son of the vanished Imam, was waiting for me at one of the tables. I would have preferred something like the al-Rawda in Damascus for the bustle, the clinking of tea tumblers and the fragrant smoke of water pipes, or perhaps the Café Havana in the same city for its lugubrious ambiance of plot and perfidy. But Mr. al-Sadr might not have felt at ease there. Now in his early fifties, he is a man of engaging modesty: clothing slightly rumpled, shoes chosen for comfort as opposed to style; open, perhaps even vulnerable in manner; an unfailing smile on his face, accentuated by the prominent cheekbones inherited from his father. He is a man troubled to this day by his father's legacy.

"My father started his social, religious, and political activities when I was very young. I remember going to the mosque with him, to ceremonies he took part in. This was a kind of indirect education for me. He said, 'I am training you for the future.'"

Imam Musa al-Sadr was more than a religious dignitary, a politician with a turban. He had a reputation as a *bon vivant*, a man who loved Persian classical music, admired women and was attracted to them.[180] His stature, his intense green eyes, convivial personality and personal magnetism drew people to him. At nearly two meters, he towered above his Lebanese admirers. Photographs show him in the midst of crowds, turban jauntily askew, with the perpetual hunch of the tall man who must bend to be heard by those around him.

Like many public figures whose lives are lived in the full glare of actuality he remained remote from his children, unfathomable as only the world of adults, with its brusque and mysterious coming and goings, its whispers and confidences and rumors of betrayal, can seem to the young.

"Whether I lived in his house or not, I had no private education with him. I almost never saw him. He came home late, and worked until dawn. I still do not completely understand my father's mission. He was like a lake. And I do not know how to swim in this lake. What was his perspective on the community, on Lebanon, on the world? All I know is this: he took no step, carried out no act outside his mission. There were no accidents; everything was thought out.

"My father did not see the elements of a situation separately, broken down into religion, politics, society. For him, everything was a single, harmonious whole. Yet the interconnections between all things were flexible, resilient. Otherwise, he would have been shattered."

In his biographical essay, *The Strange Disappearance of Imam Moussa Sadr*, Peter Theroux describes "the gifted Lebanese politician who brought the country's Shi'a community from its obscure poverty to the centre of the world's stage," as "an agent of the shah and later of Ayatollah Khomeini."[181]

Not so, says Mr. al-Sadr, the smile fading from his face. "My father's first serious political involvement was in the student movement in Tehran, against the Shah and his support for Israel," in the early 1950s. "I know of the accusations that he worked with the shah. Was it because he was building Lebanon's largest hospital, for which Iran had promised funds, in the early 1970s? Was it because of his spiritual, social and political influence in Lebanon? I know that while he was still in Iran, he interceded on behalf of imprisoned members of the MKO,[182] which then was the only militant anti-shah group with wide popular support. He was effective in gaining their release. Another person he helped was Hashemi Rafsanjani [an influential cleric who would later become President of the Islamic Republic]. My grandfather's residence was a safe house for Navab Safavi."

"If he was an agent of the shah, why did Iran begin to export 'imams' to Lebanon to neutralize him? Why did the shah invite lesser Shi'a figures to Iran, most of whom fell into the trap? Why did the Iranian Embassy in Beirut threaten to strip him of his Iranian nationality?

"I do not believe he changed sides with regard to Iran. He was himself a part of the movement that led to 1979. His intervention was critical in saving Khomeini's life. Lebanese friends who visited him without an appointment often saw Iranian clergy and lay people whom he introduced as 'my Iranian brothers resisting the shah.' And this was before 1967, when we were still living in Tyre."

Imam Musa al-Sadr's relations with his native country, and the way Islamic Iran responded when he vanished are, to this day, a source of frustration for his son. "The post-revolutionary authorities did not give his disappearance the attention it deserved. You might argue that the Iranian leadership had its own reasons; I do not accept these reasons.

"Each of Iran's power centers had its own stand. No one of them, and not one of the countries who knew him—and always spoke highly of him—did anything more than issue protests."

Sadreddin al-Sadr folded his hands, looked down at the table, then turned to me and smiled. In his smile I saw frustration and perhaps a bitterness he would be loath to admit. Around us, the Book Fair café had slowly emptied. The tables were littered with empty cups, plates, and ashtrays clogged with smouldering cigarette butts. The bitter stink of stale smoke hung in the air. We shook hands, and I walked out into the tepid, enveloping Beirut night.

At the most mortally critical moment of his life, Imam Musa had found himself alone, far from his loyal followers and associates, his friends, his family. The mighty of the Middle East, the kings, princes, chairmen, prime ministers, ayatollahs and presidents-for-life whom he had cultivated or who had cultivated him had been of no avail. Each, I was convinced, had his reasons for flattering the charismatic Shi'a leader. Each may have had his reasons for not willing to interfere with the strategy for removing him from the political arena, perhaps—if the conviction of his family that he was alive represented nothing more than faint hope—from life itself. Each may have had their reasons for desiring and working for his removal.

If Sadreddine al-Sadr is the devoted administrator of his father's enigmatic legacy, Seyyida Rabab al-Sadr, the vanished Imam's sister, is the living depository of her brother's emotional bond with his Lebanese followers. After several glancing encounters, we finally met on a bright morning in October 2001, in an empty office at the al-Zahra Vocational School in Bir Hasan. From south of the border came the distant rumble of Israeli repression of the Palestinian Intifada; rumors of the "war against terrorism" soon homing in on Lebanon filled the air. How remote that all seemed. The fresh breeze that came wafting in off the Mediterranean rustled the foliage. It took a conscious act of concentration for me to remember that I was in Beirut, a city that for the better part of two decades had seen its vital fabric violently torn asunder, a city where fault lines of religion, class and clan lurked just beneath the surface. Perhaps the blood that had flowed thick on the ground made the perfume of the hibiscus flowers so pungent, their shades of red so vivid.

Sister Rabab is a tall, dignified woman wearing *hijab*, with strong hands and the indelible al-Sadr smile. Although her English is serviceable she prefers to speak through an interpreter when discussing her vanished brother. Not only is his disappearance a still-unhealed wound upon the family, she explains, but it remains a politically charged issue in Lebanon almost twenty-five years later.

"Only God is capable of preserving him and keeping him," says Sister Rabab. "We're convinced that those who work for the sake of God and man, to serve and to contribute to humanity, have a sacred mission. Of course, anyone who works for this sacred mission must face the possibility of martyrdom."

By evoking the idea of martyrdom was Sister Rabab admitting that it had been her brother's fate? I ask.

"God forbid," she says emphatically, with an abrupt upsweep of the chin. "We've received intelligence confirming that he has been imprisoned for life in Libya. If they had wanted to assassinate him, they could have done so here in Lebanon."

"My brother was made to vanish because he called for the unity of Lebanon, for an end to the civil war. He was against dividing up the country, against settling the Palestinians permanently, against Arab meddling in Lebanese affairs. All those who stood to lose from his involvement turned against him."

"During his eighteen years in Lebanon, he set up a system to be reckoned with. The weak and the poor saw him as speaking for them; the wealthy saw him as providing an orderly framework for their business. But he never sought personal gain."

But as the tongue seeks out the aching tooth, Sister Rabab returns to the inaction of Imam Musa's self-proclaimed friends and supporters in the Arab and Islamic world in the critical days, weeks and months that followed his fateful trip.

"What we saw was a large lack of enthusiasm, coupled with ignorance. The Lebanese authorities were weak. No one would listen to them. At the first Arab summit in Damascus [the first meeting of the "Steadfastness Front"], we counted on Hafiz al-Asad, who was Imam Musa's friend. But after the Islamic Revolution, the Syrians handed the case to Iran, which deposited the file in a safe with a combination lock. This happened in Iran, not in Syria," she says, not smiling now.

"I am saying things that have not been said before. If I cannot act, I can speak. Destruction of the Imam al-Sadr 'file' goes against religion. We don't believe the people that did it are sincere in their beliefs. Of course, they were people who had no experience in authority. They could not understand the past or the future. How else could they have acted? Some were like this. Others were hypocrites who benefitted, and gave a bad name to Iran.

"Unfortunately, we do not have another Khomeini."

In that judgement many Iranians would concur.

Beneath the disappearance of Imam al-Sadr lurks another, darker question. Had the aim of his kidnappers been not only his person, but the movement he led?

"That was the goal," she says, not missing a beat. "When the leader disappeared, parasitical ideologies came into existence. Today, those who want to preserve his path and his ideas must suffer to keep them alive."

Sister Rabab declines comment on Iranian and Syrian support for the rise of Hizbullah, which emerged from the decline of Amal. "I do not want to answer," she says, with one last sad smile before we part. "But the wound remains in my heart."

Imam Musa al-Sadr's mission may have been a mystery to his son. The movement he created may have been hijacked, as his sister claims. But today, in the hard and gritty streets of the Beirut of the deprived and the downtrodden, he seemed more alive than ever. The reason is not simply the profusion of posters bearing his smiling face that dangle crazily from lamp posts and electricity pylons. Magnified by memory, fact and legend, Imam Musa's life and disappearance resonate with the occultation of the last of the Twelve Holy Imams of Shi'a doctrine, the Mahdi whose appearance at the end of days will usher in a world of divine justice.

Would Imam Musa al-Sadr, were he to reappear, do any less for a tormented Lebanon? For a region caught in a spiraling vortex of horror? Had he been, even though imperfectly, a modern-day redeemer? On consideration, the answer must be "no." For all his aura, for all the veneration of the community he almost single-handedly rescued from oblivion, for all his religious scholarship, his powers and his charisma, he was a mortal man.

Hajj-Afif Aoun, the Amal veteran at whose house near Tyre I had taken coffee one bright early winter morning, described him thus: "Generally, before he appeared, our sheikhs spoke only about heaven and hell. They preached with folded arms against what we were facing. What set him apart was that his Islam was that of life, not of funerals and mourning.

"Imam Musa was not a prophet. But he was more than a reformer. He was unique, and unequalled. His scope was broader than Khomeini's. I worship no man. I can tell you, Imam Musa was not divine. But he was a leader."

That, I concluded as my early morning Middle East Airlines flight to Paris banked westward above Beirut and out over the Mediterranean, had been reason enough to seal his disappearance if not his doom. In a region ruled by mountebanks, scoundrels and hired despots, Imam Musa al-Sadr was that most extreme and dangerous of all rarities: a whole man.

For that, he had to vanish.

6

Shattered Images

IT WAS THE WORST TIME of the year to start out on a voyage. Bitter, slanting sleet was beating down on Istanbul in early December of 2001. I made my way, head tucked into coat collar, across the square in front of Sultanahmet Mosque. Few cities on earth can be as miserable when a violent winter storm roars down the channel that separates Europe from Asia, and Istanbul was truly miserable that day.

Through the wind-whipped bare branches, the Sea of Marmara glinted steely gray, flecked with whitecaps. Europe-Asia ferries bucked and churned in the choppy swell. Across the esplanade loomed the brick-red mass of Aghia Sofia, the Church of Christ's Holy Wisdom, and beyond it, Top Kapi palace, its massive slate-gray stone walls glistening with rain in the half-light.

I looked around. Not a tourist in sight. If they had not been dissuaded by the threat of the "random Islamic terror" that was sweeping the globe, surely the rigors of an Istanbul winter had convinced those who had ventured this far to remain snug in their hotel rooms.

Even the vagabond, underage postcard hawkers who usually infest Sultanahmet Square had retreated, and huddled in one of the few teahouses still open. I was alone.

It was the middle of Ramadan, and Turks were staying home, waiting in anticipation of sundown when they would tuck into their *iftar*. In Istanbul, and in all the other cities and towns of Turkey, the strains of the daily fast had been exacerbated by economic crisis. Tens of thousands of unemployed walked the streets. The immense tents set up in public squares by prosperous merchants and local governments to serve fast breakers unable to join their families or friends now dispensed hot soup to the hungry as well. Not since the dire years that followed World War II had Turkey been brought so low. The three-party government coalition, set up by the military who rule the country and its United States patrons, had lost public support. Led by former Istanbul mayor—and moderate Islamist—Recep Tayyip Erdogan, the Justice and Development Party waited with the calm certainty that they would form the next government.

I had come here on this blustery day, the beginning of my last voyage to Syria, to track down the iconoclasts, the prey that had continued to elude me as I wandered—or perhaps had willingly let myself be led astray—through the high-walled interior spaces of history and the dusty, diverging laneways of contemporary Middle Eastern reality.

It was here that I hoped to locate the ancient gate to the Byzantine royal palace. No easy matter, for it lay buried far beneath the hill that commands the aperture of the Bosphorus. Still, I reckoned that I was near the spot where the Chalke Portal, the Gate of Bronze, would have stood. Atop it had for at least two centuries shone resplendent an immense icon of Christ. That icon represented the earth-bound empire's direct connection with God, as embodied in the person of His son.

In the eyes of the faithful, the icon did more than depict. It partook of the divine essence, symbolized the incarnation of Christ—the Word made flesh—which lies at the heart of Christian doctrine and separates it—radically—from its Abrahamic sister faiths, Judaism and Islam. By the early eighth century, however, for a vocal and increasingly influential cohort of Byzantine subjects, any attempt to represent the divine constituted nothing less than the worship of idols. Against John the Apostle, who affirms the primacy of the Word, the iconoclasts retorted with the absolute prohibition of Exodus:

> Thou shalt not make unto thee any graven image, or any likeness of anything that is in heaven above, or that is in the earth beneath, or that is in the water under the earth; thou shalt not bow down thyself to them, nor serve them ... [183]

Long lurking on the periphery of the eastern Roman state, the resentment of the doctrine of the Incarnation, and by extension the refusal of religious depiction had, by the early years of the eighth century, entered into the antechambers of the imperial court. Soon it would seize the weakened empire from within.

On my previous visits to Syria, I had become aware of a historic discontent with images. This discontent was diffuse, ill-defined, as much cultural as theological. It had existed, suggested several specialists, before the coming of Islam, particularly in the early Christian community of Antioch, which I would soon be visiting. With the arrival of the new social, political and religious message brought by Muhammad, its form and expression had become more sharply defined.

Yes, iconoclasm had been a Byzantine phenomenon, arising out of conflicting readings of Christian theology. But it had been more: the gravest in a series of conflictual dialogues that began with the seizure of Damascus by the first armies of Islam.

These historical lines of force converged in 726, in Constantinople, where I stood buffeted by the sleet. It was here that the Emperor Leo III ordered the ceremonial destruction of the great icon of Christ. The act touched off more than a century of bitter cultural conflict and internecine strife. It was an ideological victory for Islam, a victory which the caliphate, obsessed with its geostrategic interests, had been unable to capitalize on.

No one knows exactly when the demolition took place. Had Leo chosen a cold, blustery day like today to carry out the infamous act that launched the campaign for the proscription of religious images? Perhaps it was one of those fine luminous spring days I had come to know so well from the months I had lived in the City on the Bosphorus, or in the humidity of summer? The chronicles are mute; what evidence may have existed has either long been expunged or remains undiscovered.

The destruction of the image of Christ was the first great public salvo in the war over and about representation. Like any war, it had been preceded by the gathering tensions, the confrontations and the fracturing and remaking of alliances that characterize the inexorable slide toward hostilities.

Leo's action was brutal, but it carried great symbolic power. Within his palace, the emperor may well have felt himself free to act according to his convictions, writes André Grabar.[184] But he knew well that the icon above the palace portal was a symbolic "profession of faith" on the part of the all-powerful sovereign who resided there. No misinterpretation was possible. The smashing of the great icon was a public act, a declaration of policy. The crowd of onlookers, at first shocked and awed, rapidly turned hostile and erupted in protest, killing the royal delegate in charge of the operation. Stung by the outburst of *lèse majesté*, Leo ordered his troops to carry out violent reprisals.

The emperor, his absolute power challenged, could not retreat. His opponents, as events were to demonstrate, would not yield. Even if it took one hundred years, they would persevere.

The event itself could be compared with Luther posting his theses on the doors of the church at Wittenberg. "Iconoclasm saw itself as a purification of the Church," writes French cultural critic Alain Besançon. "As a return to its veritable traditions which had been corrupted by the worship of images. Such was the conviction of the emperors who took quite seriously their 'equality with the apostles.'"[185]

But there was more to Leo's initiative than a fit of pique, or a proto-Lutheran striving for purity, or the pretension of apostolic equality. It came from without, from the looming proximity of Islam. By adopting the new religion's doctrinal rigor he believed he could reverse the tide which, in the form of an Arab army, had a decade earlier crashed threateningly against the walls of the City. Iconoclasm would thus also be an attempt at spiritual vaccination.

As I made my way across the windswept square, hands thrust deep into my pockets, I thought of the hidden dynamics that had thrust the anti-iconic creed to the forefront of the emperor's agenda.

The deeper I immersed myself in the convoluted polemics, the claims and counter-claims, the skein of conjecture and the pall of obscurity that envelops the story, the more certain I became that Leo was the vector, the instrument, the temporary embodiment of a deep-seated spiritual, social and political shift long in the making. His life and career embodied the struggle between western Christianity, which had only half-successfully negotiated the shift from Greek and Roman paganism to monotheism by transposing the attributes of cthonic divinities and Olympian deities to the Holy Family and to a legion of saints, and the older Christianity of the East, which had long rejected, indeed, never accepted, the gods of the Hellenic pantheon.

These Hellenic deities migrated eastward as consorts in the armies of Alexander, and later still, as camp followers of the conquering legions of Rome, which had assimilated and Latinized them. The Macedonian's goal, when he was not hell-bent on vengeance for the depredations of the Persians against Greece, was less to assume the status of a god, although that idea pleased him greatly, than to convert the Orient to Hellenism. There were obstacles. "The Greeks," writes Ulrich Wilken, "were always ready to recognize foreign gods as their own ... (but) the Oriental peoples invariably refused to take over Greek gods and cults."[186]

Should this be even half true, the iconoclast movement, which rose from within eastern Christianity to reject the idol worship of the hellenized, crypto-pagan west would appear in a different light: that of historical continuity. As would the exemplary resistance of Muslim Asia to the Western cult of instrumentalized rationality, of which "Islamic terrorism" can be seen as but another manifestation.

Shivering, I ducked into the side portal of Sultanahmet Mosque, where an Islamic book fair was in progress in one of the dependencies. The howling Black Sea storm had overwhelmed my curiosity, not the direction I must follow.

* * *

ACROSS THE BOSPHORUS on the Asian shore, all but obscured by the low, fast-flowing clouds and sheet's of rain, lies the teeming, traffic-clogged Istanbul suburb of Kadiköy, known in Byzantine times as Chalcedon. There, in the church of St. Euphemia, the Fourth Ecumenical Council was convened in 451. Monophysitism—the doctrine that rejected the dual nature of Christ for a single divine identity—had briefly triumphed. But the emperor, Marcian, who owed his throne to the intercession of the monophysites, was determined to overcome them in the time-dishonored manner with which leaders turn on their revolutionary supporters.[187]

Chalcedon, seen from the vantage point of today, glows like a beacon radiating toward past and future with a bright and steady beam. It brought the contradictions that haunted Christianity into the full light of day, and in the process disposed of the monophysite opposition by anathema and, when that failed, by full military repression. The Fourth Council, with the most pious of intentions, also contrived to alienate the eastern provinces of the empire which, unwavering in their belief in the single nature of Christ, be it human or divine, buzzed with angry talk of religious secession and schism.

Constantinople may have been the seat of empire, but it was a relative late-comer as a center of Christian belief. The City, too, was tainted by the absolutism it had inherited from Rome, and by its original inheritance as a Hellenic colony. Far more venerable as havens of belief were the Syrian cities of Antioch, Jerusalem and to a lesser degree, Damascus, and the Egyptian metropolis of Alexandria. In that city the use of Greek had been abolished in the religious liturgy, to be replaced by the native Egyptian language, Coptic.[188] In Syria, a significant number of Christians continued to worship in Aramaic, the language said to be that of Christ. Some of them survive to this day in the fastness of their mountain villages.

As the day progressed, the rain intensified. The winter's first blizzard was sweeping across the western Russian steppes and ravaging the Balkans, trapping travellers in trains and creating highway havoc. I departed Istanbul late that evening in a downpour, heading southeastward toward Syria. From the city's main terminal my intercity bus crossed the Bosphorus Bridge, then wound down through the Asian suburbs to the Kadiköy terminal to take on passengers. All that could be seen of ancient Chalcedon through the fogged window was an array of bus agency signs, passengers with frosted breath jostling to board the bus and brightly-lit, deserted shops offering snacks for the journey.

After a brief stopover in Konya I boarded a bus for Antakya—the ancient city of Antioch. The express from Konya sped southeastward through the ancient Seljuq dominions. Sweeping across the central Anatolian steppe, the cold gusts of winter had tinted the landscape a monotonous grayish yellow; clouds pursued us across the horizon. But as we descended through the Cicilian Gates north of Tarsus, beneath looming crags alongside a tumbling stream, and out into the orange groves of Adana the air lay warm and moist across the land. From the Adana Otogar it was a two-hour journey to Antakya. I arrived after nightfall in a drizzle.

Modern boundaries in the Middle East do not express what might be considered the natural frontiers of states, contemporary or otherwise, but those of the Western powers that laid them down during and after the great upheaval of World War I. What had for centuries been the multiethnic Islamic Ottoman Empire overnight became, in 1918, a termite's nest of feuding tribal, religious, sub- or pseudo-national entities created to match the imperatives of their would-be imperial masters. At the secret negotiating sessions to subdivide the region that had earlier taken place in Paris and London and were cast in concrete at Versailles, historical affinities were ignored and subverted; cultural sensibilities tossed aside, loyalties auctioned and purchased, decisions taken that would poison the future as surely as a pestilence-ridden cadaver thrown down a well poisons the water. Any resemblance to the present, where a remake of this Sykes-Picot imperialist strategy is underway, is more than coincidental.

Ancient and prosperous cities like Aleppo overnight found themselves cut off from their natural hinterland. Syrian cities like al-Ruha—renamed Urfa—passed under the dominion of the Turkish Republic.

The fate of Antioch had been—if such is possible—more galling and ignominious. In 1939, the city was handed from Syrian jurisdiction to that of Kemalist Turkey by Syria's French rulers. Turkey, where military dictatorship legitimized its rule with a theory of racial superiority, had been leaning toward its ideological brethren, the Axis powers. Neutrality could be arranged, Ankara had let it be known, at a price. That price would be the former Ottoman administrative district known as the Sanjak of Alexandretta, with its port at Iskanderun and the city that was its crown jewel. So great was the offense to Syria's nascent national pride that to this day the region is shown on maps as Syrian territory, while the actual border is shown as a near-invisible dotted line.

I had been looking forward to a leisurely stroll along the banks of the Orontes, the river that rises at the far northern extremity of the Anti-Lebanon, flows around Homs and winds through Hama before emptying into the northeast corner of the Mediterranean. The rear door of my hotel gave directly onto the river. The next morning I ventured out into the rain. There, turbid and slugglish, between high stone banks from which poured torrents of run-off water mixed with sewage, flowed the Orontes. Even had the water been clear and fast-moving, there was no riverside promenade along which to walk. A rusty, twisted chain-link fence was all that stood between the mud-slimed streets and the indolent current below. The city, having fouled the river, had turned its back on it.

The clouds lifted only long enough for me to catch a glimpse of the mountains that tower above Antakya before the next downpour began. I hurried back across one of the bridges that span the river to the new section of town and sought refuge in the municipal museum, a concrete blockhouse that housed the priceless mosaics rescued from the dwellings of wealthy Antiocheans built during the late Roman period. Inside the museum the atmosphere was clammier than outdoors. The walls seemed to ooze a bone-chilling damp; the museum staff, huddled around battered teapots hissing away atop electric coils, seemed sullen, as though struck with catalepsy.

The mosaics proved as exuberant as the day was glum. Jewel-like and vivid, they depicted scenes from the hunt, wild and domestic creatures, luxuriant vegetation, minor demigods like Narcissus and Echo, Ganymede, or Titans like Tethys and Oceanus—all identified in Greek—who represented Venus among the seven planetary powers in the Pelasgian creation myth.[189]

That exuberance, which reflected Antioch's notoriety as a city of pleasure, stood in strange contrast to its stern reputation as a city of piety. "The Christian spirituality one finds in the sources for late antique Antioch derives its distinctive quality from the rich, sometimes uneasy blending of the Hellenic and Semitic cultures," as the historian Susan Ashbrook Haney puts it.[190]

Uneasy might be an understatement. The mosaics I saw were a barely diluted expression of a hellenizing culture transposed holus bolus into a Semitic environment. The images are secular, celebratory, festive, savage and sensual. They had been salvaged from the villas of the wealthy merchants and officials who alone could afford such luxury, not from the humble dwellings of the pious, indigenous population. What attachment to Tethys and Oceanus, or to the world that evoked them, could have existed among the Aramaic-speakers of Antioch?

Perhaps, I reflected, as I strolled along the riverbank in the drizzle, the contradiction was only apparent.

Only in the fleshpots of the Levant could the pure of heart pursue their cleansing vocation, the mosaics seemed to proclaim, almost defiantly. Only against a background of public dissolution could a fierce semi-ascetic reading of religion flourish. Antioch's peculiar character drew, as moths to a flame, the apostles Paul and Peter, and later Barnabas, the founder of the city's Christian community. A subsequent Paul, bishop of Antioch in the latter third of the third century, preached that Jesus was a man born in time from Mary and divinely inspired to a unique degree. In so doing, he had subverted the Trinity and disallowed Christ's divine nature.[191]

The daring bishop's best-known spiritual successor was Nestorius, who ascended the Patriarchal throne at Constantinople in the early fifth century. Thunderously defeated at the Third Ecumenical Council, the Nestorian doctrine of the single, human nature of Christ sought refuge farther eastward, where it thrived under the benevolent gaze of the Persian shahs and ekes out a precarious and residual existence to this day.

Antioch's stubborn opposition to the dual nature of Christ was not laid to rest for all that. It persisted from the end of the fifth century to the advent of Islam.[192] Contrarian to a fault, these cantankerous Syrians may have endured Byzantine rule, but they would not accept its doctrine.

Leo III, the iconoclast emperor, was from these parts. He had been born not far north of here, in a town known in Byzantine times as Germanicea, and now, as part of the Turkish state, called Kahraman Maras. Described as "Syrian by birth" by one chronicler, he could, an Arab source claims, "speak correctly both the Arabic and Roman [i.e., Greek] languages."[193] Germanicea then lay at the northwestern extremity of historic Syria, the region which by the fifth and sixth centuries had become a territory hostile to the official dogma of Byzantium.

Radiating outward from Antioch, hostility to icons was running at flood tide in the eastern provinces by the early years of the eighth century. As wealthy Antiocheans transferred over time their loyalties from demi-gods and minor deities to religious icons, the resentment of their Syrian subjects and inferiors toward these icons had grown apace. Shortly before Leo issued the edict that would touch off the conflict, he had received two bishops from Phrygia, to the northeast. The emissaries were so violently opposed to religious images that one had already taken the initiative, and destroyed all the icons within the limits of his diocese.[194]

But the orthodox authorities could not heap all the blame for the plague of the image breakers upon Antioch, exporter of monophysitism and hotbed of doctrinal sedition. The iconoclast emperor had been catapulted to power by men like him, hard-bitten easterners from the Byzantine military district that encompassed southern Anatolia and northern Syria. Far removed from the influence of Jews and Muslims who inveighed against Christian depiction, many inhabitants of this district held a homegrown hostility to holy images. In taking the drastic action he did, when he did, Leo III was responding as well to his clansmen, and to his first and most faithful constituents. He may well have been acting to forestall a greater calamity.

The danger to Byzantium was clear and present. Islam had been, for almost a century, under the direct influence of the Syrian Arab culture that had made straight its road to both worldly and spiritual domination. Such was its impact that it now began to exert an influence on eastern Christianity's conception of itself.

The rain was still cascading down when I left Antakya at dawn two days later. Aboard the Damascus bus the few passengers bantered in Turkish with the driver and his assistant. An hour later, when we reached the Syrian border station at Bab al-Hawa, the sky had cleared, and everyone on board switched—without missing a beat—into Arabic.

* * *

IT PLEASED ME TO STROLL of a Sunday morning down the Via Recta, the Street Called Straight, nostrils flaring at the scents of the fresh-ground coffee and spices that floated across the narrow roadway from the tiny storefronts that line it. As Friday is the official day of rest in Syria, the Muslim extremity of the long thoroughfare that begins as the Sharia Midhat Pasha is thick with the coming and going of tradesmen, customers, deliverymen, bearers bent double under their overloaded pallets, impatient taxis, swerving bicycles and tourist shop touts. But halfway along, a subtle shift takes place. The street widens out; the pace slows, the atmosphere is more relaxed. Some shops are closed. Strollers are dressed in their Sunday best, men in dark suits, ladies with uncovered heads, on their way to one of the half-dozen churches that flourish in the Christian quarter of Old Damascus.

The district that is wedged in between the Bab Sharqi, Bab Kissan and Bab Tuma ("Thomas's Gate") covers at most a dozen hectares, and two millennia of uninterrupted habitation and history. And the ancient street along which I walked is as straight today as it had been when Saul of Tarsus was struck blind by the transcendent truth of that which he had denied.

And there was a certain disciple at Damascus, named Ananias; and to him said the Lord in a vision, Ananias. And he said, Behold, I am here, Lord.

And the Lord said unto him, Arise, and go out into the street which is called Straight, and inquire in the house of Judas for one called Saul, of Tarsus: for behold, he prayeth.[195]

As the scales fell from Saul's eyes and he became transformed into Paul the Apostle, then began to preach the divinity of Jesus in the synagogues, his coreligionists rapidly turned against him. They vowed to kill him and, as in Salonica several years later, he was forced to flee for his life.

On this street in this ancient quarter had begun the extraordinary career of a man whose radical abjuration of Judaism was to embed in Christianity its irreducible anti-Judaic core. To it had come, in April, 2001, a stooped, half-crippled old man determined to travel in the path of the apostle who was his half-namesake.

It was another Sunday, bright and clear, a perfect Damascus spring day. The narrow lanes of the Old City were lined with raw police and army recruits. Posters of the Pontiff, shown either alone or in company with President Bashar al-Asad, had been plastered to walls or taped to shop windows. Overhead, helicopters hovered, to swoop low as the motorcade carrying Pope John-Paul II made its way past cheering throngs of Syrian Christians waving pennants in the Papal colors of yellow and white. His route was to carry him from the Abassiyin stadium where he had celebrated mass before a crowd of 45,000 toward his guest residence at the Greek Catholic Cathedral, and along the way he would be seen by a sizeable segment of the city's Christian minority.

Millennia-old Straight Street had never looked newer. It gleamed with a fresh coat of asphalt and new curb-stones laid on for the visit. In the midst of the dirt, decay and disrepair of Damascus, these refuse-free avenues seemed to be an illusion that would vanish no sooner than had the Papal caravan gone its way, like a carpet that unrolls, then rolls up as he who treads it passes.

All around me, the sidewalks were aflutter. Orthodox popes in their pillbox hats rushed to and fro, while Jacobite priests wearing their distinctive cowls jockeyed for the best sight lines. Girls in school frocks fidgeted excitedly, young men crowded around a cubbyhole snack bar feigning disinterest, pre-adolescent boys on scooters wearing yellow and white caps zigged, zagged and popped wheelies down the traffic-free street, an officer making a last inspection of the troops strutted down the ranks. "You there, corporal, get those men into line!" I imagined his barked command, as the somnolent conscripts snapped to attention and extended right arms to mark off the appropriate distance. On neighboring rooftops residents fidgeted in anticipation. Among them, I spotted security men muttering into their walkie-talkies.

Looking down the sinuous street that leads from Bab Tuma to the Christian quarter's churches and religious establishments, I caught sight first of the motorcycle outriders, then the official limousines accompanying the Popemobile well before they slowed to negotiate the sharp turn onto Straight Street.

The helicopters were dead overhead now, the downdraft from their rotors stirred clouds of dust as they hovered above the narrow lanes. Then the Popemobile was in front of me, turning the corner. In it, behind bullet-proof glass, stood John-Paul, bent double with age and infirmity, waving feebly to the crowd. Somewhere in the background I heard the chorus of Vivaldi's *Gloria*, adding anachronism to a scene that bordered on the surreal. People cheered, clapped. Several women wept. Children waved flags. The conscripts stood at attention, ramrod straight. Who was this ancient man? Their's not to wonder why.

Syria is a tight ship, and this was a high-profile visitor on a mission as much political as religious. The Pope's every step, every word, had been plotted, debated, weighed and evaluated, his movements choreographed to extract the maximum benefit for the Vatican, for the Syrian regime, and, accessorily, for the Christians of Syria, who account for twelve percent of the population.

Perfect harmony prevailed, of course. President al-Asad used the official welcome ceremony at Damascus airport to lash out at Israel. The remarks were predictably censured in the West as "anti-semitism," and the Pope was taken to task for not having denounced them.

Some Muslims grumbled, *sotto voce* lest they be seen as inconsiderate hosts, that His Holiness, after having apologized to the Greek Orthodox hierarchy in Athens for the sack of Constantinople during the Fourth Crusade, should also have apologized to the Syrians for the depredations of earlier Crusaders who ravished these lands with the cry of "God wills it!"

Plans had been made for John-Paul to visit the Ummayad Mosque and offer prayers there, in company with Sheik Ahmad Kuftaro, a man upon whose shoulders age and infirmity lay even more weightily than upon the Pope's. The visit—the first to a Muslim place of worship by a reigning pontiff—had taken place, the two venerable men of religion had met, exchanged greetings and meditated together, but no prayer was offered.

In Damascus, as in all of Syria, history lies heavy, but not inert, upon the land. When the second caliph, Umar, visited Jerusalem shortly after the holy city fell to the armies of Islam, he declined to pray at the Christian cathedral.

To do so, the legend goes, would have encouraged other Muslims to follow his example, and rapidly transformed the church into a mosque.

Whoever took the decision that the Pope would not offer a prayer in the Ummayad Mosque surely had Umar's precedent in mind. Perhaps it had been Monsignor Isidore Batikha, the Greek Catholic Primate of Damascus, the hands-on detail man who had negotiated the finer points of the Papal visit and had guided John-Paul to his rendezvous with the Mufti.

My first encounter with the Archbishop had been a fleeting one, a courtesy call on my initial visit to Syria. But it had been enough to persuade me that it was there that I must seek the roots of the iconoclast movement. Now, less than one week after the Pope's visit, we met again. I found the Archbishop in a state of near-collapse. His finely chiseled features were drawn, his eyes sunken and red, his wiry salt-and-pepper beard contrasted with the waxen pallor of his skin.

Clearly, our interview would have to wait. More than eight months were to pass before, finally, on a cloudy December day during the *Eid al-fitr* holiday I took a seat in his office.

The Archbishop, dressed in purple robes, heavy gold chains and jeweled pendants draped about his neck, ushered me into his chambers. While he attended to the disbursement of a small stack of gifts with an aide, I looked around the room, from the rack of episcopal staves with their mother-of-pearl filigree and finely wrought silver pommels to the black vestments draped from an easel upon which was displayed an icon of the Holy Mother. On the walls hung photographs of the Patriarch, and of the late president Hafiz al-Asad and his son and dynastic successor, Bashar. Outside the windows, the branches of the orange trees in the colonnaded courtyard sagged under the weight of ripe fruit.

As his secretary made a discreet withdrawal, Monsignor Batikha settled into the ornately carved armchair across from me. "Where were we, then? Ah yes, the iconoclasts," he began, in elegant, fluent French.

"Behind the iconoclast conflict we will find a crisis in the Church. A political crisis. To understand it, we have to go back to the Council of Chalcedon, in 451. There, Byzantium imposed its will on the three Churches of the East: the Copts, the Nestorians, and the Syriacs. The split was philosophical, between the Byzantines, who were influenced by classical Greek antiquity, and the non-Byzantines, who did not share the Greek culture of the empire."

Instead of bone-dry disputation, instead of abstruse doctrinal arcana, I was hearing a vivid account of a political battle that was to determine the fate of the Near East. The meeting with Monsignor Batikha had been well worth waiting for.

"There was a political dimension as well," he continued. "The people living in the region rejected the Byzantine occupation. It was a great empire, true enough, but one imbued with a Greek form of Christianity. Those who lived here had always refused to accept such an interpretation. To make matters worse, it was preached by Greek bishops who spoke no Arabic … which they all speak today.

"The patriarchs of Alexandria, who were Copts, and those of Antioch, who were Syriac, found the pretext they needed. The ground was ready for what I call islamization before Islam, meaning the rejection by the Eastern Churches of everything that spoke of the flesh, of the incarnation of Jesus Christ."

By now, Monsignor Batikha had my complete attention.

At the Council of Chalcedon, he explained, two powerful schools of thought collided: those who believed that Christ's humanity had been absorbed in his divinity, and those who upheld the coexistence of the human and the divine within one person. "The former came away from the Council with the charge of monophysitism hanging over their heads. It took the Church 1,500 years to discover that they had been duophysites (those who believed in the dual nature of Christ) all along."

At this point, the Monsignor laughed ironically, shaking his head. These matters, which at first, second and perhaps third glance are remote, abstruse and desperately out of phase with the temper of our times, are real, apposite and crucial to our understanding of who we are, he seemed to be saying. The events that were soon to unfold in the region, from Afghanistan to Iraq and beyond would bear him out.

"When you combine the doctrinal conflict with the forced hellenization of everything Christian, and add Byzantine military and political domination, you understand how this 'pre-Islamic' form of Christianity made it possible for the Arabs to liberate the land from its foreign occupiers, from outside domination, from all the bombast and the posturing. The excesses, the boastfulness, the self-satisfaction of the Empire are certainly among the reasons for the rise of the iconoclast movement."

What was the Byzantines' critical mistake? he asked with a rhetorical flourish. "They revealed too much of the sacred. This went squarely against what I call the Oriental mentality which prefers to conceal rather than reveal. Icons, in the final analysis, are manifestations of the incarnation: what had been invisible became incarnate; God became flesh."

"For the Orientals, icons were not mere paintings. They were the actual presence of that which they represented. Such were the forces that touched off the rebellion. Remember, the first public act of Emperor Leo III was to smash the great icon of Christ above the Chalke Gate, in Constantinople."

Here at last was a plausible perspective, humane, coherent, rooted not in Orientalist condescension, nor in the victor's desire to efface his defeated foe, nor in the erudite musings of academics, but in the very land and place where rebelliousness in matters of the spirit was (and is, as any Syrian will tell you) second nature. An article of faith, in fact. Before I traveled to Syria, I'd had a hunch that here I would find, in the rise of Islam, the key to the image crisis— and that perhaps, in the history of the image crisis, I would find keys to the astonishing success of Muhammad's new dispensation and ultimately with the West's inability to come to terms with Islam.

Of course, it would reflect well on Syria's Christian community, which for all its assertion of equal status remains a sensitive minority in a Muslim land, to claim some credit for the rise of the new faith. Did the Archbishop's analysis, when all was said and done, reflect state policy? Could it afford not to?

Still, one must take these tiny moments of sudden sharp focus when and where one finds them. On leaving his office, I strolled westward through the labyrinth of the Old City. It was midday, and the call to prayer rang out from the minaret of the Umayyad Mosque. A tiny utility vehicle, of the variety which alone can negotiate this labyrinth of cleft-like lanes buzzed by, forcing me onto the narrow, crumbling curbstone of indeterminate ancientness. From a nearby stall, blending with the exhaust fumes, floated the rich aroma of roasting nuts. Rarely, in my long stay in Damascus, had past and present seemed so richly, so inextricably joined together as they did that day.

* * *

IF THE CONFLICT BETWEEN Damascus and Constantinople had taken on the character of a holy war, it was a war that, after a century of confrontation, had reached a stalemate. Force of arms could not settle the issue. Three sieges by Arab armies had failed to capture the Byzantine capital. It may well have occurred to the protagonists that ideology and its bastard spawn, propaganda, might better influence the outcome.

When it came to depiction of the sacred and the nature of Christ, the two dispensations seemed to be on a converging course. But Byzantine iconoclasm was more than an emulation of Islam, the better to defeat it. It had its own practice, its own language, its own antecedents within Christianity, its own tortured relationship with Church doctrine and scriptural interpretation.

Constantinople had been a theatre of internal conflict ever since Christianity had supplanted Roman paganism as state doctrine. Often virulent, sometimes violent, this internal dialogue contributed powerfully to the movement to destroy religious images.

"What offended the opponents of icons in the eighth century, and what continues to offend many Christians today," writes Daniel Sahas, "is what they perceive to be a prohibition against icons and the absence of any specific justification of them in the Bible. In this respect, the iconoclasts of the eighth century were the literalists, and the forerunners of the *sola Scriptura* of the Protestant Reformation."[196]

For those who were to emerge victorious after a century of bitter struggle against the image breakers, the significance of icons far outweighed the putative biblical prohibition. Sahas, offering the classic iconophile response, argues that "by depicting God the Word in so far as He became flesh, the icon confirms the Christian belief in the incarnation, as well as in the personal character of the Godhead."[197]

The purpose of icons, runs the argument, is not to draw the attention of the worshipper to the image itself, but to raise up his spirit from the finite world to the incorruptible Kingdom of God. For the learneds and the theologians, these were convincing if not clinching propositions. For the simple believers, oft confronted with a Church hierarchy unable or ill-disposed to speak their language, the distinction may have been less clear. Or, in the case of the empire's eastern subjects, clear in its unacceptability.

Christianity, at its birth, had little patience with art, in which it recognized one of the most solid foundations of the pagan system that it abominated, and which had violently persecuted it. Figurative art was a manifestation of idolatry, of immorality. Among the early Christians, the ancient Jewish repugnance for images found new and zealous followers.[198]

Early Christianity, its rigorous neo-Judaic purism rooted in the ancient Semitic rejection of representation, disdained depiction as idol worship. But the Hellenic tradition with which it was to fuse drew its power precisely from the capacity of art to body forth the unseen. In the gathering conflict, the two were to collide.

Not the least of the paradoxes that surround and pervade the iconoclast conflict, the notion of incarnation, on which the justification of religious images was ultimately to turn, antedated Christian doctrine and could trace its lineage to paganism. Writes Alain Besançon: "Greek art brought about in unique fashion the incarnation, or rather the inhabiting of the divine in human form. Man, when he is represented, has the form of a god, and god, the form of a man."[199]

It was a curious incarnation. When he visited the ruins of Olympia in 1937, Nikos Kazantzakis described the great classical pediments displayed in the museum: "Serenely illuminated by the morning light, they still live: the centaurs, the Lapithae, Apollo, Herakles, Nike."[200]

The scenes carved onto the pediment depict an all-too-human outburst of primeval passion, of wild orgasm. The symposium, emblematic of civilization, has ended, and now the participants writhe with drunken violence. With the exception of the centaurs, those rutting half-men, half-beasts, all the others have assumed full human form. Only their posture betrays them. But, "serene in the midst of the frenzied mortals, unseen by the combatants, extending simply his right arm, stands Apollo."[201]

Apollonian calm was the godly mode; gaudy, painted anthropomorphic statuary, the human mode that stood only one remove from the bestial. This mode was certainly less than theomorphic. Behind the god-like, ethereally creamy marble of an idealized and non-existent Athenian high antiquity bleached by time of its colors lurks a vein of cruder, more brutal depiction that would not only survive well into the Christian era but go on to become the basis of representational art in the West. Whether on the pediment at Olympia, in the domestic mosaics that I had seen in Antakya, or in the southern Syrian city of Suweida it was fully visible, a testimony to the longevity and stubbornness of the pagan pantheon, where demigods at one remove, in their appetites, from the centaurs disported themselves shamelessly and carnivorous beasts savaged their hapless prey.

This is a troublesome legacy, for it suggests that more than the refined quality we attribute to Greek high classic art may be involved in creating the beliefs that lay behind Christian sacred forms, a vulgate aesthetic that the iconoclasts challenged and briefly overthrew.

Alongside the assertive and incontrovertible inheritance of Greek art stands another, understandably more attractive and more accessible yet enigmatic: that of Greek philosophy. Coexisting with a civilization regulated by dark, cthonic forces incarnated by anthropomorphic gods was a realm in which Plato could argue that the fundamental postulate upon which all art rests is that of the goodness of the world. "Created or uncreated ... the world's goodness is the principal characteristic of its beauty."[202] But "the nature of the divine makes it impossible to depict the divine. Art has reached a ceiling: it is restricted to the earthly sphere, where it accomplishes a proedeutic, educational and civic function. It prepares its own dissolution. The lover of its beauty finds support in art for his first steps, then abandons it. In this sense, we can call Plato the father of iconoclasm. Sooner or later, all the enemies of the image will invoke the platonic argument."[203]

But, adds Besançon, Plato is simultaneously the father of the iconophiles, for it is he who does full justice to man's desire to contemplate divine beauty. And with his successor Aristotle, "the exercise of the best part of man, which is his reason, must be applied to the best of all subjects, those which are eternal and immutable. Contemplation is thus the activity which is unique to virtuous reason ... Here, what Aristotle says differs not at all from Plato."[204]

It is at this precise point that we enter a zone of uncertainty, not to say cognitive dissonance. Famously, Aristotle had contrived to divorce his philosophical activities from his everyday affairs, particularly as private tutor to Alexander the Great. The forty-year-old philosopher, for instance, inspired his post-adolescent charge with the dislike of barbarians (though Alexander, as a non-Greek speaker from wildest Macedonia certainly qualified as such) and with reverence for the cult of heroes. And therein hangs a tale.

To their good fortune, Alexander did not treat all the "barbarians" he conquered on his march to the east as his tutor would have wished, that is to say, with despotic diligence. Such treatment he preferred to administer to the free Greek citizens of Thebes who had dared to resist him. Fortunate barbarians. Them he proposed to "entrust (...) to Hellenic care and protection." As cruise missiles rained down upon Baghdad, one captured a preternatural foreshadowing of the "American democracy" to be visited upon the restructured countries and subordinated peoples of the Middle East, not to say upon all those who, for whatever reason, might be "with the terrorists," that is to say, might disagree with some aspect of what is to be prescribed for them.

Nourished on Aristotelian thought, Alexander marched off to conquest. When he overcame Egypt, he sought not to mix Greek and Egyptian culture, but to "affirm his program ... that, without prejudice to the Egyptian cult, Greek ways of life, Greek gymnastics, Greek arts and literature in honour of Greek gods should in future have a home in Egypt."[205]

Those very gods were to survive, in Greek and later, in Roman colonies the collapse of Alexander's one-man imperium, as was the god-like dimension with which the Macedonian had invested himself in Persia, and which would find new expression in the icon cults of early Christianity. But never would they—nor he in the guise of a god—be welcomed, much less accepted, by the Egyptians and the Syrians.

The Alexander cult gave his emulators ideas upon which they were quick to act. "At the end of the Roman Empire, there stood in every city an icon which indiscutably and officially bodied forth a god: the statue of the emperor ... Divine Augustus was present in the statue before which the imperial subject would sacrifice."[206]

By the time Constantine the Great decided to move his capital from Rome to the city overlooking the Bosphorus, and accepted Christianity *in extremis*, Helleno-Roman paganism and Christianity had already well begun the process of intermingling that would meld them into a new hybrid culture known as Byzantine.[207] The contradictory constitutive forces of the new culture would continue to rend its fabric, culminating three hundred years later in the iconoclast outbreak, the ultimate and failed attempt by the Oriental component to assert its primacy.

The struggle against idols was broadly and deeply rooted in the Semitic heritage of Syria, but nowhere did it find such acute expression as in Judaism, the original monotheist dispensation and fertile seedbed from which both Christianity and later Islam would spring.

Yet even in a creed that strived for purity, paradox abounded. "Two themes intertwine in the Old Testament. The absolute prohibition of images and the affirmation that images of God exist."

Thus, when Aaron created the golden calf, and the people said, "These be thy gods, O Israel, which brought thee out of the land of Egypt," (Exodus 32:4), " ... the people had, strictly speaking, neither committed apostasy nor changed their God. It had wished to possess an image that would make this God visible, tangible."[208]

The biblical strictures against idolatry had one aim above all: to suppress it among the people, where the sharp line of demarcation between deity and idol, defined as the object of any worship that did not address itself to the one, sole and jealous God, tended to blur.

Eternal backsliders, the Chosen People had become in the course of their history well acquainted with the illicit fascination of false gods. "The transgression of prohibitions marks the history of Israel ... we cannot speak of a formal repudiation of the cult of the true God, but of an intermingling of this cult with idolatrous cultures. Yaveh remained the legitimate God of Israel. But other gods became associated with him ... "[209]

During the historical periods when the Jews participated fully in the civilization surrounding them, they tended to follow the general trend, if at a slight remove, associating other gods with the unnameable One. But in times of separation, withdrawal and fervor, literal and rigorous obedience to the Second Commandment became the inviolable rule.[210]

It took three centuries before the religion founded on the life and teachings of Israel's greatest false messiah became the dominant cultural and spiritual force in Syria and Mesopotamia. Throughout those centuries, a certain laxness with regard to depiction had begun, insidiously, to infect the Jews.

As Christianity consolidated its positions, and gradually usurped control of the Roman Empire from within, the people of Israel launched a series of stinging counter-offensives, accusing the followers of Jesus of idol worship. The tone became sharper with the onset of the Persian wars at the beginning of the seventh century. The Jews, for reasons not difficult to grasp, had thrown in their lot with the conquering Sassanids that in 614 sacked Jerusalem, carried off the True Cross, and massacred the Christian population.

Deprived of their Persian protectors, confronted by the the Basilieus Heraclius's cruel ultimatum—"baptism or death"—those Jews in the reconquered territories who did not convert sought refuge in rigorous orthodoxy. The lavishly decorated synagogues like the one on display in the National Museum in Damascus that had flourished in the desert city of Dura Europos were either abandoned to be buried beneath windblown desert sand, or their figurative mosaics were destroyed, to be replaced by geometric motifs.[211] No sign of weakness, no derogation from the Law could henceforth be permitted nor tolerated.

The drumfire of accusation quickened. The large number of extant Greek anti-Jewish texts to survive that period may indicate that the Jewish attack on imagery was having an effect. With the rise of Islam and the early confusion among Christians about the true nature of the new religion, the issue had become blurred. Even as Heraclius and his successors rallied to expel and defeat the Persians, they had lost the battle for the hearts and minds of the subject peoples of Syria.

That battle turned not only on military might and repression, but ideas: on the question of image worship.

* * *

LEO III THE ISAURIAN fancied himself more than an emperor. He, like the most illustrious emperors of Byzantium before him, would be high priest as well, Pope and Caesar combined. Iconoclasm was but a cynical ploy, say some scholars, a means of concentrating in the emperor's hands total control of the religious establishment. If such were the aim, he all but achieved it. One of the effects of his success was to make the geographic boundaries of the empire and of the church contiguous. Leo could thus claim it his legal prerogative to make his own religious views binding upon his subjects. The principle itself was nothing new, but it concealed a radical religious agenda, and it was being exercised by a popular ruler.

Others believe that his main motive in launching the iconoclast movement was to convert Jews and Muslims to Christianity. Had this been the case, it was a poor strategy indeed. If any Jews were considering conversion, it was to Islam. As for the Muslims, they then were, as they have been ever since and promise to remain today, notoriously unreceptive to changing religions, a capital crime under Islamic law.

Ultimately, Isaurian Byzantium's great and good fortune lay in the stars, and in the decline of the one power that could threaten it: the Damascus caliphate. The vigor of the Umayyads had long spent itself, the caliphs were increasingly seen as impious and licentious revellers and carousers, for whom the prescriptions of faith meant nothing.

By his issuance of the iconoclast edict Leo had neutralized, so he thought, the Muslims' advantage in the struggle for the souls of the Syrian believers. What he had overlooked was the bitter resistance of his new adversaries. Fresh from a military defeat of the Arabs, he and his successors would become progressively embroiled in a war of words and symbols of faith with their fellow Christians.

Matching the boundaries of the state to those of the church was Leo's master stroke. It was also a grievous strategic error, one that set up an asylum for a bitter adversary. One of the most eloquent voices to be raised against iconoclasm came from the inner circle of the caliph's court in the person of St. John Damascene, a direct descendant of Mansur, the Christian official whose alleged treason had opened the gates of Damascus to Islam one hundred years earlier. Safe in the Umayyad capital, the Damascene was free to fulminate against the rulers of Constantinople, and fulminate he did.

Never a culture given to fleeing the abstruse, Byzantium expressed social and political conflict in the language of religion. Perhaps the better to deflect attention from his very real position as a high-ranking minister to the caliph and boon companion of the wanton and dissolute Yazid II, John Damascene created for himself the persona of a man of unimpeachable learnedness, piety and fervor (although this persona may have been invented for him by his later admirers). The caliph would not have been unaware that his court minister's fierce defense of religious images could be put to good use to undermine iconoclast Byzantium's resolve in its struggle with Damascus.

John Damascene devised a complex and sophisticated strategy. Systematically, he developed the distinction to be drawn between the cult of worship, of which God can be the only object, and that of devotion (*proskynesis*, in Greek), accorded to sacred things. He argued that the icon communicates not the face, nor the identity of the divine Person, but his energy, which is transmitted via the material nature of the icon, in the manner of a sacrament. "Nature leads us toward immaterial God by causing us to travel upstream against the descending current by which it has guided the divine energy. John is in full harmony with popular devotional practice, and this is why Orthodox tradition exalts him as the most eminent defender of icons."[212]

For all his theological suasion and doctrinal brilliance, John Damascene could not alone tilt the balance toward icons. Leo's position seemed impregnable. He ignored the Pope of Rome, Gregory III, who expelled the iconoclasts from the church, and detached Italy from the Byzantine Empire.

If Leo had a soldier's attitude to imperial discipline, his son Constantine V was a man who combined theological accomplishment with an iron will and a fondness for power inherited from his father. Where Leo had been content to prepare the ground for the abolition of icons, the actual physical process of uprooting them only began in earnest with the new ruler.

The new Constantine was as clever a manipulator of religious argument as he was an able military commander. His strategy was to win over—or browbeat—the high clergy by presenting image worship as a heresy, a sharp and thorough break with the consensus established by the great church Councils. So well-constructed was his intellectual and religious argument that the efforts of an entire generation of theologians was needed to overturn it.[213]

The Council of 754, summoned by Constantine, sealed the victory of iconoclasm which now stood unchallenged. Offenders against the New Order would henceforth be delivered over to the secular arm for chastisement. The condemnation of image worship was now unequivocal and absolute:

> Supported by the Holy Scriptures and the Fathers, we declare unanimously in the name of the Holy Trinity, that there shall be rejected and removed and cursed out of the Christian Church every likeness which is made out of any material whatever by the evil art of painters. Whoever in future dares to make such a thing or to venerate it, or set it up in a church or in a private house, or possess it in secret, shall, if bishop, priest or deacon, be deposed, if monk or layman, anathematized and become liable to be tried by the secular laws as an adversary of God and an enemy of the doctrines handed down by the Fathers.

The Council's decree ended with a ringing tribute to "New Constantine and the most pious, many years! ... You have destroyed all idolatry." Finally, anathema was proclaimed against the Patriarch Germanus, "worshipper of wood" and against Mansur, that is, John Damascene, "inclined to Muhammedanism, the enemy of the Empire, the teacher of impiety, the perverter of the scriptures."[214]

According to the icon-worshippers upon whose accounts the only surviving history of the era is drawn, the anti-icon campaign was violent. "Images were broken, burned, painted over and exposed to many insults ... Many image-worshippers were executed, tortured or imprisoned."

Little wonder that Constantine V soon came to be known by his foes and victims as Copronymous, "he whose name is excrement." The emperor's campaign of terror against holy images had proven devastatingly effective. But in the end it earned him nothing but the scatological execration that has followed him down through history. Worse, the luck of the Isaurians was soon to turn.

His son Leo IV the Khazar (for Constantine V had married a woman from the mysterious tribe that had converted *en masse* to Judaism only to vanish) was a pusillanimous young man who took for a wife Irene the Athenian. Here, alarm bells should be ringing in attentive readers' minds. In choosing a woman from Athens, the young emperor's advisers failed to notice—or noticed only too well—his new consort's sympathy for the icons. Surreptitiously and with duplicity the ancient pagan school of Athens seemed to have stretched its hand into the future to bring the iconoclasts down. On the death of the fourth Leo in 780, rule of the Empire was entrusted to Irene.

Seven years later, yet another Council was convened, this time in Nicea. It reestablished image worship and heaped anathema and opprobrium upon the heads of the iconoclasts. And in a devastating blow to the image fighters, it ordered the restoration of icons to churches and strengthened the influence of the monasteries in the religious and political life of the empire.

Soon, with the ascension to the throne of yet another Leo, the iconoclasts once again seized state power. But their enemies had become more determined, and ideologically more sophisticated. The icon smashers had, since the beginning of the conflict, succeeded in polarizing the debate: the only choice was between idolatry, which no Christian could countenance, and icon-smashing.

Now, however, the defenders of icons came not only upon an argument that would lay the initiative in their hands, but upon a champion who would carry the battle to the iconoclast diehards. Nicephorus I, who assumed the patriarchal throne at the beginning of the ninth century, after seventy-five years of bitter internal religious and civil strife, held that the icon was not a natural image of the prototype. It was, instead, an artificial image which did not partake of the nature of the prototype; a mere imitation.

In his reasoning, says Besançon, Nicephorus followed Aristotle. "Is the glorious transformation of the body at the Resurrection accidental or substantial? If it is the former, then it cannot be total. If it is one of substance, then Christ's humanity will have vanished. That would be monophysitism. The human nature of Christ was not altered in the Transfiguration. It was 'renewed,' not transformed. It must be admitted that the flesh, corruptible, mortal, circumscribed, is capable of a divine 'way of being.'"

All of which sent things straight back to the solid ground of the Council of Chalcedon: the union of the two natures, with neither confusion nor separation. But what then of the divine nature? "If it cannot be represented, is it Christ whom we see in the icon, or only his human nature?"[215]

This was a delicate matter. It was to be elegantly resolved by Theodore, abbot of the monastery of Studion in Constantinople. The monastery had been a perpetual thorn in the side of the iconoclast emperors not only because of its wealth, but of its spiritual influence. "In Christ, the invisible becomes visible," the abbot asserted. "That which we see in the icon is his very person. In other words, his *hypostasis*—his personal existence—and not his nature. Such is the key to the icon problem ... The incarnation had not produced generic Man, but a particular man, the man from Nazareth."[216]

Though once again overcome by the iconoclast restoration, the icon worshippers now, thanks to the work of Nicephorus and Abbot Theodore, wielded the doctrinal weapons that would stiffen their already fierce resistance. Though the the image breakers held state power, their ideological monopoly, powerful in appearance, had been undermined. Worse for them, their campaign to root out the influence of the monasteries, those repositories of belief that the victorious iconophiles claimed fueled icon worship, had failed.

When, on March 11, 843, a council convoked by Theodora, who ruled the empire as regent on behalf of her minor son Michael, ended its deliberations, a solemn liturgy was celebrated in the cathedral of St. Sophia. After more than a century of internecine strife, the iconoclast movement had been finally struck down.

But had it in the end? The stylized, idealized form of the Byzantine icon had been transformed by the lengthy crisis. Bodies became elongated, faces sunken, gone was the spontaneity that once animated the primitive icons of Syria and Egypt, and earlier, the vivid mosaics of Antioch and Suweida. It was as though the style finally adopted—a style that has remained virtually unchanged ever since—was the result of a compromise between the full humanity that was Christ's and the symbolic abstractions that iconoclasm had been prepared to tolerate. The compromise, says Besançon, was justified by the place that the icon chooses to represent: neither entirely heaven, nor entirely earth, but in the mystically contemplated intermediate space of the Transfiguration.

"But the truest, least expungeable traces of the iconoclast mentality can be found in the incapacity of the icon to depict the world of the profane ... A totally sacral, cultish art created around itself a desert."[217]

The defeat of iconoclasm was not the end of the matter. Having lain dormant for seven hundred years, the intense loathing of religious images and what they had come to represent in the hegemony of Catholic Rome was revitalized by the Protestant reformation. Across northern Europe, from Germany through the Netherlands and into Calvinist Geneva, statues, paintings and other devotional artifacts were stripped from churches. The connection with Islam had become tenuous. Though the Ottomans thought they recognized in Luther a soul brother, their advances were hardly reciprocated. And when they were, alliances and arrangements were grounded in *realpolitik*.

European civilization had emerged as the world's dominant cultural force. Islam had long forfeited its primacy and its once unstoppable impetus. Soon it would come under a sustained counterattack that has shown no signs of abating.

* * *

RETURNING TO DAMASCUS via Turkey at the end of Ramadan, I turned once again toward the Old City in search of the trail of the iconoclasts. Could they would still be lurking there, in the dark crevices between the ancient buildings, in the shadows where light never shines, in the crumbling, yellowed pages of forgotten manuscripts, in the frayed memories of elderly men?

Caliph al-Walid, we recall, had invited—or instructed—the Christians to relocate from their original house of worship in the heart of the city. The ruler and his half-brother Umar II, who was to follow him two years after his death, in 717, had made a courageous effort to right the listing Umayyad ship of state by building monuments pleasing to God and by summoning the Byzantines to a "dialogue of civilizations." But at home, they preferred that their Christian subjects adopt a rather more humble profile.

Confronted with the inevitable fact of the new mosque-to-be, the Christian hierarchy packed its altar pieces, its icons and its holy vestments, and withdrew, *intra muros*, toward the eastern quarter. Meanwhile, block by massive stone block, the Basilica of St. John was being deconstructed to make room for the monumental structure that would be erected in its stead.

Islam would not, however, entirely supplant Christianity in Damascus nor in Syria, and certainly not cause the community to vanish. The ambiguous nature of the fall—or capture—of the ancient city, the numerical strength of the Christians, the vital role assumed by Christian scholars, scribes, book-keepers and civil servants in creating a new structure for the Islamic state, not to mention the day-to-day tenacity of the Christians themselves as they went about their lives huddled in the shadow of the mosque, would see to that.

Al-Walid proved intractable but as good as his word. The new houses of worship were constructed along the Via Recta, in the sector known as Bab Tuma. While the stones and mud brick of those first churches have disappeared, the institutions they housed are still very much alive, and in some cases all but unchanged.

The two main denominations, the Greek Orthodox and the Greek Catholics, both legatees of Byzantium, abjured iconoclasm and welcomed the Orthodox restoration of holy pictures when it finally came, on February 19, 842, after 116 years of rule by the image breakers. But a smaller, and elder denomination called Syrian (the adjective indicates denomination, not nationality) Orthodox—colloquially known as Jacobites—held a much more ambiguous position.

I had first encountered this quintessentially Oriental community several years before, in the city of Mardin in south-eastern Turkey. There I had visited the monastery of Deyrul Zafaran, the massive saffron-toned stone complex that for centuries had been the see of the Syrian Patriarchate. But the deepest roots of the Syrian Church were to be found in Antioch, where it claims to have been founded by Saint Peter in 37 CE.

Two days before the New Year I arrived at the portal of the Syrian Orthodox Cathedral. "The Patriarch will see you now," said the sacristan as he escorted me into the formal reception room of the parish hall that abutted the church. There, in an elaborately carved armchair at the far end of the room, sat His Holiness Ignatius Zakka I Iwas, the diminutive white-bearded man who exercises supreme religious authority over the world's estimated three million Syrian Orthodox faithful, a congregation scattered from the Indian state of Kerala via the Middle East to the suburbs of Pittsburg, Sao Paulo and Sydney.

His ceremonial vestments were of brightest scarlet, over which he wore a black cloak. From his neck hung a massive gold cross. The customary words of welcome disposed of and coffee served, for this was Damascus and some things could not be unduly hurried though other audiences were to follow, we got down to the business at hand. And His Holiness was nothing if not businesslike, even expeditive.

"Please," he began, with the kind of smile that bespoke paternalistic admonition, "do not call us Jacobites." I had earlier let the word drop, innocently enough I believed. "That is what they called us, the Byzantines who thought they could destroy us. Jacob Baradeus was only one of the many men of God who labored to preserve the faith."

As in most matters theological in the vast repository of strife-ridden dogmatic disputation that forms the chronicle of organized religion, there are at least two versions of the Baradeus story. The first, that of the official institution, as explained by Patriarch Ignatius Zakka, has God raising up "an indefatigable man called Yacub ... to defend the church."[218]

Through the intercession of the Empress Theodora, who was herself the daughter of a Syrian priest and wife of the Emperor Justinian, this Baradeus was consecrated bishop in Constantinople, in 544. "Following his consecration, Mor Yacub traveled far and wide, vigorously organizing the affairs of the church."[219] Due to the indefatigable efforts of Bishop Jacob, the church was able to withstand the "heavy blows of Byzantine persecution" and hew to the ancestral faith.

When the Byzantines, at the Seventh Ecumenical Council—that which under Irene the Athenian brought an end to the first iconoclast period—described the Syrian Orthodox Church as "Jacobite," their intention was not to praise Bishop Jacob, but to degrade the church itself, which has formally repudiated the title.[220]

But Philip K. Hitti's monumental *History of the Arabs* describes Baradeus as the "monophysite bishop" of Edessa. "So zealous was this Jacob in the propagation of the faith that the Syrian Monophysite Church became known after him as Jacobite."[221]

Who to believe?

Today, harmony reigns amongst the Christians of the East, Patriarch Ignatius explained. But it was not always thus. "Divergences between us and the Greeks began with the Council of Chalcedon. We thought the Council had adopted a Nestorian doctrine [the Nestorians believed that Christ's nature was exclusively human]; they thought we denied His humanity. Now, after much consultation, we have one doctrine and one faith, that Christ was man and God, and that his two natures are combined in one person."

It sounded a bit too easy. Could this curious survival not be the last refuge of monophysitism, the ultimate retrenchment of an iconoclasm that dare not speak its name?

"Do you believe in religious images?" I asked, taking the direct approach.

"When it comes to the use of icons, we are not like the Greek Orthodox," came the Patriarch's reply, confirming by way of non-denial. "We were far away from the icon wars. At that time, we already lived under Islam, and they—the Muslims—did not accept images, as you know. As a result, we rarely used holy pictures in our churches. Even today, we depict only Christ, the Holy Mother, and our patron saints." I thought back to the magnificent monastery in Mardin which for centuries had served as the seat of the Syrian Church. There I had seen only a handful of pictures; nothing that could approach the exuberant and colorful displays that plaster every square centimeter of Greek Orthodox church walls from Ochrid to Istanbul by way of Sofia and Salonica.

"It was relatively easy for Islam to tear the Nestorians away from Christianity, for they believed, as the Muslims do, that Christ had only a human nature. They were closer to Islamic belief than we were. But, let me tell you that we were persecuted for centuries by Byzantium. We were happy to be far removed from the Byzantines. We were closer to the Muslims than to them!"

The past is past, he concluded with a sigh. "Today, we have friendly relations with the Greek Church. More than twenty of our monks have graduated from theological schools in Greece. But when we speak of history, we should declare all the facts."

Those "facts" had left me more uncertain than ever before. One man's monophysite was another's iconoclast. The seditious tentacles of imagery had slowly re-infiltrated the crumbling edifice of doctrinal purity.

7

The Meridian

THE SUN WAS SETTING as the Antakya coach pulled into the Harasta depot on the northern fringes of Damascus. Ramadan would soon be over. Tempers sharpened by a month of fasting and lack of sleep had reached hair-trigger sensitivity. Two taxi drivers competing for space under a narrow viaduct leaped from their cars and began to flail at one another while the horns of other taxis, eager to reach home to break the fast, blared in impatient anger.

My last sojourn in Syria would, I hope, shed light on the controversy from the other side of the civilizational divide I had set out to explore, the Muslim side. For it was here that the combination of state power and religious fervor created a force that would confront Christianity as it had never before been confronted: by measuring it against its own principles. Between my first voyage to Syria nearly two years earlier and today, a time of measuring had come once again. The molecules in the air had begun to thicken, to rearrange themselves in ways ill imagined.

The reign of the first four successors to Muhammad, Abu Bakr, Umar, Uthman and 'Ali, had been—according to the conventional wisdom of Sunni Islam—a period of enlightened governance inspired by the example of the state the Prophet had founded in Medina. However, under the Umayyad caliphate, a prosperous, globalizing Islamic society where wealth and power, not piety, became supreme values, provided the first practical test of the new doctrine.

The Damascene caliphs, following in the footsteps of Mu'awiyah and his dissolute son Yazid, disdained no earthly pleasures. Their court echoed with poetry and song, wine from the vineyards of al-Ghuta flowed freely. The Empire was expanding vigorously, reaching as far as the Indus, the depths of

Central Asia and the shores of the Atlantic; new wealth flowed into the city. Its population soared.

Alongside the worldly, often dissolute behavior of the caliphs and their wealthy retinue, there survived intact a substantial core of pious believers. As the grip of Islam over the centrifugal forces in Arab social life began to loosen, supplanted by relationships founded on domination, pietists accused the rulers of neglecting divine law, of overlooking the Qur'anic injunctions, of worldliness and debauchery, of substituting force for compassion, power for justice.

In Islamic tradition, every century witnesses the appearance among believers of a renewer, a *mab'uth*, "he who is sent" to reinvigorate the faith. Such a man, some historians say, was Umar II, who ruled over the Empire for three years, between 717 and 720.[222] One hundred years had elapsed since Muhammad's migration to Medina. The second Umar's ascent to the throne seemed touched by the finger of the prophetic.

The new caliph's piety, a throwback to that of his namesake, stood in stark contrast to the licentiousness of his Umayyad predecessors that had so enraged the devout, and handed a powerful anti-regime argument to detractors. Here was a caliph who went about in patched clothing and mingled with his subjects. So humble was his demeanor that petitioners often could not recognize him in the crowded hall where he held audience. During his brief reign, the practice inaugurated by Mu'awiyah of cursing 'Ali, his defeated arch-enemy, from the pulpit at Friday prayers was abolished.

So intense was the piety of the ruler that he placed the state's robust finances at risk as he promulgated fiscal measures to attract new converts. By encouraging the Empire's numerous non-Muslim subjects to adopt Islam his measures deprived the treasury of a substantial source of income from payment of the land tax that was incumbent on all non-Muslims.

The policy had an impact not only upon the caliphate's non-Muslim subjects, but on relations between Damascus and Byzantium. Leo III had one year earlier ascended to the imperial throne and broken the Arab siege of Constantinople. Not without help from divine intercession in the form of a terrible storm that destroyed the Arab fleet on its return to Syria, say some sources,[223] nor without a direct command from Umar II, who ordered his generals to abandon their encirclement of the City. Not again, until that fateful May of 1453 when it fell to Sultan Fatih Mehmet, the Ottoman conqueror, would an Islamic army threaten the Second Rome.

While Umar II, a man under the influence of the clerical establishment, had indeed abandoned the military campaign against Byzantium, he apparently proposed to continue by other, perhaps more subtle means. Where arms had failed, he chose politics. One of Umar's few surviving edicts, communicated via the time-trusted method of chains of authority, enjoins his representatives to deal harshly with the visual appurtenances of Christianity in his realm:

"I hold that Abd er-Rahman bin Thawban, who held it from his father, that Umar bin Abd-al-Afiz [Umar II] wrote to one of his governors: leave not one single cross to be shown without breaking and destroying it ... "[224]

Whether the edict was enforced or not remains unclear; it did indicate that attacks on Christianity, if not on Christians, were becoming more frequent among the Muslim devout, and that idolatry was their focus. These attacks must have been particularly telling in eastern Asia Minor, homeland of Byzantium's influential monophysite population.

Umar's measure may have provided the occasion for direct communication between the caliph and the emperor which some historians speculate actually took place. Others argue, without convincing evidence, that Umar attempted to bring about the conversion to Islam of his Christian counterpart. One source attributes to the Isaurian a spirited defense of the cross that was later to become and article of iconoclast faith: "We honor the cross because of the suffering of that Word of God incarnate borne thereon, as we have learned from a commandment of God to Moses, and from the prediction of the Prophets. As for pictures, we do not give them like respect, not having received in Holy scriptures any commandment whatsoever with regard to this."[225]

There is some reason to doubt the accuracy of Leo's protestations. As a destroyer of images of Christ which were His literal incarnation, the chief iconoclast could not have it both ways, could not pay lip service to the Word of God incarnate while smashing His incarnate image at the Chalke Portal in Constantinople.

The curious dialogue of civilizations between the Damascus caliphate and Byzantine Constantinople sharpened with the accession of Umar's successor Yazid II. The new ruler, a younger brother of the illustrious al-Walid, builder of mosques and monuments, proved every bit as dissolute as *his* namesake Yazid, accursed by the Shi'a for the murder of Imam Hussein. It was to this wastrel that we owe the event that arguably precipitated the iconoclast crisis: an edict ordering the destruction of sacred images in all Christian churches under the jurisdiction of the caliphate.

It is hard to imagine a character further removed from the saintly Umar II. Not only was Umar's younger brother, the new ruler of Damascus, a libertine, he was a superstitious man of shallow belief, easily influenced and more easily guided by soothsayers, predicators and diviners. The edict itself has not survived, but it is described by a certain John of Jerusalem, in his report to the

Ecumenical Council which, convening in Nicea in 787, temporarily overturned iconoclasm. Like most anti-iconoclast documents, it is perhaps better understood as propaganda:

When Omar [Umar] had died, he was succeeded by Yazid, a frivolous and fickle man. Now, there was in Tiberias a certain leader of the lawless Jews, who was a sorcerer and the instrument of soul-destroying demons, called Tessarakontapechys [Forty-Cubits-High] … Being informed of the frivolity of the ruler Yazid, this wicked Jew went to him and attempted to make some prophecies. Having in this manner gained the tyrant's favor, he said: 'I wish, O Caliph, on account of the good will I have towards you, to suggest a certain method, easy to accomplish by means of which you will win an extension of your life and will remain here to rule for thirty years, if you put what I say into effect.' Won over by the promise of longevity, the senseless tyrant replied: 'Anything you suggest to me I shall readily do … ' Whereupon, the Jewish sorcerer said to him: 'Give an order without delay or postponement that an encyclical letter be issued throughout your dominions to the effect that every kind of pictorial representation, be it on boards or in wall-mosaic or on holy vessels or altar cloths, or anything of the sort that is found in Christian churches should be obliterated and entirely destroyed; not only these, but also all the effigies that are set up as decoration in the market-places of cities.' It was a devilish plot on the part of the false prophet to have added 'all effigies' because he tried to avoid suspicion of being hostile to us [Christians]. The wicked tyrant was easily persuaded by him and set out emissaries throughout his dominions to pull down all the holy icons and other images. And in this fashion he denuded God's churches … before this plague had reached our country. And since the God-loving Christians took flight so as not to destroy holy icons with their own hands, the emirs who had been charged with this task imposed it on accursed Jews and miserable Arabs. And so they burnt the holy icons, and some churches were whitewashed, while others they scraped down. When the unworthy bishop of Nakoleia [Advisor to Leo III] and his followers heard of this, they imitated the lawless Jews and infidel Arabs and set about insulting the churches of God … [226]

Whatever the accuracy of John of Jerusalem's account, the soothsayer's words had proven to be empty blandishments. Instead of the thirty-year reign he had been promised, Yazid died in 724. The effect of the edict on the Christians of the caliphate was short-lived. Its secondary impact, however, that on the Byzantine state, may have been dramatic. Two years later, after smashing the great icon in Constantinople, Leo III issued his own iconoclast edict.

While no cause-effect relationship can be decisively established between the anti-Christian—and anti-iconic—initiatives of Umar II and Yazid II and their Byzantine counterparts, and while some scholars strongly deny that a connection exists, it seems improbable in the extreme that events in the Umayyad state were not closely observed and understood in Constantinople, and vice-versa. They were the two super-powers of the day, one the guardian of a creaky but politically sophisticated edifice, the other fresh, brash, aggressive and self-assured in its reach. Whether the respective sovereigns actually corresponded seems the lesser issue. The dialogue, now military, now religious, now symbolic, that had been unfolding since the establishment of Umayyad power in Damascus in 661, quickened.

Within both the feuding empires deep currents were fashioning a future that was to radically alter both. In Byzantium an iconoclast dynasty had come to power and would wield it, with short interruptions, for a century. In the Islamic world, Umayyad rule would last but twenty-five years longer. Deep within its bowels, the legacy of impiety and aristocratic usurpation, the smouldering revolt of the partisans of 'Ali, and Arab exclusivism had created contradictions that the Damascus caliphate, for all its brilliance, could not resolve. Neither could Abassid Baghdad nor Ottoman Istanbul. Attempts at Islamic revival in the twentieth century may yet have proven unsuccessful, but they also indicate an acute grasp of the task at hand.

* * *

AS I RANGED THE ALLEYS of Old Damascus or pored over learned texts in the reading room of the French Institute for Oriental Studies, I had begun to experience feelings of acute frustration. Western scholars could ill-afford to ignore the impact of Islam on Christian perceptions of images, or upon the outbreak of the iconoclast conflict. But it was becoming clear to me that an Islamic view of the lawfulness of images had not been represented with the same thoroughness as were the conflicting views on the subject from within Christianity, or Judaism. Of course, I had to admit that the Arab-language sources which were by definition inaccessible to me might hold that which I sought: a voice from within Islam that would speak on its own terms and in its own vocabulary.

For the Qur'an, the crucial prohibition is against "idols." Not only, like strong drink and games of chance, do they direct man away from what must be his primary focus, the Oneness of God, but standing implicitly as partners or surrogates, they deny that Oneness. Islam allows of few greater transgressions. " ... And there is none comparable unto Him."[227]

The prohibition against depiction in early Islam may derive from the Qur'anic passages on Solomon, the King-Prophet whose patronage of art was legendary and whose artisans were equally so, perhaps including *jinn*, those unseen beings who dwell in the same realm as the angels and are reputed to be made of fire. Two aspects of the Solomon story, argues the Islamic art historian Oleg Grabar, are pertinent to the Islamic attitude toward art, while in partial contradiction with each other.

"One is that a work of art is something to wonder about, to be amazed by ... The other implication is that a work of art is a falsehood, a lie ... "[228] Were that to be true, the work of the artist would be not only suspect, but dangerously subversive of divine order.

Over time, an Islamic canon emerged, drawn upon the life of Muhammad, whose non-revelatory sayings and daily acts form the basis of a complex and ramified structure based on emulation and reasoning by analogy. By applying the rules that could be derived from this structure, believers could take guidance for their own lives and for the life of the community.

One of the conclusions that was arrived at by many traditional threads of interpretation and validation was that artists, on the day of the Final Judgement, would be summoned by God to breathe life into their creation. If they failed to do so, the eternal flames of Hell would be theirs.[229] For they would have been a party to the worst of lies by presenting the work of their imagination or depictive powers as a simulacrum of divine creation.

But these were abstract considerations. Meanwhile, the voice I had hoped for had not materialized. Time—and my already oft-extended visa—was running out. A few days before my departure from Damascus, the telephone rang. Seyyid Ridwan Majdalawi was on the line. Our last meeting had taken place weeks earlier, on a cold, windy day at Grand Mufti Ahmad Kouftaro's residence on the outskirts of al-Ghuta. As we parted then, he had promised to find someone through whom he could speak.

"When we can meet?" he asked, short of breath. "The man, I find him."

If he had found the man, I had found the voice.

Or, more properly, the voice had found me.

"I will come for you in one hour."

My Syrian sojourn was drawing to a close. I had no more appointments. This was the one I had been expecting.

"I'll be waiting."

Seyyid Ridwan's much traveled pick-up shuddered to a stop at the sidewalk where I stood waiting for it in a patch of winter sunlight. I climbed in, and we roared off. Within two minutes, though my companion had offered nothing but greetings and a handshake, I intuited our destination. We were heading west, across town, toward the slopes of Jabal Qassiun. Fifteen minutes later we had arrived at the main entrance to the raw concrete mass of the Abu Nur Foundation, made our way through the main entrance and to the elevator. We got out at the fourth floor.

"The man," as Seyyid Ridwan called him, was expecting us. His name was Ibrahim, he was a specialist in the teaching of Arabic to foreigners and worked full time at the Foundation. Ibrahim, a compact, gray-haired fifty, wore a tweed jacket over a wool sweater, and a head-hugging knit wool skullcap of the kind affected by the devout. His thick-lensed, horn-rimmed spectacles made him look faintly owl-like.

We shook hands, and sat down around Ibrahim's desk. Glasses of tea appeared. From the adjoining common room came the murmur of students offering midday prayers. The peculiar odor of piety, a mingling of the smells of closed rooms and old socks, pervaded the place. The atmosphere was propitious, the exchanged pleasantries calculated to establish a climate of mutual obligation. The discussion could begin, far from the ceremonial niceties of Damascus's Christian establishments.

Seyyid Ridwan pulled out a sheaf of typed notes. Speaking now in Arabic, with Ibrahim translating, he explained how Islamic tradition had come to prohibit depiction of living creatures. "The sons of Adam were righteous men. But when one of their brothers died, the Devil whispered in their ear: 'I can make for you an image of the dead which you can place in your temple.' So the Devil made the statue, which resembled the dead man. The sons of Adam died, and as they did, the Devil made an image of each, and placed it in the temple.

"People began to stray from God, they began to fight. They asked themselves, 'Why worship a God we cannot see?' The Devil whispered, 'these are your gods,' and the people began to worship them."

"Then came Abraham," continued Seyyid Ridwan, warming to the subject. "The Qur'an relates the story of his confrontation with the idol worshippers. One day he went to the temple and smashed all but the largest idol. When the people saw what had happened they asked, 'Who did this?' Having heard Abraham deprecating the idols, they brought him before them and questioned him. To open their minds to his message, he said, 'The largest of them did this.' They realized that their idols could do nothing. They had wronged themselves. The Devil came to them, and tried to return them to error."

"You see," said Seyyid Ridwan, "in the Qur'an Allah has taught us the way of dialogue. 'Ask the greatest idol,' Abraham challenged them. 'He cannot speak,' the people replied. 'Why then do you worship them in place of Allah?' But dispute got the upper hand, and they decided to burn Abraham to protect their gods."

The story snapped into sharp focus.

The place was Urfa, the dusty ocher-tinted town in what is today south-eastern Turkey where the ur-Patriarch of three faiths had stopped, according to local legend, on his way to Canaan. There, atop the pyre, as the flames licked at the prophet's feet, God intervened, saying "O fire, be coolness and peace for Abraham."[230] Then, according to local legend, the flames were transformed into water, and the logs into fish: the same water that fills the sacred pool in the Halilurrahman Dergah, in which swim hundreds of thousands of sacred carp, the living embodiment in perpetuity of the burning logs. Urfa was where Bediuzzaman Saïd Nursi had died in 1960, and where his empty grave remained. It was a town, and a place, I knew well.

"When people turn their backs on divine teaching and become enslaved by the capriciousness of their senses," continued Seyyid Ridwan, "it is only natural that they turn to idols. Moses called upon people to forsake the Golden Calf. Jesus prohibited idol worship, and so did Muhammad. Let me tell you two *hadith*, among many:

"Before the emigration to Medina [622 CE, the event that marks the beginning of the Muslim calendar] Ali stood atop Muhammad's shoulders to cast down an idol that sat atop the Ka'aba," the black stone of meteoric origin that stands at the center of the Muslim universe, and toward which all believers must turn when they pray. "Ali said, 'it broke like glass.' Then they departed."

"Later, when he returned victorious to Mecca, God's messenger walked into the holy house and destroyed the idols surrounding the Ka'aba. There were more than 400 of them, and each tribe had its own special deity.

"So, you see, Islam prohibits everything that distracts man from worship of Allah. If he worships such things and turns away from Allah, he will be the loser."

He paused, perhaps for dramatic effect, then shuffled his papers.

"All of us have one or more gods inside us. In the past, humans would place effigies of these gods before them. And if they'd had no idols, they would have created them, even out of dates to be eaten. Those were material gods. But in today's world, man has immaterial gods within him that he bows down before."

If I had hoped for a detailed, analytical description of the way in which *hadith* prohibit figuration, a kind of Islamic version of iconoclasm, I was to be disappointed. There were to be no references to the footnoted erudition of generations of Byzantinologists and art historians.

As Seyyid Ridwan gained momentum, to the satisfaction of Ibrahim the interpreter, those hopes were rapidly receding. I thought back to my frustration at not finding in Damascus a Muslim voice to discuss the question of image worship. Now, having found that voice, I found myself grumbling inwardly because my hosts' method was not that of the very Western academics whose arguments and whose methodologies I had found increasingly glib, dissatisfying and sterile.

I felt cornered, trapped between my Westerner's culturally determined expectations of a dispassionate overview that hewed to the standard and generally accepted parameters of learned discourse, complete with the verbal equivalent of references, and the self-imposed duty that had brought me to Syria in the first place: to open myself to, to accept another, perhaps—even hopefully—antithetical view. On my neck I felt the glacial breath of intellectual paralysis. My physical reflexes were operating in default mode, pen jotting squiggled words on the ruled pages of my notebook. But cognitive gridlock loomed.

I shivered. Put down my pen. Reached for my glass of tea.

Perhaps it was the cold.

Muslim thinkers like Ridwan Majdalawi had their own ways of ordering the world, and these ways did not follow the contours of the Western scholarly method, though at times they intersected it. He, and I assumed many like him, were by no means the primitive mullahs of the sort one could stumble upon in the dusty, impoverished Qur'anic schools of Pakistan or Afghanistan, imparting a narrow, rigorous Islamism.

No. These Syrians, these Palestinians, were men of sophistication, evolving within a tradition that had either not accepted—or had perhaps rejected—the Western verdict brought down against it, that of irrelevance and hostility to the modern age and its ways. Instead of modernizing Islam, they were interested in Islamizing modernity.

Beginning with a question about the Islamic view of representational art, Seyyid Ridwan's argument had quickly swerved toward the theological, away from the modalities I imagined were decisive, to finalities of the sort that "white science" systematically and dismissively shrugs off, those which it hastens to consign to the realm of irrationality, superstition and the anti-modern.

The transition was swift, sharp.

I found myself transported into a self-contained universe driven not by the old, familiar materialist skepticism, but informed by belief. A universe no less absolute and all-encompassing than the one, built of rational certainty but ultimately unverifiable by the scientific method, that we inhabit. Could my host's reasoning have been far distant from that of the Byzantine erudites who endlessly debated the legitimacy of depicting the sacred? Or of their Muslim opposites who scolded them for their sophistries? Or from our own, which bends necessity to its own unavowed imperatives ? Lurking beneath these half-formed, fleeting thoughts lay the question that strikes if not fear, then a sense of heightened vulnerability, into the heart of any Westerner in the Middle East: "What if he's right?"

The tea was tepid by now, and a bit too sweet. Nevertheless, I drained my glass, picked up the pen I had laid upon the desktop, and resumed my jotting.

"But there are also idols within us, false gods. We cannot see them. They are our desires, our caprices," he said. His smile made me feel certain that he had intuited my disarray. Seyyid Ridwan and I had spent too much time together.

"In our time, we should break the idols that are within us, and not mistake them for heavenly teachings. The love of money and property is one such idol, and so is the pursuit of material pleasure if we seek it in an illicit way."

"When man refuses to break these idols, when he continues to worship them, Allah will place a seal upon his heart and upon his senses, and he will lose the way of truth."

My first impulse was to believe that Seyyid Ridwan spoke from the experience of his heart. Our cross-town conversations of months before flashed through my mind. But no. His eyes, and the measured calm of his voice redirected my attention.

In the distance, down some dark corridor, I thought I head the metallic clang of a door closing. Perhaps it had only been the wind.

Now. In a clammy office in a religious institution in Damascus, a new definition of iconoclasm stared me in the face. It was a definition, I realized with a shock, apposite to our era. Not unlike the Christian world prior to the outbreak of the iconoclast conflict, the idols we worship—such was being implied, though my hosts were far too considerate to state it outright—accompany our every waking moment as painted images once did, surround us like prison walls built of winking television monitors or computer screens. Even these could be too readily dismissed and disconnected. The idols of which he spoke are now embedded within us, so perfectly internalized, assimilated into consciousness that they seem of a piece with it.

Unlike the idols Abraham and later Muhammad smashed, unlike the icon atop the Chalke Gate demolished by Leo III, unlike the lurid tableaux ripped from churches by Luther, Calvin and their emulators, today's idols—if Seyyid Ridwan's definition is right—will not be so easily extirpated.

Like pesticide residues, they have become systemic, and can now be found in every cell of the body. Like virtual DNA. No decontamination program currently available will have an effect; no filter, no matter how fine its mesh, can separate them out; no membrane can block their osmotic power; no chemical agent can cause them to precipitate, no nanotechnology is minute enough or swift enough to track down and destroy them.

Should this be so, we, as in the oft-repeated Qur'anic warning, are already the greater losers. But I was not being counselled to accept, as a man of Western culture, an ascetic regimen of self-denial and abasement. With such regimens Islam has no truck. Divine law, argued Seyyid Ridwan, was more than enough to regulate these matters. That is to say: the limits, which are known, must be applied and respected.

That, on the eve of the iconoclast outburst, was an imperative upon which all three of the great monotheistic dispensations could concur. While matters of doctrine and dogma divided them, often mortally for all—or because of—their proximity, their attachment to the law made them co-inhabitants of the same spiritual universe.

No longer. Those whom Muslims like Ridwan Majdalawi are challenging to an informed exchange of views operate from an intellectual tradition and a culture that, seen from the Islamic vantage point, might well meet the definition of idolatry. A tradition and a culture in thrall to powerful but invisible inner gods.

If I had heard him correctly, and I think I had, the kind of iconoclast movement that would take on these concealed graven images was now, as far as the West was concerned, on the civilizational agenda. A meridian had been reached. The looming tragedy was that we, in the West had become blinded by our infatuation with idols, our intoxication by them, but did not appreciate it, could not anticipate it, did not know it—or, if we intuited it, could not articulate it. Ridwan Majdalawi's was the method of dialogue. Others, less formally schooled than he, would be far less inclined toward patience, exchange, understanding. They would be hard, ruthless, unforgiving men, up from the hard-scrabble schools of poverty, desperation and oppression, men steeped in humiliation prepared to wield their thirst for the fight against misbelief, disbelief and unbelief like knives. Men for whom the Qur'an would yield less of its compassion, much more of its resolve.

In the cultural offensive the West has thrust since the beginning of the nineteenth century upon the Islamic world, the latest and most inglorious episode of which is the current campaign to refashion once more its heartland and ultimately to bend it to our consuming Western will, we will be seen as idol-worshippers. Accurately and justifiably, our civilization will be perceived as a lurching giant intoxicated with the images of our perfected selves, longing for annihilation, yearning for the oblivion that is death.

Notes

PREFACE

1. Philip Hitti, *The History of the Arabs From the Earliest Times to the Present* (New York: St. Martin's Press, 1970), 87.

CHAPTER 1

2. A.A. Vasiliev, *History of the Byzantine Empire 324–1453* (Madison: University of Wisconsin Press, 1958), 176.

3. Ibid., 194.

4. Hitti, *History of the Arabs*, 195.

5. Ibid., 155.

6. Quoted in Hitti, *History of the Arabs*, 150.

7. Ibid., 152.

8. Wilferd Madelung, *The Succession to Muhammad: A Study of the Early Caliphate* (Cambridge: Cambridge University Press, 1997), 61.

9. Ibid., 184.

10. Ibid., 197.

11. Hitti, *History of the Arabs*, 180.

12. Ibid.

13. "La majorité des annalistes musulmans ne peut … s'empêcher de rendre un hommage involontaire au souverain remarquable, au plus éminent peut-être des politiques de l'Islam, qui, en substituant à l'oligarchie théocratique, inaugurée par Mahomet, maintenue par Omer, un gouvernement régulier et organisé contribua plus que personne … à asseoir la domination du Qoran" (Henri Lammens, S.J. *Études sur le regne du calife Omaïyade Mo'awia 1e* [Beyrouth: Université St. Joseph, 1908], 65).

14. "Quatre circonstances—disait plus tard Mo'awia—n'ont donné la supériorité sur 'Ali. Je cachais soigneusement mes projets, lui les affichait publiquement. Mes troupes étaient mieux équipées et plus dociles; les siennes, très médiocres, ne songeaient qu'à la rebellion. Pendant la journée du Chameau, je l'ai laissé débattre avec ses ennemis. Si ses derniers triomphaient, ils se montreraients, j'en avais la certitude, plus accomodants que lui; si 'Ali l'emportait, ce serait au dépens de son prestige. Enfin, je possédais dans un plus haut degré les sympathies de Qoraiches" (Ibid., 124).

15. Madelung, *Succession to Muhammad*, 16.

16. Hitti, *History of the Arabs*, 182.

17. Ibid., 197.

18. "En définitif, l'Islam peut se féliciter des succès omaiyades: le triomphe de 'Ali eut perpé-tué l'anarchie en son sein; ses hériteront des qualités négatives du père" (Lammens, *Études sur le regne,* 146).

19. *Crescent International,* Feb. 1–15, 2002.

CHAPTER 2

20. Jorge Luis Borges, *The Aleph and Other Stories 1933–1969,* edited and translated by Norman Thomas di Giovanni (New York: Dutton, 1978), 23, 29.

21. Hitti, *History of the Arabs,* 221.

22. Afif Bahnassi, *La grande mosquée omeyyad à Damas: le premier chef d'oeuvre de l'art musulman* (Damas: Tlass, 1990), 49.

23. Ibid.

24. Finbar Barry Flood, *The Great Mosque of Damascus: Studies on the Makings of an Umayyad Visual Culture* (Leiden: Brill, 2001), 5.

25. Brigid Keenan, *Damas* (Paris: Éditions Place des Victoires, 2000), 27.

26. Flood, *Great Mosque of Damascus,* 20.

27. Ibid., 13.

28. Ibid., 4.

29. Ibid., 1.

30. Hitti, *History of the Arabs,* 286.

31. Bahnassi, *La grande mosquée omeyyad,* 29.

32. Éric Geoffroy, "La Syrie, terre des prophètes" in *Les Derviches tourneurs de Damas. Liturgie soufie de la Grande Mosquée des Omeyyades,* Le Chant du monde, 34.

33. Ibid., 39.

34. Bahnassi, *La grande mosquée omeyyad,* 118.

35. Ibid.

36. Flood, *Great Mosque of Damascus,* 34.

37. Anne-Marie Bianquis, "La Ghouta, un paradis entre montage et steppe" in *Damas: Miroir brisé d'un Orient arabe,* dirigé par Anne-Marie Bianquis, avec la collaboration d'Elizabeth Picard, *Éditions Autrement* Série Monde, HS N° 65 (1993):18.

38. Ibid., 26.

39. Ibid., 21.

40. Ibid., 23.

41. Hitti, *History of the Arabs,* 689.

CHAPTER 3

42. Patrick Seale, *Asad of Syria: The Struggle for the Middle East,* with the assistance of Maureen McConville (Berkeley: University of California Press, 1989), 42.

43. *Syria 2000: Geopolitical and Economic Yearbook* (Damascus: Nice Publications, 2001), 33.

44. Interview with a source intimately connected with the Egyptian Muslim Brotherhood.

45. Raymond A. Hinnebusch, *Authoritarian Power and State Formation in Baathist Syria: Army, Party and Peasant* (Boulder: Westview Press, 1990), 146.

46. Seale, *Asad of Syria,* 475–480. Seale writes that al-Hindawi may have been an Israeli double agent.

47. Robert W. Olson, *The Ba'th and Syria, 1947 to 1982: The Evolution of Ideology, Party and State. From the French Mandate to the Era of Hafiz al-Asad* (Princeton: The Kingston Press, 1982), 3.

48. Alain Gresh, "Crimes et mensonges d'une 'libération'" in *Le Monde Diplomatique* (mai 2003):14.

49. *Syria 2000*, 33.

50. Ibid., 319.

51. Ibid., 321.

52. Ibid., 316.

53. Ibid., 325.

54. Ibid., 327.

55. Ibid., 329.

56. Hinnebusch, *Authoritarian Power and State Formation*, 81.

57. For a detailed analysis of the ideological role of the West in the creation of Israel, see Thierry Hentsch, "L'Ombre de l'Occident dans le conflit israélo-palestinien" in *Relations* Numéro 676 (mai 2001):32–34.

58. Ummar Abd-Allah, *The Islamic Struggle in Syria*, foreword and postscript by Hamid Algar (Berkeley: Mizan Press, 1983), 29.

59. Hinnebusch, *Authoritarian Power and State Formation*, 83.

60. Abd-Allah, *Islamic Struggle in Syria*, 21.

61. Ibid., 90.

62. Ibid., 95.

63. Ibid., 93.

64. Patrick Seale, *The Struggle for Syria: A Study of Post-War Arab Politics 1945–1958* (London: I. B. Tauris, 1965, 1986), 287.

65. Ibid., 290.

66. Anthony Shadid, *Legacy of the Prophet: Despots, Democrats and the New Politics of Islam* (Boulder: Westview, 2001), 54.

67. Quoted in Shadid, *Legacy of the Prophet*, 59.

68. Abd-Allah, *Islamic Struggle in Syria*, 109.

69. Ibid.

70. Olson, *Baath and Syria*, 61.

71. Abd-Allah, *Islamic Struggle in Syria*, 48.

72. Seale, *Struggle for Syria*, 351.

73. From the foreword to Abd-Allah, *Islamic Struggle in Syria*, 11.

74. Ibid., 183.

75. Ibid., 189.

76. Ibid., 213.

77. Ibid., 214.

78. Robert Fisk, *Pity the Nation: The Abduction of Lebanon* (New York: Atheneum, 1990), 179.

79. Seale, *Struggle for Syria*, 319.

80. Abd-Allah, *Islamic Struggle in Syria*, 192.

81. Fisk, *Pity the Nation*, 186.

82. Seale, *Struggle for Syria,* 332.
83. Hinnebusch, *Authoritarian Power and State Formation,* 297.
84. Abd-Allah, *Islamic Struggle in Syria,* 193.

CHAPTER 4
85. Hitti, *History of the Arabs,* 647.
86. Ibid., 183.
87. Ibid., 441.
88. Interview in *Salam Iran,* a film by Jean-Daniel Lafond (Montréal: Information, 2002).
89. Yann Richard, *L'Islam chi'ite* (Paris: Fayard, 1991), 56.
90. Hitti, *History of the Arabs,* 443.
91. Ibid., 618.
92. David Fromkin, *A Peace to End All Peace: The Fall of the Ottoman Empire and the Creation of the Modern Middle East* (New York: Avon Books, 1989), 75.
93. Ibid., 195.
94. Ibid, 193.
95. Ibid.
96. Ibid., 315.
97. Ibid., 335.
98. Ibid.
99. Ibid., 394.
100. Ibid., 397.
101. Phillip S. Khoury, *Syria and the French Mandate: The Politics of Arab Nationalism, 1920–1945* (Princeton: Princeton University Press, 1987), 37.
102. Ibid., 38.
103. Fromkin, *Peace to End All Peace,* 437.
104. Khoury, *Syria and the French Mandate,* 41.
105. Derek Hopwood, *Syria 1945–1986: Politics and Society* (London: Unwin Hyman, 1988), 22.
106. Ibid., 100.
107. Ibid.
108. Seale, *Asad of Syria,* 10.
109. Daniel Pipes, *Greater Syria: The History of an Ambition* (New York: Oxford, 1990), 161.
110. Khoury, *Syria and the French Mandate,* 101.
111. Ibid., 102.
112. Jacques Weurleusse, *Le Pays des Alaouites* (Tours: Institut français de Damas, 1940), 56.
113. Ibid, 55.
114. Seale, *Asad of Syria,* 6.
115. Ibid., 7.
116. Khoury, *Syria and the French Mandate,* 151.
117. Moroccan Islamic feminist Fatima Mernissi explores the brief career of Sitt al-Mulk in her *Forgotten Queens of Islam,* translated by Mary Jo Lakeland (Minneapolis: University of Minnesota Press, 1993), 161–178.

118. Mernissi, *Forgotten Queens of Islam,* 162.

119. Quoted in Mernissi, *Forgotten Queens of Islam,* 169.

120. Malise Ruthven, *Islam in the World* (New York: Oxford University Press, 1984), 214.

121. Quoted in Mernissi, *Forgotten Queens of Islam,* 166.

122. Ruthven, *Islam in the World,* 214.

123. The Druze coexisted in peace with their Christian Maronite neighbors in Mount Lebanon until the mid-nineteenth century when a Maronite peasant revolt that may have been instigated by France touched off a Druze pre-emptive massacre. More than 10,000 died in less than one month. The troubles spread as far afield as Damascus, where there were more than 5,000 Christian deaths, the worst pogrom in the city's multi-millennial history. Recently, in Lebanon, the Druze under the leadership of the Jumblatt clan, has had an active role in support for the Palestinian cause. See Ruthven, *Islam in the World,* 216–217.

124. Mernissi, *Forgotten Queens of Islam,* 164.

125. Khoury, *Syria and the French Mandate,* 152.

126. Ibid., 153.

127. Ibid., 154.

128. Ibid., 159.

129. Ibid., 56.

130. Ibid., 164.

131. Ibid., 166.

132. Ibid., 173.

133. Ibid., 177.

134. Ibid., 178.

135. Alice Polleau, "Journal d'une française pendant la révolte syrienne" quoted in Lenka Bokova, "L'insurrection syrienne contre le mandat" in *Damas: Miroir brisé d'un Orient arabe,* dirigé par Anne-Marie Bianquis, avec la collaboration d'Elizabeth Picard, *Éditions Autrement* Série Monde. HS Nº 65, (1993):81. My translation.

136. Khoury, *Syria and the French Mandate,* 201.

CHAPTER 5

137. Hitti, *History of the Arabs,* 190.

138. Ali Shariati, *Martyrdom,* translated by Laleh Bakhtiar and Husayn Salih (Tehran: Abu-Dharr Foundation, n.d.), 107.

139. Seale, *Struggle for Syria,* 173.

140. Interview with Saddredin al-Sadr, Beirut, December 2001.

141. Hizbullah was not alone in its victorious campaign against the Israeli army and its proxy occupation forces, the South Lebanese Army. The Lebanese Communist Party, the Syrian Social Nationalist Party and Amal all contributed martyrs to the cause.

142. Peter Theroux, *The Strange Disappearance of Imam Moussa Sadr* (London: Weidenfeld & Nicholson, 1987), 42.

143. Ibid., 44.

144. Yann Richard, "Ayatollah Kashani: Precursor of the Islamic Republic?" in *Religion and Politics in Iran,* edited by Nikki R. Keddie (New Haven: Yale University Press, 1983), 108.

145. Fisk, *Pity the Nation,* 115.

146. Jean-Pierre Digard, Bernard Hourcade, Yann Richard, *L'Iran au Xxe siècle* (Paris: Fayard, 1996), 132.

147. Majed Halawi, *A Lebanon Defied—Musa al-Sadr and the Shi'a Community* (Boulder: Westview Press, 1992), 122.

148. Madelung, *Succession to Muhammad,* 84.

149. Ruthven, *Islam in the World,* 183.

150. Halawi, *Lebanon Defied,* 123.

151. Augustus Richard Norton, *Amal and the Shi'a: Struggle for the Soul of Lebanon* (Austin: University of Texas Press, 1987), 39.

152. Theroux, *Strange Disappearance,* 14–15.

153. Quoted in Theroux, *Strange Disappearance,* 5.

154. Halawi, *Lebanon Defied,* 163.

155. Theroux, *Strange Disappearance,* 19.

156. Norton, *Amal and the Shi'a,* 43.

157. Quoted in Norton, *Amal and the Shi'a,* 46.

158. Halawi, *Lebanon Defied,* 159.

159. Quoted in *Beirut Daily Star,* July 16, 1974.

160. Conversation with Mr. Hajj-Afif Aoun, Tyre, December 2000.

161. Theroux, *Strange Disappearance,* 48.

162. Norton, *Amal and the Shi'a,* 49.

163. Theroux, *Strange Disappearance,* 48.

164. Halawi, *Lebanon Defied,* 203–210.

165. Norton, *Amal and the Shi'a,* 49.

166. Fisk, *Pity the Nation,* 557.

167. Joseph Alaghal, "Hizbullah's Gradual Integration in the Libanese Public Sphere" *Sharqiyat* vol. 13, no. 1 (2001):33–59.

168. Fisk, *Pity the Nation,* 227.

169. Quoted in Norton, *Amal and the Shi'a,* 168.

170. See *Persona Non Grata: The expulsion of Civilians from Israeli-Occupied Lebanon* (New York: Human Rights Watch, 1999).

171. Jeffrey Goldberg, "In the Party of God" *The New Yorker,* October 14, 2002.

172. Alaghal, "Hizbullah's Gradual Integration", op cit.

173. *Beirut Daily Star,* June 16, 1974.

174. Norton, *Amal and the Shi'a,* 55.

175. Theroux, *Strange Disappearance,* 61.

176. Ibid., 79.

177. Ibid., 80.

178. Ibid., 66.

179. Ibid., 95.

180. Conversation with Robert Fisk, Beirut, December 2000.

181. Theroux, *Strange Disappearance,* 4.

182. The MKO, acronym for the Mujahidin Khalk Organization (People's Mujahidin), founded in the early 1960s, favored a blend of Marxism and Islam. After having been defeated in its attempt to seize power after the Islamic Revolution of 1979, its founder Masud Rajavi fled Iran and took up residence in France. In 1986, the organization was expelled from France and given shelter by Saddam Hussein. The militia, integrated into the Iraqi armed forces, signed a separate cease-fire with United States military authorities. It can be expected to provide "freedom fighters" for the American campaign against the Islamic Republic.

CHAPTER 6

183. Holy Bible, King James Version (New York: Ivy Books, 1991), Exodus 20:4–5.

184. André Grabar, *L'iconoclasme byzantin. Dossier archéologique* (Paris: Collège de France, 1957), 133.

185. Alain Besançon, *L'image interdite* (Paris: Gallimard, 1994), 233.

186. Ulrich Wilcken, *Alexander the Great*, translated by G.C. Richards (New York: Norton, 1967), 307.

187. Vasiliev, *History of the Byzantine Empire*, 105.

188. Ibid.

189. Robert Graves, *The Greek Myths* (London: Penguin Books, 1962), 27.

190. Susan Ashbrook Haney, *Antioch and Christianity in Antioch—The Lost Ancient City* (Princeton: Princeton University Press, 2000), 43.

191. Ibid., 42.

192. Ibid., 20.

193. Vasiliev, *History of the Byzantine Empire*, 234.

194. Grabar, *L'iconoclasme byzantin*, 94.

195. Holy Bible, King James Version, Acts 9:11.

196. Daniel J. Sahas, *Icon and Logos: Sources in Eighth-century Iconoclasm* (Toronto: University of Toronto Press, 1986), 13.

197. Ibid., 6.

198. Charles Diehl, *Manuel d'art byzantin* 2 volumes (Paris: Librairie Auguste Picard, 1925), 1.

199. Besançon, *L'image interdite*, 36.

200. Nikos Kazantzakis, *Journey to the Morea* (New York: Simon and Schuster, 1964), 64.

201. Ibid., 65.

202. Bescançon, 71.

203. Ibid., 72.

204. Ibid., 74.

205. Wilken, 117.

206. Bescançon, 113.

207. Vasiliev, *History of the Byzantine Empire*, 43.

208. Besançon, *L'image interdite*, 124.

209. Ibid., 128–130.

210. Ibid., 143.

211. Grabar, *L'iconoclasme byzantin*, 99–100.

212. Bescançon, *L'image interdite,* 240–241.

213. Bescançon, 236.

214. Vasiliev, *History of the Byzantine Empire,* 261.

215. Besançon, *L'image interdite,* 243–244.

216. Ibid., 244.

217. Ibid., 269.

218. Mar Ignatius Zakka I Iwas, *The Syrian Orthodox Church of Antioch at a Glance,* translated into English by Emmanuel H. Bismarji (Allepo: 1983), 41.

219. Ibid., 41.

220. Ibid., 42.

221. Hitti, *History of the Arabs,* 79.

CHAPTER 7

222. Hitti, *History of the Arabs,* 222.

223. Ibid., 203.

224. Grabar, *L'iconoclasme byzantin,* 105.

225. A. Jeffrey, "Ghevond's text of the correspondence between 'Umar II and Leo III," HThR 37 (1944): 322 in *Anthology of Texts in Translation,* 182.

226. Cyril Mango, *The Art of the Byzantine Empire, 312–1453. Sources and Documents* (New York: Prentice-Hall Inc., 1972), 182.

227. Ibid., cxii.

228. Oleg Grabar, "Art and Culture in the Islamic World" in *Islam: Arts and Architecture* (Cologne: Könemann, 2000), 38.

229. Ibid., 39.

230. Qur'an, XXI, 69.

Index